WORD/INFORMATION PROCESSING

Essential Concepts
SECOND EDITION

Marilyn K. Popyk

Gregg Division/McGraw-Hill Book Company
New York Atlanta Dallas St. Louis
San Francisco Auckland Bogotá Guatemala
Hamburg Lisbon London
Madrid Mexico Milan Montreal New Delhi
Panama Paris San Juan São Paulo Singapore
Sydney Tokyo Toronto

Sponsoring Editor: Roberta Mantus
Editing Supervisor: Curt Berkowitz
Design Supervisor/Cover Designer: Nancy Axelrod
Production Supervisor: S. Steven Canaris

Developmental Editors: Morton Redner and Winifred Davis
Photo Editor: Rosemarie Rossi
Photo Researcher: Lorinda Morris
Text Designer: Delgado Design
Cover Photographer: Wolfson Photography, Inc.
Technical Studio: Graphic Media N/Y

DEDICATION

To my mother Rose Toki Popyk
And in Memory of my father Walter Popyk

Library of Congress Cataloging-in-Publication Data

Popyk, Marilyn K.
  Word/information processing.

  Rev. ed. of: Word processing essential concepts.
© 1983.
  Includes index.
  1. Word processing.   I. Popyk, Marilyn K.
Word processing, essential concepts.
II. Title.
HF5548.115.P67   1986   652'.5   86-7414
ISBN 0-07-050593-4

Some of the line art in this book was created electronically.

The manuscript for this book was prepared electronically.

Word/Information Processing: Essential Concepts, Second Edition

Copyright © 1986, 1983 by McGraw-Hill, Inc. All rights reserved. Printed in the United States of America. Except as permitted under the United States Copyright Act of 1976, no part of this publication may be reproduced or distributed in any form or by any means, or stored in a data base or retrieval system, without the prior written permission of the publisher. Portions of this work are taken from Marilyn K. Popyk's *Word Processing and Information Systems*, Second Edition, copyright © 1986, 1983 by McGraw-Hill, Inc.

    3 4 5 6 7 8 9 0   VNHVNH   8 9 3 2 1 0 9 8 7

ISBN 0-07-050593-4

Contents

About the Author vi   About the Reviewers vii   Photo Credits viii
A Message to the Student ix

Chapter 1 The Changing Office   1

Technology and You 2   **Technology and the Office** 3
Setting the Stage: Three Key Inventions 3

Information and the Office 11
Managing Business Information: The Goal of the Office 11
Information Defined 11   Problems of Increased Paperwork 12
Productivity in the Office 13

The Information Processing Cycle 15
Input 15   Processing 16   Output 18
Distribution/Communication 18   Storage and Retrieval 19

The Role of Word Processing in Information Processing 19
The Development of Word Processing Equipment 19
People: The Key Element in Information Processing 21

Chapter Summary 22   Information Processing Vocabulary 23
Chapter Questions 23   Case Study 24

Chapter 2 Documents   25

Processing Information 26   **Distributing Information** 27
Kinds of Business Communications 27
Correspondence 28   Reports 29   Statistical Tables 29
Forms 29   Other Documents 31

Classes of Documents in Information Processing 32
Short Documents 32   Repetitive Documents 32   Boilerplate 33
Lengthy, Text-Edited Documents 35

Business Applications of Information Processing 36
Law 36   Health Care 37   Banking 38   Insurance 39   Retail 40
Restaurants 41   Manufacturing 41   Distribution 42   Other Fields 43

Chapter Summary 44   Information Processing Vocabulary 45
Chapter Questions 45   Case Study 46

Chapter 3 Input   47

Methods of Document Creation 48
Longhand 49   Shorthand 49   Typed Rough Draft 51
Keyboarding 51   Machine Dictation 52

iii

Voice Storage Media 53
Internal Storage Media 53   Discrete Media 54

Dictation and Transcription Machines 57
Portable Dictation Units 58   Desk-Top Dictation Machines 59
Central Recording Systems 60   Computer-Aided Transcription 63
Optical Character Reader 6   Image Processing 64   Voice Processing 65

Chapter Summary 67   Information Processing Vocabulary 68
Chapter Questions 69   Case Study 69

Chapter 4 Word Processing Equipment 71

What is a Word Processor? 72   Components of a Word Processor 73
Keyboard 74   Central Processing Unit (CPU) 76   Storage 79
Printer 83   Display (Monitor) 83

Blind Equipment 90
The Beginning of Modern Word Processing 90   Improvements 92
Blind Word Processing Today 93   Linear Display Word Processors 95

Display Word Processors 96
How to Use Display Word Processors 98
What Display Word Processors Can Do 101

Word Processing Systems Configurations 103
Standalones 103   Clustered Systems 104   Time-Sharing Systems 106

Chapter Summary 108   Information Processing Vocabulary 109
Chapter Questions 109   Case Study 110

Chapter 5 Microcomputers and Software 112

Computers 113
Mainframe 113   Minicomputer 114   Microcomputer 114

Software 119
Disk Operating Systems 120   Development Software 122
Applications Software 123

The Computer Connection 132
The Personal Computer Link 133   PC Networks 134

Chapter Summary 135   Information Processing Vocabulary 136
Chapter Questions 137   Case Study 137

Chapter 6 Information Systems 139

Output 140
Soft Copy 140   Printers 140   Reprographics 144

Distribution/Communication 150
The U.S. Postal Service 150   Electronic Data Communications 151
Transmission Systems 157   Electronic Audio Communications 163
Teleconferencing 163

Storage and Retrieval 164
Storage of Paper and Magnetic Media 164   Micrographics 165
Optical (Laser) Disks 169   Image Processing 171
Microimage Transmission 171   Data Base Management Systems 171
Online Information Services 173   Records Management Systems 173
Information Management 174

Chapter Summary 174   **Information Processing Vocabulary** 178
Chapter Questions 179   **Case Study** 180

Chapter 7 Integrated Information Processing and Office Environment and Organization 181

Integrated Information Processing 182
The Systems Approach: Integrated Information Systems 182
The Executive Workstation 183
The Changing Information Processing Cycle 185   Computer Security 187
Technology Takes a Quantum Leap 189   Technology Changes Lives 191

Ergonomics 192
Office Furniture 193   Equipment Design 194   Lighting 194
Noise Control 194   Temperature 195   Humidity 195
Office Landscaping and Design 195   Health Issues in the Office 196
The Balance Between People and Equipment 197

Office Organization 198
Matching the System to the Need 198
Information Processing in a Traditional Setting 199
Decentralized Information Processing 201
Centralized Information Processing 204   Peopleware 208

Chapter Summary 208   **Information Processing Vocabulary** 210
Chapter Questions 210   **Case Study** 211

Chapter 8 Careers 212

Productivity 213
Work Procedures and Methods 213   Measuring Productivity 214

Careers 215
Differences That Affect the Employee 215
Careers in Information Processing 216
Onward and Upward 223   Toward Change and Growth 223

Chapter Summary 224   **Information Processing Vocabulary** 226
Chapter Questions 226   **Case Study** 227

Glossary 228   **Index** 241

About the Author

Marilyn K. Popyk served as Director and Instructor of Word Processing Programs at Henry Ford Community College in Dearborn, Michigan. In addition to teaching, Ms. Popyk has done considerable curriculum development work. Her accomplishments include the development and implementation of a two-year degree program and a one-year certificate of proficiency program in word processing, and the creation of course materials, visuals, and document tasks for new courses in word processing concepts and applications.

Ms. Popyk has been employed as an Educational Consultant for Wang Laboratories, Inc., in Lowell, Massachusetts. And as an independent consultant, she has created and conducted in-house microcomputer training programs for colleges, universities, and corporations. The author of several journal articles, Ms. Popyk also served as Educational Consultant for the State of Michigan Secondary and Postsecondary Divisions, Vocational Department. She has conducted numerous seminars and workshops for education and industry in information/word processing and is affiliated with many educational and professional associations including the Association of Information Systems Professionals (AISP), the American Society for Training and Development (ASTD), the American Vocational Association (AVA), the National Business Education Association (NBEA), and the American Association of Women in Community and Junior Colleges (AAWCJC).

Ms. Popyk received both her B.S. and her M.Ed. degrees from Wayne State University in Detroit, Michigan.

About the Reviewers

Ruby F. Barker is Associate Professor of the General Business and Marketing Department at Tarleton State University in Stephenville, Texas. She is a member of the National Business Education Association and the Southwest Administrative Services Association.

David R. Cosky is Assistant Professor of Secretarial Science and Office Automation at Gloucester County College in Sewell, New Jersey, where he coauthored the Word Processing/Office Automation courses and curriculum. He is a member of Phi Delta Kappa, Delta Pi Epsilon, the National Business Education Association, the South Jersey Business Education Association, and the Association of Information Systems Professionals.

Ronald G. Kapper is Professor of Office Careers at the College of DuPage in Glen Ellyn, Illinois. He is past chair of the Educator's Advisory Council of the Association of Information Systems Professionals and past president of the Chicago Area Business Educators Association. He is currently serving on the Board of Directors of the Illinois Business Education Association and is a member of numerous other professional and educational organizations. Mr. Kapper was named the Most Outstanding Member of the Chicago Chapter of the Association of Information Systems Professionals for two consecutive years.

Barbara M. Rodriguez is the National Coordinator of Office Support Systems at Arthur Young & Company in New York City. In addition to being a charter member and past president of the New York City Chapter of the Association of Information Systems Professionals, Ms. Rodriguez has conducted seminars and workshops on implementation and management of office systems and word processing for AISP Syntopicans, the Administrative Management Society, and the American Management Association. She is also a member of numerous professional organizations.

Joan Tiller is Director of Vocational Education at Valencia Community College in Orlando, Florida. Ms. Tiller has served on the Board of Florida Business Education Association and was a recipient of the Outstanding Postsecondary Business Educator Award from the Florida Business Education Association. She is also a member of the Florida Council on Vocational Education, the Florida Vocational Education Association, the American Vocational Association, the National Business Education Association, and Delta Pi Epsilon.

Photo Credits

Original text photographs by Dennis Barna and Will Faller as indicated below. Other photographs reproduced with permission of the following:

Page 2: Bob Rogers Photography (left); Cathering Ursillo/Photo Researchers (right). **Page 4:** The Bettmann Archive (left); Honeywell, Inc. (right). **Page 5:** AT&T (top two); ComData Corporation (third from top); Northern Telecom (bottom). **Page 7:** IBM Corporation. **Page 13:** Yan Lukas/Photo Researchers. **Page 14:** Burroughs Corporation. **Page 20:** Dennis Barna (top, bottom left, and middle left); Will Faller (middle right and bottom right). **Page 22:** *Office Administration and Automation.* **Page 27:** Frank Siteman—The Picture Cube. **Page 37:** Will Faller. **Page 38:** NCR Corporation. **Page 39:** Dennis Barna. **Page 40:** NCR Corporation. **Page 42:** Hewlett-Packard Company. **Page 50:** Will Faller. **Page 53:** Will Faller. **Page 54:** Dennis Barna. **Page 56:** Dennis Barna. **Page 58:** Dictaphone Corporation, Rye, N.Y. **Page 59:** Will Faller. **Page 61:** Dictaphone Corporation, Rye, N.Y. **Page 64:** IBM Corporation (right); Stenograph Corporation (left). **Page 65:** Wang Laboratories, Inc. **Page 66:** Interstate Voice Products. **Page 75:** Dennis Barna. **Page 78:** Intel Corporation. **Page 81:** Dennis Barna. **Page 82:** IBM Corporation. **Page 84:** IBM Corporation. **Page 86:** NCR Corporation. **Page 89:** CPT Corporation (top left and right); Lanier Business Products (bottom). **Page 91:** IBM Corporation. **Page 92:** IBM Corporation. **Page 93:** The Canon Corporation. **Page 95:** Royal Business Machines, Inc. **Page 96:** Dennis Barna. **Page 97:** Burroughs Corporation (top right); Digital Equipment Corporation (top left); Epson (bottom right); Lanier Business Products (bottom left). **Page 99:** Will Faller. **Page 100:** Will Faller. **Page 114:** Sperry Corporation. **Page 115:** Will Faller. **Page 116:** IBM Corporation (left); Lockheed Corporation (center); Hewlett-Packard Company (right). **Page 117:** Philip Amdal/Microsoft Corporation. **Page 119:** QIC Research, Inc. (left); Anderson Jacobson, Inc. (right). **Page 128:** Radio Shack, A Division of Tandy Corporation. **Page 132:** Hewlett-Packard Company. **Page 141:** Qume Corporation. **Page 142:** Diablo Systems, Inc. (top); Hewlett-Packard Company (bottom). **Page 143:** Benson, Inc. (top); Texas Instruments, Inc. (middle); Qume Corporation (bottom). **Page 144:** Michael Business Machines. **Page 145:** A. B. Dick Company. **Page 146:** Xerox Corporation. **Page 148:** Varityper. **Page 149:** Will Faller. **Page 151:** INTELPOST. **Page 152:** Western Union. **Page 159:** ComData Corporation. **Page 161:** Bell Laboratories. **Page 162:** Sperry Corporation (top); Systems Compatibility Corporation, Chicago (bottom). **Page 163:** AT&T/Bell Laboratories. **Page 165:** Misco (bottom); Ring King Visibles, Inc. (top). **Page 166:** Brian Griffin (top); Microseal Corporation (bottom). **Page 167:** 3M Office Systems. **Page 169:** 3M Office Systems. **Page 170:** Dennis Barna. **Page 184:** IBM Corporation (top); Xerox Corporation (bottom left); Lanier Business Products (bottom right). **Page 190:** Radio Shack, A Division of Tandy Corporation. **Page 193:** Data-Mate (left); Will Faller (right). **Page 194:** Ring King Visibles, Inc. **Page 195:** Burroughs Corporation. **Page 198:** Will Faller. **Page 199:** Will Faller. **Page 202:** Hewlett-Packard Company. **Page 205:** Western Union. **Page 213:** Will Faller. **Page 216:** Genicom Corporation. **Page 218:** Will Faller. **Page 220:** Genicom Corporation. **Page 223:** Will Faller.

A Message to the Student

With *Word/Information Processing: Essential Concepts,* Second Edition, you are about to embark on an informative tour of today's modern business office and the office of tomorrow. Like most people who begin something exciting, you are probably curious and a little nervous about the events to come. You may be perplexed about some of the new machines that make office work more efficient. These machines—word processing and related types of information processing equipment—are simply tools for doing a job. In this book you'll learn what these tools can do and why they're important—indeed essential—to the kinds and the quantity of work performed in today's offices.

Business offices vary in style. Some are very fast-paced and occasionally frantic environments; some are quiet and subdued; some are formal; some are more relaxed; still others balance a fast-paced style with a relaxed atmosphere. One thing all offices have in common, however, is that they have all been affected by developments in the world of electronics. In *Word/Information Processing: Essential Concepts,* you'll learn about many of those developments and about some of the specific ways in which they have changed office work.

Chapters 1, 2, and 3 deal with the way technology has affected our professional lives and office procedures. The way we work and the tools we work with are discussed. These chapters also explore the way information is processed in an office setting, the kinds of documents and information produced in that environment, and the variety of methods used to create business correspondence.

Chapters 4 and 5 deal with equipment and software and discuss the impact that word processing equipment, microcomputer technology, and software have had on the modern office. These chapters contain a description of how documents are processed using word processing equipment, as well as an overview of business applications software used with microcomputers. They also include information on the categories of computers and the various methods used to configure these systems.

The business of the modern office is in processing information. Chapter 6 is concerned with the various methods by which information is printed, reproduced, communicated and distributed, and stored and retrieved.

Chapters 7 and 8 deal with tying together all the concepts in Chapter 6 and showing how the new automated office relates to the employee. Information dealing with ergonomic issues, office organization, and employee productivity is included. Descriptions of different kinds of jobs relating to the automated office are also provided.

Word/Information Processing: Essential Concepts has been designed to be "user friendly"—that is, it has been designed with you, the reader, in mind. Its purpose is to give you the greatest amount of information in the clearest and most easily understood manner. Several design features make this possible. Each chapter is broken up into small sections preceded by headings that give you the gist of the information presented at a glance. Realistic situations are provided in the text to give you examples of and to clarify important concepts. Throughout the book you'll find charts, diagrams, photographs, and other illustrations that identify equipment, procedures, systems, and specific documents described in the text. Further, you will notice that certain words and phrases are printed in italic type. These are key terms in word and information processing. They are not only defined within the sentence or paragraph in which they are used, but they are defined again in the back of the book in a glossary that you will find helpful when you want to quickly review a term.

Following each chapter, a summary, vocabulary list, and set of questions will help you review the most important concepts presented. A case study after each chapter will give you an opportunity to apply what you've learned to a realistic situation.

Your future as an information processing employee is inevitably linked in some way to modern technology. *Word/Information Processing: Essential Concepts* has been developed to help you become familiar with that technology and thereby to help you acquire the confidence that will enable you to achieve your career goals. Think of this book as your own modern office companion, one that you can use—and keep using—as a source for basic office information.

Marilyn K. Popyk

CHAPTER 1

The Changing Office

Waking up to the sound of music from her digital clock radio, Marcy Lundquist, an administrative assistant, reaches for the remote control unit near her bed and turns on the TV set. After watching the morning news, she gets out of bed, showers, dresses, and goes to the kitchen of her apartment. There she pours a glass of orange juice, butters a roll, and puts a cup of water into her microwave oven. About two minutes later, the water is boiling. Marcy adds a spoonful of freeze-dried coffee to the cup of hot water and begins eating. After this quick breakfast, she gathers her coat and attaché case, turns on the automatic security alarm that will protect her apartment while she is away, and leaves for work.

One hundred years ago the morning routine of a typical office worker would have been quite different from Marcy's. The inventions Marcy takes for granted, such as the digital clock radio, remote-control television, and microwave oven, simply did not exist. These inventions, all fairly recent, affect the daily lives of working people today—people like you.

TECHNOLOGY AND YOU

If you stop to think about it, you can recognize the effect of modern technology on almost every aspect of your daily life. For example, you may be one of millions of people who owns a pocket calculator. These devices instantly perform mathematical operations that are a routine part of your personal finances, hobbies, or shopping. With a pocket calculator, you can quickly balance your checkbook or personal budget. You can compare unit prices at the supermarket or department store, figure out proportions of ingredients when you cook, and yardages of material when you sew. You can also compute batting averages, hiking distances, and measurement conversions for distances, weight, height, and temperature. The daily opportunities for using a pocket calculator are almost limitless.

You are also likely to come into contact with new technology

Computers have become a part of our everyday lives.

The Changing Office

and procedures in doing your personal banking. *Automatic tellers* let you deposit money, withdraw cash, and review the balance of your account—all without coming in contact with another person. You can find these automatic tellers at various locations in your community. Sometimes they are installed in factories, supermarkets, and offices so that workers can do their banking on the premises.

If you are one of the increasing number of people who have a home computer, you may be able to pay your bills without ever writing a personal check. Several kinds of home computers let you communicate directly with a bank computer which will transfer money from your own account to a creditor's account automatically.

No doubt you are familiar with other electronic inventions that have appeared in recent years. These include electronic car ignitions, portable miniature radios and cassette players, video recording machines, instant replay devices used in televised sports events, electronically controlled traffic lights, and digital wristwatches. Some of these are luxuries; all help make your daily life more enjoyable, comfortable, or safe.

TECHNOLOGY AND THE OFFICE

Just as these new inventions have changed your personal life, so have they changed the way work is done in offices. The office of today is almost certain to contain machines that did not exist decades or even a few years ago. It is important to know about these new machines—what they are, how they work. Learning about them will be one of your main goals in this book.

Setting the Stage: Three Key Inventions

Since the late nineteenth century, three inventions in particular have contributed to a revolution in office practices. These three inventions are the typewriter, the telephone, and the computer. Let's take a look at all three.

The Typewriter. Imagine yourself visiting an office in the mid-1800s, with its big wooden desks, quill pens, and inkstands—and no air-conditioning.

All correspondence is written by hand—by men. Women have not yet entered the work force. Information moves around, in, and out of the office at a rate extremely slow by today's standards. Businessmen trust most daily transactions to memory. A small number of office clerks and people who function as secretaries are responsible for items that have to be committed to paper. Letters are dictated by one person directly to another. Documents are copied by hand at an average speed of ten words

Contrast the nineteenth century office with the office of today.

a minute. The file cabinet is not yet a necessity, so papers are stacked on desks, stuck on desktop spikes, or tacked to the wall. But all this is about to change.

From 1820 to 1860, inventors in Europe and the United States developed several versions of a machine with a keyboard that an operator could use to print a letter. C. L. Sholes, a Milwaukee newspaperman, devised the best of these typing machines and in 1869 received the fifty-second patent issued for a typewriter. It was Sholes' machine that F. Remington and Sons bought and mass-produced, beginning in 1875.

Picture yourself as an office clerk in the 1870s, copying documents by hand all day with a pen you dip in an inkwell. One day your boss tells you he is getting in some new machines called typewriters that turn out printed documents at least three times faster than any clerk can produce by hand. Suddenly your training and experience are made obsolete by a new invention that makes a tremendous racket with clackety-clack keystrokes and a ringing bell.

You might have reacted the way many office workers did in the late nineteenth century. They resisted the change—even protested. But typewritten documents were so much easier to read and faster to produce that nothing could stop the typewriter from becoming an indispensable office tool.

By 1900 typewriters were less bulky. They could print upper- and lowercase letters, as well as numbers and a few special symbols. By that time, inventors and manufacturers had agreed on a standard keyboard arrangement of three rows of letters and a top row of numbers. Once manufacturers *standardized* keyboard design, trained typists could move from one office to an-

The Changing Office

other, easily transferring their skills to any kind of typewriter. (*Standardization* of equipment is the process by which manufacturers agree on a basic design for a specific piece of equipment.)

The Telephone. It is so common now to pick up a phone and dial that you might wonder what life was like before Alexander Graham Bell invented the telephone in 1876. Before that, people communicated by word of mouth—one person talking to another person—or by letter. Information traveled slowly; the greater the distance, the longer it took to get there. News about the Gold Rush in California, for example, took several days to reach the east coast by mail. A letter sent by ship from Europe might not reach the United States for six weeks.

There was a quicker way to transmit information before the telephone. It was the telegraph, invented in 1846 by Samuel Morse. By 1866, telegraph lines connected every part of the United States and even extended across the Atlantic. In general, the telegraph was mainly used by governments, newspapers, and large businesses. It was not practical for offices and homes.

The telephone had two advantages over the telegraph: It was less expensive, and it was direct voice communication instead of Morse code. This meant that no special operator was needed, and phones could be placed everywhere, between any two points, close together or far apart. Not only people in the same building or city, but also those in different cities and even countries could communicate with each other almost instantly—at the speed of electricity. All this meant a huge increase in the amount of information people could exchange.

Since its development in the 1880s, the telephone has evolved into one of the most important pieces of office equipment. Today it is used for much more than person-to-person voice communication. Executives telephone recorded dictation to secretaries who are free to transcribe it at a later, more convenient time. Businesses communicate written and graphic information over telephone lines. Telephones and other electronic systems are linked together in networks to provide countless more ways to exchange information that we discuss in later chapters.

The Computer. In 1890 the Census Bureau in Washington, D.C., had a problem. It had taken ten years to count and classify everyone living in the United States when the 1880 census was taken. But by 1890 the country had grown 25 percent. Until then the Bureau had used handwritten data sheets. That method would have to be replaced. The Census Bureau held a

The evolution of the telephone can be seen in its changing shape.

Technology and the Office

contest to see who could come up with the best technological solution to its problem. The winner was Dr. Herman Hollerith, a statistician from Buffalo, New York. He designed an electromechanical machine that could be set in action by punched cards. His device came to be known as the "census machine." Instead of taking ten years to complete, using Hollerith's machine, the 1890 census was finished in three years.

Hollerith was not the first person to design an automatic counting machine. For years mathematicians and inventors had tossed around ideas for a machine to solve complicated mathematical problems. But Hollerith's was one of the models that helped spur the development of the kinds of computers now used by businesses. In fact, Hollerith redesigned his equipment for use in business and founded a company that later merged with others to form what became International Business Machines (IBM).

During World War II, developments in mathematics and science made it possible to build a computer that led to the ones we use today—although you would not know it to look at it. It was a giant piece of equipment named the Electronic Numerical Integrator and Computer (ENIAC). It took up several rooms, and its operators had to climb up on ladders to run it. The first business computer was installed in 1954. In the next two decades over 100,000 computers were in use in the United States alone. More compact, versatile, and less expensive models were introduced.

Equipment was miniaturized, that is, manufacturers found new ways to get more electronic capability into less space. (*Miniaturization* is the ability to make very powerful parts in very small sizes.) Then came a technological development of great significance: the *microprocessor* (*micro* means small; the *processor* provides the ability to calculate). Also called a *microchip*, it is made of silicon (an element in sand). While philosophers considered such far-fetched ideas as how many angels can dance on the head of a pin, in our modern world today, a microchip is just as impossible to imagine. It is not much larger than the head of a pin. Yet electronics engineers measure its information processing capabilities in millions of instructions per second (MIPS)—more than 200 times more than ENIAC, which weighed 30 tons.

Not only are microchips small, but they operate on a fraction of the electricity it takes to run bigger equipment. This gave manufacturers the opportunity to design portable, less expensive equipment with a wider variety of applications. In 1977 Apple Computers became the first company to introduce for

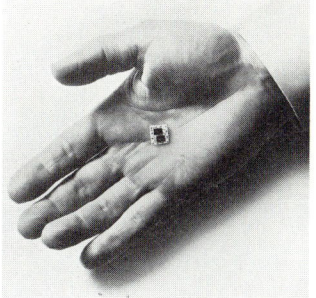

Tiny silicon chips can outperform the huge old ENIAC computer.

mass marketing a microcomputer it called a personal computer, small enough to fit on a desk. To give you an idea of how far miniaturization has come, the personal computers sold today are as powerful as the most powerful computer made twenty years ago.

Computers are still used to solve the complex mathematical problems for which they were originally designed. However, they have acquired thousands of other applications in science, medicine, industry, and business. Business could not exist today as we know it without computers to process data for such things as payrolls, customer account information, and inventory records.

The Changing Office

In many offices you will find evidence of equipment and procedures that have either developed from these three pieces of equipment—the typewriter, the telephone, and the computer—or expanded the use of the basic instruments. The dictating machine, for instance, was developed after the phonograph and was based on its technology. Thomas A. Edison did not consider his first recording device to be practical for office use, but in 1888 Alexander Graham Bell and others introduced a modified version of it designed as an office dictation machine.

With the invention of the dictation machine, offices had a

choice of two methods for recording spoken words: shorthand and, of course, the dictating machine. Both methods have advantages. Shorthand offers the advantages of speed, flexibility, and confidentiality. A good stenographer can take dictation almost as fast as the author can speak, and can understand or verify during dictation any of the author's speech patterns that might be hard to understand if they were transcribed from a dictating machine.

The dictating machine's advantages include flexibility and ease of use. The machine can be used at any time that is convenient. It requires very little skill to operate, and transcribing recorded dictation does not require the same type or degree of training that shorthand does. In recent years the dictating machine, combined with other kinds of automated equipment, has played an important part in changing office procedures.

Not only is it necessary to produce documents in an office, it is necessary to reproduce them. Carbon paper came into use at about the same time the typewriter became an office tool. Before that, documents had to be copied by hand, one at a time. This was a time-consuming task unless many copies were required. In that case the original document was sent out to be engraved on a plate, then printed in the same way newspapers or magazines were printed.

In the 1960s came the photocopier, a machine that copied documents by photography. The photocopier revolutionized the copying process. For the first time you could reproduce information quickly and cheaply, copying not only typewritten and handwritten documents but other printed material as well.

Ways Technology Is Used. Continuing improvements have made it possible for the telephone, typewriter, computer, dictating machine, and photocopier to serve the ever-increasing needs of business for specialized ways of handling information. For example, the telephone has evolved from a one-to-one, person-to-person, or station-to-station link to one in which switchboards can link several parties or offices together for conference calls. On some telephones, merely pressing one digit instantly connects you with a person or office whose number you frequently dial. You can also speak by phone to people who are traveling by car, train, or airplane, or even to someone who is walking on the street if that person has the proper kind of phone receiver. Many of these changes were brought about by improvements in computer technology.

When electricity was added to the manual typewriter, the result was the electric typewriter, which is faster and more versatile than manual machines. Today, coupling microprocessor chips with the electric typewriter has created a new class of typewriters called *electronic* typewriters, which have special features to aid the work of the typist.

Office Automation. Essentially the same kinds of office tasks are being performed today that were performed in the past. Improved equipment, however, permits you to streamline the flow of work at the same time it provides a greater choice of ways in which to get the work done. The key word is *automation*. Automation is the system of production that uses "self-acting," or automatic machines.

This improved equipment makes more efficient methods of work possible, which in turn create a new kind of office environment—often referred to as the *automated* or *electronic office*. The automated office uses new technologies such as the electronic typewriter and the computer to make office work faster and more accurate. New machines improve on older models' speed and ease of operation; and many of these machines can be made to interact with each other to bring about even greater efficiency in office work.

Business organizations must have timely information to perform effectively. In the past our economic growth has been based largely on industry and manufacturing. Now new growth is coming from businesses that sell services rather than goods. Some of these businesses sell information directly to their customers; others use information to provide some other service more efficiently. Whatever service a company provides, its success will depend on how well the company manages its information. For this reason, the percentage of people employed in office work will continue to grow. Office automation encompasses six major technologies:

>**data processing** Information in numeric form usually calculated by a computer.
>
>**word processing** Information in text form—words and numbers.
>
>**graphics** Information that may be in the form of numbers and words, then keyed into a computer and displayed on a screen in a graph, chart, table, or other visual form that makes it easier to understand.
>
>**image** Information in the form of pictures. Here an actual picture or photograph is taken, entered into the computer, and shown on a screen.
>
>**voice** The processing of information in the form of spoken words.

The six major technologies of office automation can function effectively only so far as the people using them function effectively.

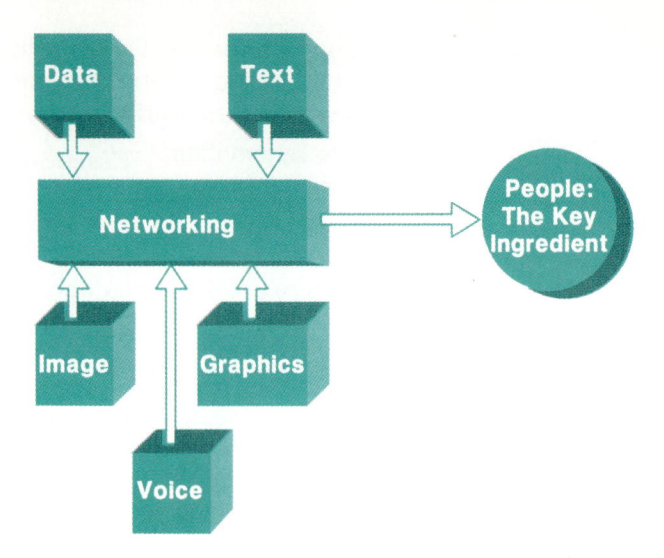

networking The linking together electronically of computer and other office equipment for processing data, words, graphics, image, and voice. "Networking" the equipment of various technologies, so that people and machines can communicate and interact, further expands the possibilities for processing and managing information.

Throughout this textbook, we explore each of these technologies and look at how office automation helps you become a more efficient and productive office employee.

Information is only valuable if it can be communicated easily and quickly to the people who need it. Technology too is useful only if it can be applied and easily used to help people. Making people more productive through the use of technology is the major goal of office automation. Whatever equipment a company uses, whatever information it processes, people are the key ingredient. They make the decisions and act on the information.

Office equipment has changed so much since the mid-nineteenth century that it has changed the office environment. Offices are not the static work places they once were. Today's office is an exciting, changing place. Manufacturers now offer businesses such a wide array of equipment that you are bound to find differences from one office to the next. If you work in the same office for any length of time, you are almost certain to see continual changes in the systems you use and probably in your style of working, too. You might, for instance, one day find yourself working at home instead of in an office, sitting in front of a machine that has a keyboard like a typewriter and a screen like a television set. You may use this machine to communicate with someone who also works for your company but who lives and works in another city or state.

INFORMATION AND THE OFFICE

As new and improved equipment keeps appearing in offices, you may pause and wonder why. Why keep creating new ways to do things? What is wrong with the old and regular way of doing business? These are the same questions many clerks and stenographers asked in the 1870s when the typewriter was introduced to offices. Why, people asked, do we need this machine when things are going along very well as they are? To answer these questions, it is necessary to look first at the basic function of business offices.

Managing Business Information: The Goal of the Office

Even if you have never worked in an office yourself, you probably know someone who has. You know that most offices have a similar look to them—there are desks, chairs, telephones, and at least one typewriter. But what do you know about the work that all offices have in common?

Regardless of size, all business offices manage information of one kind or another. This usually involves originating, processing, reproducing, filing, and storing information as well as communicating and distributing it to people who need or want it.

Information Defined

Of course, to say that all business offices manage information is a fairly broad statement. To understand why it is an important one, let's define information. *Information* is the orderly and useful arrangement of facts, or *data*, so that they are accurate, timely, complete, and concise. To create information, you start with facts or data that you classify or organize.

Let's assume that you want to take a vacation. You might have some idea about where you want to go and how to get there. You send for travel brochures, maps, airline schedules, and rates. You get a list of hotels. You listen to weather forecasts. You figure out how much you have to spend.

So far, these items are separate, unrelated facts. It is up to you to organize them and give them some meaning. You have to convert the facts to information that you can use to make a decision.

You might separate places at the seashore from those in the mountains, warm places from cold, or places you can drive to from those so far you have to go by air, and so on. Once you have

Information and the Office

sorted your facts, you will probably find that making a decision is easy. If you were a travel agent, your customers would pay you to do this for them. Part of your business activities, then, would be managing travel information.

In the business world, data is processed in much the same way to create information that then may be used by employees and clients. For example, suppose you took a phone message from Martin Chase for Delores Manning, who is out of the office. You take certain data from Mr. Chase including his name, who the message is for (Ms. Manning), the message itself, the date and time of the call, and Mr. Chase's phone number. Before you hang up, you doublecheck to make sure the data you have is accurate.

As you receive the data from Mr. Chase, you transfer it to a phone message form that organizes it in a useful way. The message form has a place for the date and time, the name of the person the message is for, the name of the person who called, the phone number of the person who called, the message, and the name of the person who took the message. When Ms. Manning returns to the office, she receives the filled-out form which conveys information that is accurate, timely, concise, and complete.

Problems of Increased Paperwork

The success of a business depends in part on how efficiently it manages the information that is important to it. As the amount of information increases, businesses occasionally find themselves searching for ways to keep paperwork under control. Business offices in the United States create a staggering amount of information on paper every day—more than 600 million computer printouts, 234 million photocopies, and 76 million letters, according to a New York consulting firm. Eastman Kodak Company estimates that the number of documents handled by an average employee is more than 4,000 pieces—or two full file drawers—per year, and growing.

This increase in the amount of information we handle is due in large part to the ability of machines to create and process it. An IBM study shows that the cost of a typical data processing transaction has fallen from $14.54 in 1955 to 4¢ today. It also took over 900 times longer in 1955 to process a single transaction than it does now. Computers have reduced the time we spend on each transaction from 375 to .4 seconds. The transactions surveyed by IBM included payroll, maintaining files, calculations, referring to tables, and preparing reports.

You might think that automation would reduce the number of office jobs available. But the U.S. Bureau of Labor Statistics es-

The number of office jobs continues to grow.

timates that the number of white-collar office workers in the United States will rise from 37.9 million in the 1970s to over 55 million in the 1990s. In short, the management of information does and will continue to depend on people—those who operate the machines and those who reach the decisions that make the information useful.

Productivity in the Office

In the office, *productivity* refers to the output per employee. A productive office is one in which people produce accurate, timely, concise, and complete information of a particular type in an appropriate form at the lowest possible cost and make it available to those who need it.

Productivity is greatly affected by the kinds of equipment and methods available to help employees do their work. For this reason managers look to automation as a way of increasing office productivity. You have already seen examples of how machines can speed the processing of information. An inexpensive pocket calculator can do mathematical problems that would take a per-

Information and the Office

son trained in math much longer to complete, while a large computer can handle with astonishing speed the work of an army of clerks.

As automated equipment and methods make it easier to perform routine tasks faster, office workers have more time to take on more challenging and creative work. This has important implications for your career. Many office workers today rarely use a typewriter. You will more likely produce correspondence on a word processor—electronic equipment that makes it possible to keyboard and revise a document more quickly than you could on any typewriter. This will give you time for administrative responsibilities that no machine could do, interesting things such as organizing meetings for the boss and correlating information from other departments.

The new equipment has also changed life in the office for executives. A national sales director who used to spend endless hours creating a budget using a pencil, paper, and a calculator can now do the same thing faster and more simply on a desk-top computer. The manager keyboards the numbers for the budget. Then by pressing a few keys, the computer makes the calculation and displays the results on the screen instantly. This gives the director time to meet personally with members of the sales force and spend more time developing marketing techniques for the company's products.

New equipment has also changed the design of offices, stimulating a concern for the relationship of employees to their working environment. New kinds of office equipment require new kinds of office furniture and new ways of organizing space so that the work can be done efficiently and comfortably. The

Modern office design is open and inviting.

amount of space that was adequate for a standard electric typewriter is probably not adequate for more up-to-date equipment. Some offices have grown quieter because the equipment has become quieter, and thick partitions between cubicles or work areas are no longer necessary. Other factors such as the kind of lighting in an office, the arrangement of work areas, the location of machines, and the quality of air in an office are being carefully considered by office planners in an effort to improve the interaction of people and machines.

In general, executives have begun to pay more attention to the office as an environment to be managed. They view it as a place where people, equipment, a group of functions, and appropriate procedures can be organized to produce accurate, timely, complete, and concise information at low cost.

THE INFORMATION PROCESSING CYCLE

The way an office is organized to handle information is called its system for *information processing*. By coordinating equipment, people, and procedures, the information processing system is used to make sure that needed information is received by office workers, managers, and customers.

The *information processing cycle* consists of a regular sequence of five steps, or stages, that recur frequently in the processing of typical types of information in offices, such as letters and memos. The stages in the information processing cycle are:

> **input**
> **processing**
> **output**
> **distribution/communication**
> **storage and retrieval**

Let's take a closer look at this cycle by following a specific example as it goes through each of these stages.

Input

Juan Serantino, an underwriting agent at the Mutual Insurance Company, receives an application for a life insurance policy from Margaret Chan. The application is a printed form that has been filled out by Ms. Chan.

To the Mutual Insurance Company, this application is a form of input. *Input* consists of facts or data that are entered into a system for processing. Input can come into the office from outside, or it can be originated within the office. It can come in several forms: *numeric* data, such as Ms. Chan's age and the date of her birth (for instance, "10/6/50" for October 6, 1950); *alphabetic* data such as *F* for "female" and *S* for "single"; and *alphanumeric* data such as Ms. Chan's address.

Information processing cycle.

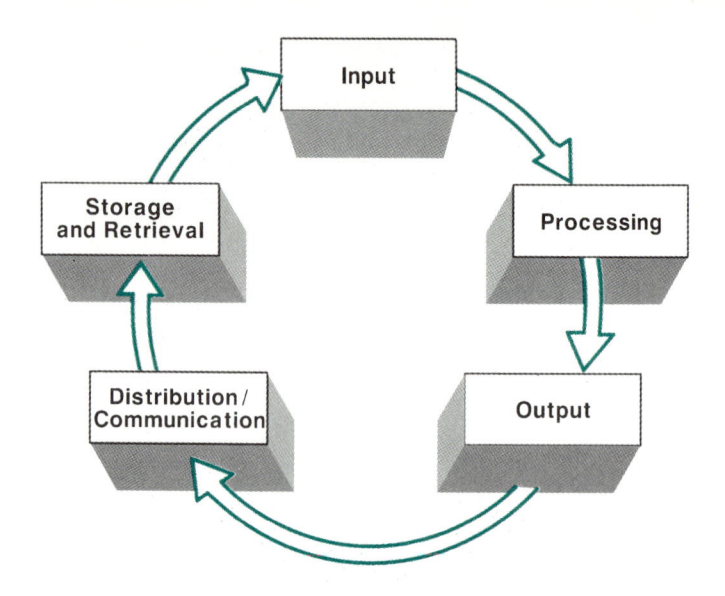

In another office, input might be in the form of *graphics* such as charts and graphs. An electronics company, for example, might have input in the form of bar charts showing industry-wide sales growth in such consumer areas as watches and earphones.

A large percentage of the paper input received in an office is in the form of *images*—photocopies, pictures, signatures, and logos. In the personnel department of a company, standard personnel data includes photocopies of résumés, acceptance letters, letters of recommendation, contract agreements, and corporate waivers.

Still another kind of input is *voice*. This might be dictation for a letter, a recording of a business meeting, or a telephoned order for a product.

Thus, input, the first stage in the information processing cycle, can consist of almost any facts or data that come into the office or that originate in the office. Depending on its type, input will be processed manually or with the help of electronic equipment.

Processing

The second stage of the information processing cycle is known as the *processing* stage. In the processing stage, input is organized to become information. It may be sorted, classified, or edited. Sales reports, for example, may be sorted by geographic region and further classified according to the type of product sold. Input may be subjected to mathematical calculations or

The Changing Office

other logical processes. It may be summarized, checked, and so on.

In the processing stage Mr. Serantino goes over Ms. Chan's application, verifies the facts or data it contains, and applies certain prescribed rules that Mutual has for processing insurance policies.

In many offices machines play an important role in the processing stage of the cycle. Depending on the kind of input, two kinds of machine processing may occur: *data* processing and *word* processing.

Data processing is usually done by a computer, which carries out mathematical and other logical manipulations on numbers or other symbols fed into it. (A company's payroll can be prepared by a data processing system.) The instructions as to how to process the data are known as the *program*, which can be stored in the computer.

In its broadest sense, *word processing* is a total system of personnel, procedures, and equipment designed to handle business communications efficiently and economically. In a narrower sense, word processing involves the manipulation of alphabetic and numeric characters to serve various communication purposes. The alphabetic characters are often in the form of *text*—words and sentences.

Word processing can be done on several kinds of machines, which have in common the fact that they all have keyboards, much like a standard typewriter keyboard. They also all have a central processing unit—the "brains" of the operation—which allows keystrokes to be recorded and stored.

Words and numbers are recorded, or entered into the word processing equipment, by *keyboarding*—pressing the keys. Unlike typewriting, keyboarding does not assume that a final printed copy is produced as the operator presses the keys. In keyboarding, the characters do not appear immediately as printed characters on paper. Further, certain production steps such as setting margins, backspacing, and aligning characters in columns are carried out automatically according to a program that is stored in the machine.

In processing Ms. Chan's application, Mr. Serantino will use both data and word processing functions. He will probably use the data processing functions of the company's computer to determine if Ms. Chan has ever applied for an insurance policy from Mutual before. Once this check has been made, and if Mr. Serantino finds that Ms. Chan has never before applied for a policy, he may obtain calculations of how much risk Mutual will take on if it insures someone of Ms. Chan's age, medical history, and occupation.

At this point, Mr. Serantino will have a formal policy prepared for Ms. Chan. Assembling the text of Ms. Chan's policy is a job for word processing equipment. An insurance policy consists of paragraphs of text that state what the insurance company will do under specified circumstances. Many of these paragraphs are the same from policy to policy. These paragraphs can be stored in word processors, retrieved easily, and inserted into a policy for a specific person.

Output

Once the policy has been assembled, it enters the third stage of the information processing cycle, known as *output*. At the output stage a readable form of copy is produced. This copy may be typed, or it may be produced on a printer attached to word processing equipment. In some offices this stage includes typesetting and printing of documents.

Output also includes the making of multiple copies, although sometimes the only output is a corrected typewritten copy with a carbon. The number of copies and the method of reproduction (called *reprographics*) depend on how many people must receive the information, what kinds of duplication equipment the office has, and the cost of duplicating the information.

In the case of Ms. Chan's insurance policy, four copies will be made—two for Ms. Chan (one of which she will sign and return), one for Mutual's Records Department, and one for Mr. Serantino's files. These copies will be produced on a carbon pack policy form consisting of five preprinted forms (one original and four copies), interleaved with carbon paper and bound at the top and perforated. The operator keys in the command to print, and the information pertaining to Ms. Chan's policy is printed in the appropriate places on the policy form. When the entire form has been printed, the operator removes the carbon pack from the printer, tears it along the perforated line at the top, and removes the carbon paper. The copies are then ready for distribution.

Distribution/Communication

Distribution of information is the fourth step in the information processing cycle. The purpose of this step is to make sure that the information is *communicated* to the people who need it. Before automated equipment was available, distribution usually consisted of giving people their copies by interoffice mail, messenger service, or the postal system. Today you can distribute information in different ways depending on the form in which it is needed and where the recipients are located. Ms. Chan's policy will probably be sent to the Records Department of Mutual Insurance Company by interoffice mail and to Ms. Chan via the U.S. Postal Service.

Storage and Retrieval

The fifth stage of the processing cycle, *storage and retrieval*, includes all records management activities in an office, such as storing, retrieving, and maintaining files. If you worked in the Records Department of Mutual Insurance Company, you would have the copy of Ms. Chan's policy to put in the file for new or pending policyholders. Depending on the kind of equipment Mutual has, you might file a paper copy of the policy, such as a carbon copy or a photocopy, or you may keep a copy on a form of magnetic media. Some offices now have machines that produce miniature copies on film.

You have now followed a document through the five stages of the information processing cycle. The document followed an established and commonly recurring path. The term *work flow* refers to this path from the start to the finish of a task. Beginning with Ms. Chan's application form, you observed the logical flow of information from an input stage, to a processing stage, to an output stage, to a distribution stage, and finally to a storage and retrieval stage. Since these stages are constantly being repeated in the office and since what is stored may be retrieved and processed again, the whole operation can be viewed as a cycle.

THE ROLE OF WORD PROCESSING IN INFORMATION PROCESSING

As information is cycled through its five stages, various parts of the information processing system are used. As you have seen, information processing includes both word processing and data processing. It includes ways to communicate, store, and retrieve information. It also includes administrative support—other secretarial functions (such as organizing meetings) that are necessary to ensure the availability of information.

The term *word/information processing* is sometimes used to describe the information processing system. This term indicates that although word processing is only a part of the whole, it is a vital part—because information in the form of words is the primary way we communicate with each other.

The Development of Word Processing Equipment

Word processing began in 1964 when IBM used the term to introduce its Magnetic Tape Selectric Typewriter, or MT/ST. IBM's machine was essentially a Selectric typewriter that recorded keystrokes on magnetic tape like a tape recorder records voice or music. If you made a typing error, you could correct it by recording a new keystroke over the wrong one on the tape. It was therefore possible to create a perfect, error-free tape. Then you could print as many perfect copies as you needed by simply turning a knob. The MT/ST printed about 180 words a minute—faster than almost anyone can type. Clearly it was a dramatic advance beyond the typewriter.

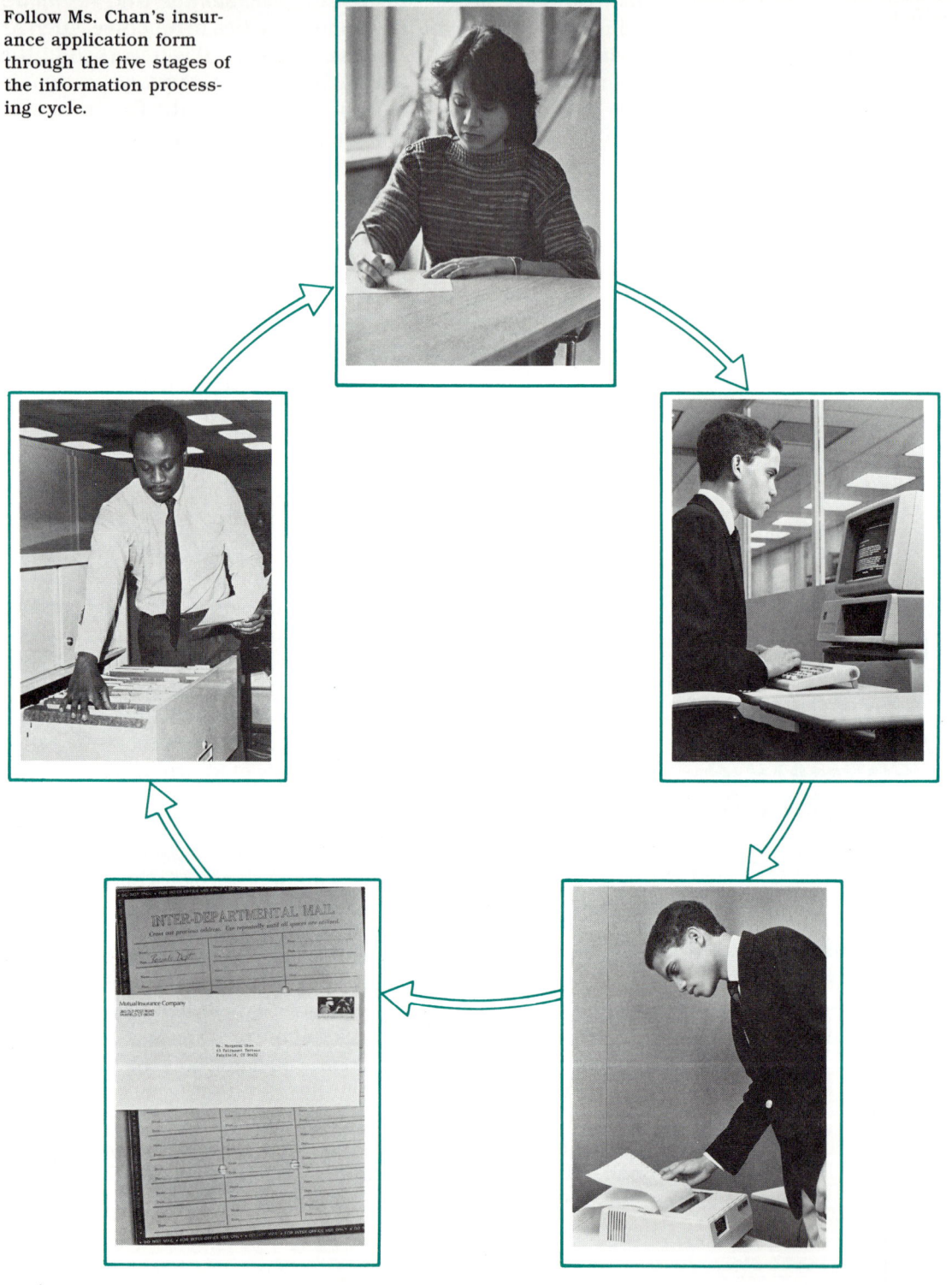

Follow Ms. Chan's insurance application form through the five stages of the information processing cycle.

The Changing Office

Other manufacturers, or *vendors*, soon introduced word processors and added their own technological improvements. The *magnetic media* that record keystrokes took on new forms, such as tape cassettes, cards, and disks. This made it possible to store more documents in less space. By far the most important word processing innovation was the video display terminal (VDT). A video display has a special tube designed to show clear, readable text. The scientific name for it is a cathode-ray tube and, in fact, a video display is often called a *CRT*.

When you keyboard words and numbers, the text you see on the screen is called the *soft copy*. You can store the soft copy of a document on a flexible plastic magnetic disk, sometimes called a *floppy diskette*.

Once you keyboard the text of a document, you can manipulate the soft copy on the screen—changing, deleting, rearranging, and inserting new text—until it is exactly the way you want it. When the document is correct, you can press one or two keys to store it indefinitely on disk or print it on paper. The paper copy is called a *hard copy*.

So far we have discussed a computer that processes data and a word processor, that is, a computer that processes words. The microcomputer, or personal computer, changed this, since it can be used to process data and words equally well. A microcomputer can perform word processing functions if word processing software (a word processing program) is used with it.

There are already more than half a million word processors in offices around the nation. Their capabilities are proving useful in a wide variety of office situations.

People: The Key Element in Information Processing

Up-to-date equipment plays an important role in the information processing cycle, but it is only a helping role. The most vital role is played by the people who originate information and handle it as it goes through the various stages of the cycle. The office workers, after all, are the ones who decide the best way to arrange the information, the best way to have copies made, and the best way to store information so that it can be retrieved when needed. In making these decisions, office workers must be aware of the need for productivity. They must understand how to carry out tasks in the most efficient and profitable way, regardless of the kind of equipment that is available. "Good people," as one writer put it, "are your most valuable resource." The new ideas they pump into an organization are its lifeblood. Their ability to put concepts to work is the substance of its success.

This book is designed to help you become one of those "good

New equipment is displayed at conventions and trade fairs.

people"—to make you familiar with the concepts and equipment associated with information processing. The more fully you understand the new and changing office environment, the better you will be at your job.

CHAPTER SUMMARY

- Everyone is affected by new products of technology.
- New office machines allow many jobs to be done faster than they were done in the past.
- The typewriter, telephone, and computer are three inventions that have radically changed the nature of office work.
- Office automation means the use of new technologies, including computers, word processors, and high-speed photocopiers, to make office work more efficient.
- Information is most useful when it is accurate, timely, concise, and complete.
- The success of any business depends in large part on its ability to manage information.
- A productive office is one in which people produce useful information in an appropriate form, at the lowest possible cost, and make it available to those who need it.
- Information processing refers to a system of people, procedures, and equipment organized to carry out the information-handling functions of the office.
- The information processing cycle has five stages: input, processing, output, distribution/communication, and storage and retrieval.

Office automation encompasses six major technologies: data processing, word processing, graphics, image, voice, and networking. These technologies are illustrated here.

Data processing is performed on mainframe computers (above) and microcomputers (below) as well.

Word processing can also be performed on equipment especially designed for word processing, called *dedicated word processors.*

It might take a lengthy explanation in words to express the idea conveyed in this one graphic image on the screen.

Using the human voice to process information can range from simply speaking on the telephone to bypassing the keyboard and speaking directly to the computer.

An image processor photographs an image, converts the image to signals that a computer can understand, and then displays the image on the screen.

The computers in this office are linked together, or *networked*.

This is the PPG Industries building in Pittsburgh, Pennsylvania. It was one of the first buildings constructed to accommodate an electronic network. All the cabling and wiring necessary to link all the electronic equipment in the building were done as part of the construction work.

- Word processing is concerned with the manipulation of text—that is, words and sentences. Through a system of trained personnel, specific procedures, and automated equipment, word processing puts business communications into readable form.
- Information that has been processed and has reached the storage and retrieval stage can be recycled to become an element in the creation of new information.
- Since people play a vital role in the information processing system, it is important for today's office workers to be familiar with automated equipment and new procedures.

INFORMATION PROCESSING VOCABULARY

automation
data
data processing
information
information
  processing cycle
input
keyboarding

micro
miniaturization
office automation
output
productivity
standardization
word processing
work flow

CHAPTER QUESTIONS

1. Think about some of the ways in which technology affects your daily life. How might your life be different without modern technology? Give a few specific examples.
2. One complaint often heard about machines is that they put many people out of work. Since 1875 many work-saving machines have been introduced into offices, yet the number of people employed in offices has increased. How do you explain this fact?
3. What were some of the advantages that machines brought to office work in the late 1800s and early 1900s?
4. Why might office workers be reluctant to welcome new office machines? What advice would you give them?
5. Beginning in the 1870s, standardization became more and more important in offices. What advantages did it offer? Is standardization important today?
6. Why is productivity so necessary in the modern office? What are some of the factors that affect productivity?

7. What is the relationship between facts or data and information?
8. Automated equipment is important in today's offices. But people are important, too. Why is the physical and psychological well-being of workers important to office managers today?
9. How does the flow of information into and out of an office resemble a cycle?
10. What is the relationship between information processing and word processing?

CASE STUDY

The Malamud Advertising Agency is a small company that develops advertising for department stores, hardware stores, and card shops. Its staff consists of a president, an account executive (who functions the way a sales representative does), a secretary, and a copywriter. The office has two electric typewriters and a small photocopier.

The president and the account executive spend much of their time outside the office, meeting with current and potential clients. After these meetings, the president and the account executive call the secretary and dictate correspondence, such as follow-up letters. Often, the secretary has to interrupt other work to take their calls, transcribing the information they give in shorthand. The secretary also performs administrative and recordkeeping duties for the company. Contracts for new business are drawn up and typed by the secretary. Each contract has many paragraphs, some of which are repeated from contract to contract.

Every new ad campaign begins with a meeting of the president, the account executive, and the copywriter. The secretary types the new advertising copy, which may go through several drafts before it is mailed to the client. Copies are made of all contracts, correspondence, and advertising copy, and filed away.

Based on your understanding of the information processing cycle, identify the sources of information input and information output for the Malamud agency.

CHAPTER 2

Documents

Sam Parker reaches into his in-basket and pulls out the stack of mail his secretary has brought in earlier. There are two interoffice memos and two letters. As he expects, both memos contain brief announcements of upcoming meetings, one with the Sales Department, the other with Publicity. Mr. Parker notes the dates on his desk calendar and then turns his attention to the two letters. The first is a short letter from a customer, requesting information. Mr. Parker makes a note to himself to respond as soon as possible. The second letter, from a data processing consultant he met with last week, consists of a ten-page legal agreement. Mr. Parker looks it over briefly, checks his watch, and sets the agreement aside. He has a meeting to attend.

Every day businesspeople across the country send and receive vast amounts of information. They communicate with the public and with other people in business. Some of these communications are simple, brief memos, and some are as complicated as the lengthy legal agreement Mr. Parker will have to examine later.

PROCESSING INFORMATION

Much of this business communication occurs in offices throughout the country. Consequently, regardless of the size or nature of the company's business, the modern office is an information management center where speed, efficiency, and accuracy are three keys to success. The more quickly and efficiently incoming information is processed, distributed, and acted on, the more successful the business is likely to be.

Consider, for example, the use of marketing information in product development and sales. Fizz-Pop and Flavor-Rite are two soft-drink producers in direct competition with each other. Both companies conduct periodic marketing surveys to learn more about consumer preferences. Fizz-Pop, however, has a far more efficient information processing system than Flavor-Rite. Survey information is immediately channeled into the system when it comes into Fizz-Pop's Marketing Department, whereas at Flavor-Rite, surveys are piled on top of a file cabinet until someone can get around to acting on them. At Fizz-Pop, survey findings are handled by secretaries using word processors and a computer; at Flavor-Rite, a team of people work together to tabulate the findings by hand. The printing of the findings is also computerized at Fizz-Pop, while its competitor has to rely on handfed copying machines. Because Fizz-Pop can compile and print its survey findings more quickly and accurately than its competitor, Fizz-Pop's management is able to act on this information with greater speed. As a result of its greater efficiency, Fizz-Pop discovered two months earlier than Flavor-Rite that consumers do not want caffeine in their drinks.

Fizz-Pop immediately set out to design a new ad campaign stressing the fact that its cola was caffeine-free. Within three months after these findings were made known to Fizz-Pop management, the very first television and print ads appeared. Flavor-Rite, on the other hand, was so late in finding the public attitudes toward caffeine that on the day the Fizz-Pop television ads appeared nationwide, Flavor-Rite managers were just beginning to debate whether they should research a way to develop its products without caffeine. By processing information more efficiently than its competitor, Fizz-Pop could make decisions in a timely manner and maximize sales—and profits.

Documents

DISTRIBUTING INFORMATION

Businesses use many kinds of written and oral communication in distributing information. For example, Fizz-Pop research results were distributed by a combination of letters, preprinted survey forms, interoffice memos, and detailed reports. Regional managers in California and Chicago received copies of the survey findings and immediately telephoned the central office in New York City to discuss their reactions. A series of face-to-face meetings or general conferences involving representatives from the company's research, sales, and marketing departments were held. Decisions made at these meetings were translated into a formal proposal, which was then sent to the company president for final approval. The president, in turn, penciled in several changes before having the revised document distributed to the appropriate people.

KINDS OF BUSINESS COMMUNICATIONS

You know that employees in an office deal with a great variety of communications daily. Letters are received, memos dictated, and so on. All these forms of communication that convey information are called *documents*. Although in information processing a document is sometimes distinguished from simple correspondence as being longer and more complex, this book does not make that distinction. For our purposes, a document is any business communication that contains information.

Documents can be divided into a number of categories. These include correspondence, reports, statistical tables, and forms. Sometimes these categories overlap. For instance, a statistical table may appear in a report. The various categories can best be understood, however, if they are looked at separately.

Having face-to-face meetings can help people reach a decision.

Kinds of Business Communications 27

Correspondence

The most common written business communication is correspondence—letters and memos. Since much of this book deals with the creation, processing, distribution, and storage of correspondence, let's take a close look at the two main types.

Letters. Business letters serve many purposes in the modern office. Depending on the nature of the particular business, letters may be sent to customers and clients, suppliers, manufacturers, government agencies, contractors, or just about any organization, company, or individual. Some letters are intended to obtain information, others to provide it. Letters are used to express gratitude for, or dissatisfaction with, services rendered; to prompt customers to pay their bills; to generate new business; or just to "stay in touch." Sometimes a brief letter serves as a cover letter to accompany more lengthy documents.

Although most business letters are no longer than one to three typewritten pages, some do run longer. The author of a letter may create his or her document by dictating it to a secretary skilled in shorthand, by writing it in longhand, or composing it at a keyboard (typewriter or word processor), or dictating it into a machine. In general, the amount of revision required in preparing a letter is relatively small, usually involving only minor wording changes or corrections.

Memos. Memos, like business letters, serve various purposes in an office. However, while letters are generally directed to people or organizations outside the company, memos normally are used for communication within a company. Interoffice memos may be sent from one floor to another, from one office to another, or from one branch of a company to another.

Each memo is about a specific topic. It may serve to set up a meeting, request information, confirm a decision, or announce a policy change. In general, memos are shorter and less formal than letters, although this is not always the case. The author of a memo prepares it in the same way a letter is prepared: dictating it to a secretary, writing it in longhand, composing it at a keyboard, or dictating it into a machine. The amount of revision involved in preparing a memo is usually minor.

Just as most companies have letterhead stationery, so do most have printed forms for memos.

Reports

Many of the decisions made within a company are based on reports. Reports may be as short as a few pages or as long as 100 or more pages. They may be as technical as a pharmaceutical company's detailed analysis of a new drug or as simple as a sales representative's summary of a sales call.

The main purpose of a report is to present facts, and for this reason accuracy in preparation is crucial. Reports must also be prepared clearly for the reader's comprehension. It is not uncommon for a report to go through several drafts in order to achieve both accuracy and clarity. In any of these drafts the author may decide to revise content or language or even undertake a major reorganization. The longer and more complex a report is, the more time is usually required to prepare a final copy.

The author of a report may dictate to a secretary or into a machine, compose at a keyboard, or write in longhand. Often the author's own words are combined with excerpts from other documents or sources. A government research report on urban crime, for example, might include a statistical table that appeared in a newspaper or magazine article. A corporation's annual report to stockholders usually contains a chart showing the company's yearly figures and earnings growth.

Statistical Tables

If you have ever had to type a table with long columns of numeric data, you know how difficult it can be. Each statistical entry must be correctly placed on the page. Decimals must be carefully aligned and groups of figures must be precisely spaced. Although word processing can help make some of those tasks easier, painstaking proofreading of statistical tables is still essential to ensure accuracy.

A complex report may require heavy revision.

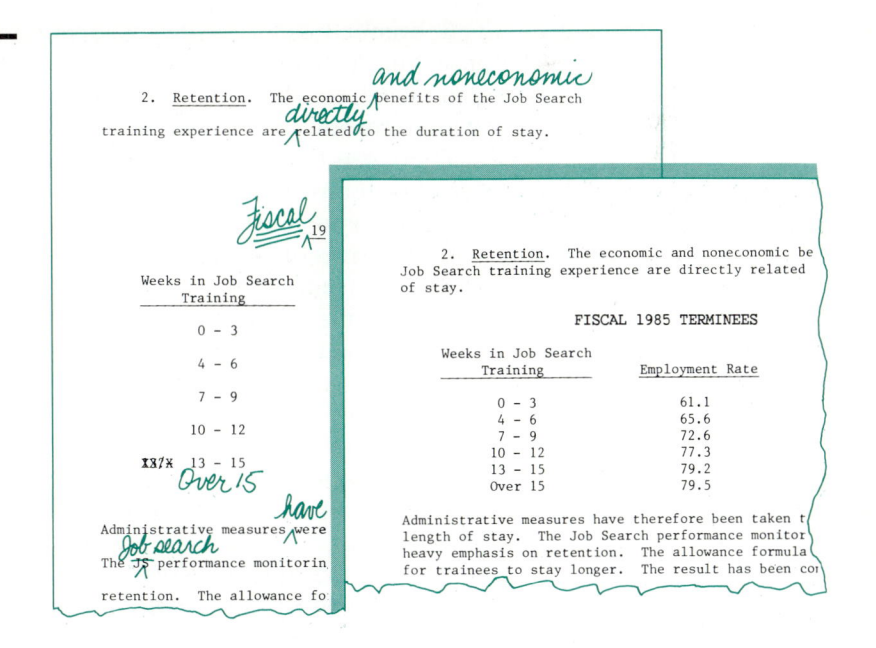

FISCAL 1985 TERMINEES

Weeks in Job Search Training	Employment Rate
0 - 3	61.1
4 - 6	65.6
7 - 9	72.6
10 - 12	77.3
13 - 15	79.2
Over 15	79.5

Kinds of Business Communications

29

The author of a statistical table usually prepares the document by hand. Other methods of creation, such as dictation or keyboarding, would be either too awkward or too time-consuming.

Statistical tables are common in almost every field. Product sales reports, for example, tabulate sales figures by region and date. Brokerage houses and other financial institutions compile statistics about stocks and bonds, earnings and dividends, interest and mortgage rates. Medical researchers prepare statistical reports detailing the results of laboratory experiments. As you will learn, office automation has done much to facilitate the processing of these varied and frequently complex documents.

Forms

You are well acquainted with forms. They are a familiar part of everyone's daily life.

> "Fill out these forms in triplicate and leave them at the desk."
>
> "Please complete and mail this form no later than . . .."
>
> "The top copy of the enclosed form should be returned to the Department of . . ."

Order forms, tax forms, application forms, insurance claims forms—sometimes it seems that almost everything people do these days requires a form of one kind or another. Indeed, in some offices that is not too far from the truth, because the paperwork handled by certain businesses consists *mainly* of forms.

In businesses forms are most commonly used to standardize and simplify the way in which certain kinds of information are processed. Product invoices and supply requisition forms are two examples of this kind of document.

There are two stages in the preparation of forms. First, the form itself has to be developed. Forms may then be photocopied or printed in sizable quantities. Sometimes, of course, preprinted forms are simply purchased from an office supply company. These forms may be packaged with carbon sheets or with paper having a carbon backing, allowing the user to make multiple copies at the same time the top, original form is being filled out.

The second stage in working with forms is filling them out. Once a form has been created and reproduced, either within the office or outside, the expectation is that it will be filled out—information will be inserted in the blanks.

In filling out forms, accuracy and neatness are essential. Care in completing and proofreading them is a must. Imagine, for example, a purchase order processed by an agricultural ma-

Forms are standardized to simplify information processing.

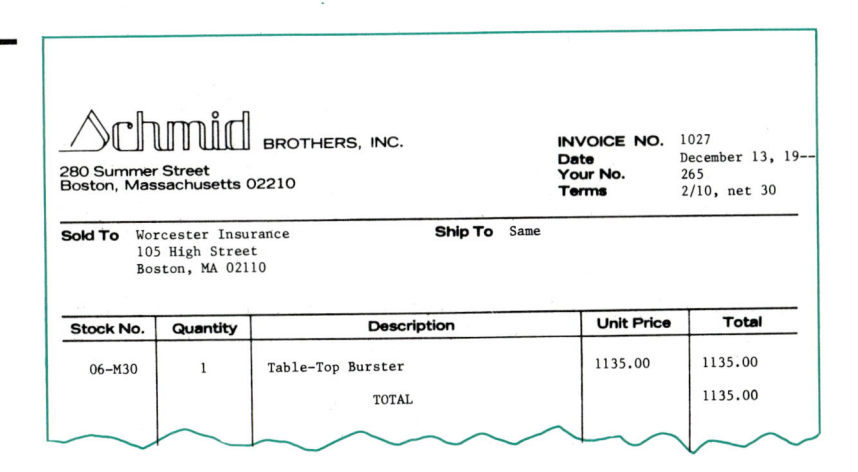

Schmid BROTHERS, INC.
280 Summer Street
Boston, Massachusetts 02210

INVOICE NO. 1027
Date December 13, 19--
Your No. 265
Terms 2/10, net 30

Sold To Worcester Insurance
         105 High Street
         Boston, MA 02110

Ship To Same

Stock No.	Quantity	Description	Unit Price	Total
06-M30	1	Table-Top Burster	1135.00	1135.00
		TOTAL		1135.00

chinery manufacturer that calls for an order of 100 tractors when 10 was the number intended. There are software packages of forms that can be purchased. Standard forms appear on the screen. The secretary keys in the fill-ins only, and the forms with the fill-ins are printed out.

Other Documents

In addition to correspondence, reports, forms, and the other documents already described, every office has a variety of miscellaneous paperwork. Envelopes, for instance, must be addressed in order to distribute correspondence. Accuracy is clearly essential here, since an incorrectly addressed letter will arrive late or not at all. For larger envelopes and packages, mailing labels must be prepared and then attached.

Small index cards or file cards are other kinds of documents. Most libraries, for example, record the titles and authors of books on such cards. Many businesses keep a master card file of clients or of specialized products or services. A reference book publisher may keep a card file of new technical terms and their meanings.

Envelopes, labels, cards—all these must be carefully and neatly prepared. Alignment can be a problem with such documents—particularly because smaller items often tend to slip in a typewriter—and typing them may take longer than expected.

Word processing technology has eliminated many of the difficulties associated with preparing most kinds of documents. This new equipment has many advantages. Because documents can be recorded and stored in a word processing system, corrections and revisions can be made quickly and easily without having to rekeyboard the entire document. Word processors can also align whole columns of words, numbers, and decimals in a fraction of the time it would take on a standard electric

Kinds of Business Communications

typewriter. Dozens of envelopes can be addressed flawlessly with just a few keystrokes. Forms, reports, and other documents can be created, formatted, revised, stored, and retrieved with remarkable speed and efficiency.

CLASSES OF DOCUMENTS IN INFORMATION PROCESSING

The same kinds of documents are being produced in today's offices that were produced years ago. Letters, memos, and reports are still the common types of business communications. However, modern word processing equipment has brought about a profound change in how these documents are handled. Consequently, it is helpful to classify them in a manner somewhat different from the way it was done in the past. The categories that follow are based not on the purpose of the documents but on their manner of preparation.

Short Documents

Most of the correspondence produced in business offices is so brief and straightforward that it takes very little time to create. A short letter changing an appointment, for example, or a one-paragraph memo complimenting an employee on a job well done would normally require little revision, if any. Furthermore, such documents represent "one-time" correspondence. Unlike reports or statistical tables, these particular documents would not ordinarily be needed a second time. For this reason they need not be stored in a word processing system, although a file copy of the correspondence would be kept.

Repetitive Documents

Many documents that businesses distribute contain duplicate information or *repetitive text*. For example, suppose the Harrison Electronics Company plans to move its headquarters to a new building across town. The company may send out hundreds of letters to its clients, announcing the upcoming move and giving the new business address. Each of the letters in this mass mailing would contain the same information. The only items that would differ from one letter to the next would be the name and address of the person to whom the letter is addressed and the salutation. These items that differ from letter to letter are called *variables*.

A letter like the one announcing Harrison Electronics' move is said to have few variables and many *constants*. The constants are the repetitive text, that is, those parts of the document that do not change—in this case, the entire body of the letter. The variables may be only the addressee's name and address and the salutation (as in the Harrison Electronics letter).

Repetitive text is perhaps most familiar to us in standard

Some kinds of correspondence require more variables than others.

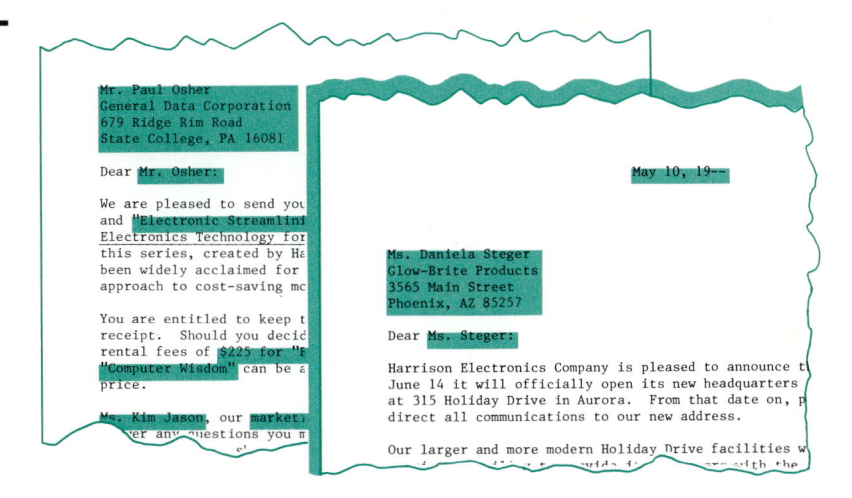

form letters. Charitable organizations soliciting contributions, for example, often send out form letters. So do various companies attempting to sell vacation real estate through direct-mail advertising. These kinds of form letters contain few variables.

On the other hand, some kinds of form letters have many variables. A letter intended to collect payment for goods or services rendered, for instance, might list in detail the exact amounts owed by the addressee. These amounts would be variable parts of the document, as would the dates due. The rest of the body of the letter would remain constant.

There are many kinds of standard, or form, documents in use, and the proportion of variables to constants in them varies. Some invoices, financial statements, and legal agreements contain many variables, while others contain only a few.

Word processing has vastly simplified the production of repetitive text. Preparing large quantities of individually typed repetitive documents once required hours of tedious and costly labor. No more. Today, word processing systems can be used to generate virtually unlimited quantities of such documents—each one an original—by means of a few keystrokes. Furthermore, depending on the capabilities of the particular system, a stored document and a stored mailing list of names and addresses can be automatically combined. In other words, the same letter can be produced countless times, with each document bearing the name and address of a different person.

Boilerplate

The Dansworth Chemical Company manufactures a wide range of products for use in industry. Every day Dansworth receives dozens of requests for information about its products. Some of these requests are for comprehensive technical data, some are

Boilerplate paragraphs are keyed for use in letters and other documents.

just for cost information, and some are for both. Many of the requests relate to several of Dansworth's products.

Word processing has greatly improved Dansworth's efficiency in handling all these requests. Detailed information about each of the company's products has been written and stored in the word processing system. This information is in the form of very specific paragraphs. One paragraph, for example, focuses on how a particular product is used. Another deals with its technical composition. A third presents cost and availability information.

Any Dansworth employee who is answering a customer's letter simply selects the particular stored paragraphs needed and indicates which ones to use. At the same time the employee specifies the order in which the paragraphs should appear. He or she can compile a document that is, in effect, custom-made to answer the particular customer's needs. The employee does this not by keyboarding the entire text but by making only the keystrokes that will retrieve the paragraphs needed.

Creating a "new" document by combining stored paragraphs, sometimes with new material added, is known in word processing as *document assembly*. The stored text itself is called *boilerplate*.

The advantage of boilerplate is that any number or combination of stored paragraphs can be used in a document, and they

34   Documents

can be arranged in any sequence. In addition, new information can be combined with boilerplate paragraphs to produce an infinite variety of new documents. Thus, as in the case of Dansworth Chemical Company, great amounts of tailor-made correspondence can be generated rapidly and efficiently, at a very great saving per letter.

Boilerplate has many uses. Contracts, wills, financial agreements, and customer service letters are just a few of the kinds of documents that can use boilerplate paragraphs stored in a word processing system.

Lengthy, Text-Edited Documents

Kathy Cardella is head of the customer service department of Wallace International, a plastics manufacturer. Last year Ms. Cardella reorganized her department to improve its productivity. This month she is working on a report explaining the effects of the reorganization.

Kathy Cardella's report is typical of the kind of long, factual documents prepared in almost every kind of business. Such documents vary greatly in content, format, and complexity, but they generally share certain characteristics.

First, instead of having just one author, they may have several. Ms. Cardella's report, for example, will contain sections written by the three managers who report to her. These managers will work closely with her in originating and processing the final document. Any of the four authors may decide to insert or delete material or rearrange paragraphs or pages. Furthermore, one author's changes frequently trigger another's.

Second, reports and other such lengthy documents often pick up parts of other documents or previous reports. Ms. Cardella may, for instance, choose to compare her efficiency data with that contained in a report she prepared two years ago. Sometimes such picked-up material is used intact; in other cases it may be updated or edited.

Third, lengthy documents frequently contain charts, statistical tables, and the like. Ms. Cardella's report will include a breakdown of job functions in her department and the approximate number of hours per week required to perform each job. In addition, the report will contain about a dozen footnotes referring the reader to certain management texts.

Because word processing allows documents to be revised or reorganized without complete rekeyboarding, Ms. Cardella's report can be prepared much more quickly and efficiently than it could have been some years ago. In fact, the more revision cycles the report has to go through, and the more people who contribute to the content, the greater will be the benefits derived from word processing.

Ms. Cardella's report is just one example of a lengthy, text-edited document. Other similar documents are legal briefs, manuscripts for publication, construction proposals, and product analyses.

BUSINESS APPLICATIONS OF INFORMATION PROCESSING

Today information processing technology is being used in almost every kind of business to improve efficiency and increase productivity. Word processors are being used to produce a great many specialized documents such as real estate agreements, case histories of patients, and forms for loans. When word processing is combined with other information processing technologies such as data processing and electronic communication, the result is a powerful system which puts accurate and timely information in the hands of those who need it to make business decisions. Let's take a look at how some professions and businesses combine word processing equipment with other office automation technologies.

Law

Large and small law firms alike have found that word processing can help attorneys save a great deal of time in handling their paperwork. There are a number of reasons for this:

- Legal documents are often long and intricate.
- Because legal documents are binding on the parties who sign them, the documents must be error-free.
- Legal documents frequently require substantial revision and several drafts before final approval.
- Many legal documents contain large sections of standardized text.

Word processing equipment is ideally suited to handle long, complex documents that (1) require much revision, (2) often make use of boilerplate paragraphs, and (3) must be free of errors.

Attorneys are now using *online data bases* (electronic libraries) to help them gather information and prepare legal cases. Using a word processor connected by telephone to a central computer, an attorney can search a data base of court precedents and retrieve in a matter of minutes information that would once have taken a clerk months of reading to find. (Information processing and the electronic technologies that help attorneys and their secretaries work more efficiently and productively are examined in more detail later.)

Let us consider the law office of Durkin, McDonnell, & Clifton, a medium-sized firm that handles general legal work using a

Many law firms are using electronic equipment.

word processing system. When a lengthy legal document needs processing and time is limited, several secretaries may work on the same document together. Each secretary keyboards and stores a different section. When the entire document is keyboarded, one secretary assembles it all in proper order. With word processing, even when there are errors or revisions, it is rarely necessary to rekeyboard an entire document. Before the final document is printed, a proofreader reads it for accuracy.

Wills, contracts, and other legal documents usually contain standardized text. Word processing is ideally suited for the preparation of these documents. The attorney who asks for the document indicates beforehand the boilerplate that is wanted. The secretary recalls the text from a disk and then inserts names, dates, and other variables.

Health Care

Word processing has many applications in a health care organization. About four out of five documents prepared in a hospital word processing center are based on doctors' dictation. Physicians dictate medical histories, examination findings, and discharge summaries for their patients' records. Most of these documents do not require revision and do not contain standardized text.

With a few keystrokes an operator can enter, and a doctor can later review on the screen, information about a patient's treatment history. The data is easily stored and retrieved for updating.

Operators maintain special lists of difficult medical terms, hard-to-spell names of drugs, and often-used phrases. Each word or phrase has its own code name. To insert an entry from this list in a document, the operator enters the code with one or two keystrokes. This not only saves time but reduces the possi-

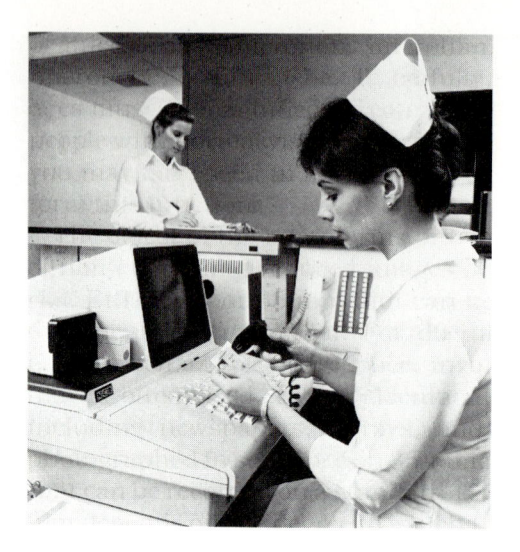

A doctor's office can benefit from technology. In addition to a word processor, the nurse in this photograph is using an electronic scanning device which eliminates the need for keyboarding.

bility of error in a profession where complete and accurate records are absolutely essential.

This makes it easier for doctors, nurses, and other medical personnel to keep track of and calculate the time spent on each patient for billing purposes. It also makes it easier to use the information for reporting insurance claims and maintaining the hospital's own financial records.

Doctors often report to a hospital only a few days a week. When a hospital needs to communicate patient information to a doctor outside the hospital, a word processing terminal, or some other type of VDT, can be connected using telephone lines from the hospital to a terminal in a doctor's office. This gives the doctor access to continually updated medical records of patients at any number of hospitals.

Banking

It is understandable that banks use word processing extensively because they must deal with a large volume of paperwork. All financial transactions have to be confirmed by documentation of one kind or another. Letters and statements have to be sent out to depositors. Various statistical records must be originated and kept up to date. Because of the large amount and variety of paperwork that major banks handle, a number of them have integrated data processing and word processing into a comprehensive information processing system.

A frequently produced document in a bank is a one-page customer letter composed of boilerplate paragraphs combined with variables. Letters like this are commonly sent out in a mass

Documents

mailing at the end of a fiscal period. The ability of word processing equipment to recall previously stored text and then change that text rapidly into original but basically repetitive correspondence has been of great benefit to bankers.

Insurance

Like banking, the insurance business uses documentation to record its many transactions. The result is a huge volume of paperwork that must be processed with speed and accuracy.

In a large insurance company, word processing applications vary somewhat from department to department. To illustrate, let's consider Unitron Mutual. Unitron has three principal departments: Marketing, Legal, and Claims.

Unitron's Marketing Department uses word processing to produce standardized letters that are mass-mailed to potential customers. The Marketing Department also generates newsletters, procedural announcements, and various employee communications.

Unitron's Legal Department, on the other hand, uses word processing in some of the same ways that the law firm of Durkin, McDonnell, & Clifton uses it. The department also prepares reports for use by company employees. These documents, which often go through many drafts, make full use of the capabilities of word processing.

The Claims Department at Unitron handles correspondence with policyholders. A typical letter will report an accident and

Word processing is important to insurance companies.

Business Applications of Information Processing

ask for insurance coverage. Although variables may differ from one claim to another, the procedures are usually the same. Using word processors, operators assemble paragraphs of boilerplate to answer these letters.

Retail

You are shopping in a newly opened indoor suburban mall. You see a sweater you like in the window of a shop that is a branch of a nationwide chain of stores. You go in, ask for the sweater, and pay the cashier for it. The cashier uses a small keyboard on the *point-of-sale terminal* to key in the price of the sweater as well as additional coded data printed on the price tag. The point-of-sale terminal, or POS, displays on a small screen the amount you are to receive in change. The POS may look like an up-to-date version of the traditional cash register, but it is a lot more.

Office automation is now in the retail store. Point-of-sale terminals give retailers the information they need enough ahead of time to make correct merchandising and business decisions. Along with the price on the price tag is coded data about key business indicators such as:

- What items are selling.
- At which stores.
- What kind of advertising works best.
- Whether customers are responding to a particular coupon or discount offer.
- What sizes, colors, and styles are running out of stock in the warehouse and need to be reordered.

The data entered into a point-of-sale terminal is sent to a central computer for processing.

Documents

The data captured by a POS terminal is transmitted to a central computer in the headquarters office for processing. Linked data and word processing systems are used to calculate and store financial information and produce the correspondence needed for purchasing and billing customers. By correctly analyzing the information they generate, retailers can use POS terminals to detect and evaluate shifts in consumer behavior and to anticipate future buying trends. The POS terminal has become an essential tool in managing a retail business competitively in today's merchandising environment. The number of stores that use POS terminals will continue to grow.

Restaurants

Did you ever walk into a restaurant, order a medium roast beef sandwich and receive instead a hot luncheon plate with very, very rare roast beef covered with gravy? How many times have you picked up a check at the end of a meal and found that you could not read it? That will happen increasingly less often now that restaurants are using computer terminals. Fast-food chains were the first to switch to computers.

The idea is simple. You give your order to the person behind the counter. Instead of jotting it down quickly with a pencil on a pad or calling it into the kitchen, he or she keyboards your order on a computer terminal. There is no need to spell out each word of the order. Instead, every item on the menu has a key that corresponds to it on the keyboard. The person serving pushes one key first that identifies your table for the computer, and then one key for each item. There are extra keys for such things as "rare," "medium," "mayonnaise," and so on.

At the same time the server is keying in your order, in the kitchen a machine connected to the computer prints it out for the cook. A blinking light tells the server when your order is ready and it is simply picked up at a serving window. To receive the check, the server presses the keys that tell the computer to add up the cost of every item, calculate the tax (if any), and print out your check.

A computer printout from a restaurant.

Manufacturing

Rapidly expanding markets and marketing opportunities, rising costs, constant vendor and supply uncertainty, explosive new technologies, increasing government regulation, and endless foreign and domestic competition have placed the manufacturing industry in a state of radical change. Customized data and word processing systems have helped many manufacturers with their problems.

Computerized systems provide companies with easily accessible, up-to-the-minute manufacturing information. Product

Business Applications of Information Processing

Computers are used in manufacturing environments.

information such as part numbers, bills-of-material, inventory availability, production schedules, routings, plant information, work-in-process status, finished goods location, and scheduled shipping information can all be obtained, assessed, and used by management when making necessary business decisions. Manufacturing information such as material requirements and the resources available further help management develop production and material planning reports. With telecommunications capabilities such as cables, telephone lines, and communications satellites, information can be sent from one location to another, anywhere in the world. This up-to-the-minute information can be channeled throughout the company to the people who need it to make engineering, production, material, and financial decisions.

Distribution

You do not usually walk into a factory, select a product off the assembly line, pay for it, and take it home. As a rule, manufacturers do not sell directly to customers. First the product must be shipped to a warehouse, often in a different part of the country or the world.

Today it is no longer enough for a company to manufacture a superior product and then sit back and expect to make a profit. Distribution—getting the product from the factory to the store—is essential. The distribution process involves a number of factors that companies must consider and deal with successfully.

In a continually changing marketplace, managers need to

Documents

know if material and labor costs are low enough to compete yet high enough to realize a profit. A plant manager has to know how a product is selling and precisely how many are in the warehouses. A retailer may call a salesperson to ask if a shipment left the factory on time. A salesperson in the field may call headquarters to ask about a customer's credit rating—or risk losing the sale to a competitor. This kind of information must be available at a moment's notice.

In an automated distribution system, every department and office is linked to the system with a computerized terminal. For example, each time a salesperson gets an order, data about the order is keyboarded. When an order leaves the warehouse, an operator at the warehouse keyboards and enters that information as well. Instantly the central computer calculates the new inventory level and alerts managers who may then adjust the production schedule. Order entry and data reporting can be initiated and the information accessed from any location in the world.

Just as we explained earlier with POS terminals, automated distribution systems tell a company a lot more than just how many products have moved off the shelf. These systems provide valuable information about sales and profits by customer, supplier, product, product line, salesperson, and region. This information can also serve as the basis for directing sales efforts, developing promotional strategies, designing new products, and ultimately increasing company profits.

Other Fields

Besides the kinds of businesses and industries discussed, many other companies have put word processing equipment and various other office automation technologies and machinery to effective use. In the publishing industry lengthy, text-edited documents such as book manuscripts and industry surveys, along with repetitive documents such as letters of rejection and marketing letters, increasingly are being handled with greater efficiency than ever before.

In government, word processing technology has been used to prepare proposals, regulations, specifications, budgets, and numerous other documents. Standardized information that will be used or revised at a later date can be stored as boilerplate and retrieved as often as needed. In education, everything from dissertations to examinations, and student orientation information falls within the province of word processing.

Associations and membership organizations such as the American Red Cross, the United Way, the Grocery Manufacturers of America, Inc., the California Almond Growers Exchange, and many, many more utilize office automation systems for a variety of functions including fund raising, membership drives, records management, accounting, seminar and convention management, and calendar management to keep event agendas up-to-date.

As a matter of fact, there isn't an industry that hasn't been touched by automation in one way or another. Just think about it for a minute. The travel agent helps you plan your trip to an exotic island in minutes by using a terminal hooked to a computer. You even leave with the airline tickets in your hand. The hotel clerk keys in your name and instantaneously retrieves your home address, company affiliation, room number, length of stay, check-out plan, messages, and meeting commitments.

As you can see from our brief overview, office automation technologies have had an affect on every industry. We see these changes in our own lives, not only in where and how we work but also in the tools we use. From all appearances, career opportunities in the office automation field will continue to expand.

CHAPTER SUMMARY

- People in business send and receive large amounts of information.
- The modern office is an information management center where speed, efficiency, and accuracy are keys to success.
- The more quickly and efficiently information is processed, distributed, and acted on, the more profitable a business is likely to be.
- Businesses use many forms of communication, including letters, preprinted forms, reports, memos, and telephone calls.
- Business letters and memos serve a number of purposes. However, while letters are generally directed to people or organizations outside a company, memos are normally used for communication within a company.
- Decisions made within a company are often based on reports—documents whose principal purpose is to present facts. Reports may be written by more than one person and may require several drafts.
- Forms are used in business to save time and to standardize the way in which certain information is transmitted.
- Office automation has done much to improve the processing of correspondence, forms, statistical tables, and other business documents.

- Because of the unique capabilities of word processing equipment, the documents produced in an information processing environment are classified into special groups: short documents; repetitive documents; boilerplate; and lengthy, text-edited documents.
- Word processing has greatly simplified the production of repetitive text.
- Boilerplate has a number of advantages: (1) Any number or combination of stored paragraphs can be used; (2) these paragraphs can be arranged in any sequence; and (3) they can be combined with variables to create an infinite variety of new documents.
- The more revision cycles a report or other document has to go through and the more people who contribute to the document's content, the greater will be the benefits derived from word processing.
- Office automation technology—such as word and data processing—can be used in nearly every kind of business to increase efficiency and productivity. It is used widely in law, health care, banking, insurance, retailing, restaurants, manufacturing, publishing, government, and education.

INFORMATION PROCESSING VOCABULARY

boilerplate
constant
document
document assembly

point-of-sale terminal
repetitive text
variable

CHAPTER QUESTIONS

1. How can speed and efficiency in information processing contribute to a company's profitability? Give a specific example.
2. Describe five purposes for which business letters may be written. Do you think word processing can help accomplish these purposes more efficiently? Why or why not?
3. Why are documents classified into special groups in word processing?
4. Which of the following types of documents would a word processing system generally be more helpful in producing: a one-paragraph memo setting up a departmental meeting or a monthly summary of regional sales figures? Explain the reasons for your answer.

5. What are three common examples of variable information in a form letter?
6. Why would the capability of a word processing system to combine automatically a stored document with a mailing list be a significant time-saver?
7. In what ways can boilerplate be used to create "new" documents? Can you think of an example of a boilerplate document you have seen recently?
8. What characteristics do lengthy, text-edited documents generally have in common?
9. Why is word processing particularly useful to law firms?
10. Compare the kinds of documents produced in the fields of banking, health care, and insurance. In what ways would word processing applications in these fields be the same? How would they differ?

CASE STUDY

The Stoner Press is a large company that specializes in publishing books on engineering and technology and in producing audiovisual materials. Stoner generates a wide range of documents. For example, its Marketing Department frequently purchases mailing lists and sends out advertising pieces to every name on the list. This same department also creates advertising copy, which must be approved by both the Editorial and Sales Departments before it can be used.

Stoner's Customer Service Department sends out correspondence in response to customer inquiries and complaints. Much of this correspondence contains the same basic information. Customer Service also sends brief memos to department heads when a particular Stoner publication draws an unusual amount of response.

Of course, most of Stoner's document preparation occurs in the Editorial Department, which handles the company's long, highly technical manuscripts. In addition to managing the development and revision of these manuscripts, Stoner's editors correspond frequently with authors, freelancers, and experts in the field.

Stoner is seriously considering installing a word processing system. Do you think this is a sound idea? Why or why not? Which of the documents produced by Stoner's various departments would fall into the special document groups in word processing (that is, short documents; repetitive documents; boilerplate; or lengthy, text-edited documents)?

CHAPTER 3
Input

After examining an X ray in her office at Midvale General Hospital, Dr. Mary Rodriguez picks up her phone, calls an extension in the hospital, and dictates a report on her findings. At the other end of the telephone line, her report is automatically tape-recorded. Later an employee in Midvale's information processing center will play back the recording and use an electronic keyboard to input the doctor's words. One copy of the report, which is stored in the computer's memory, will be printed and placed in the X-rayed patient's medical file.

Dr. Rodriguez specializes in pediatrics, but when she dictates a report she is an *author*. In information processing, the person who creates a document—who in a sense "writes" it—is called the *author, word originator, or principal*. In this book, we refer to the document creator as the author. Since word processing is used in many kinds of work settings, the author may be a production supervisor writing an evaluation of a factory worker's performance, a scientist preparing a paper about the results of a research project, a personnel worker reporting on salary levels within a company, or a secretary composing a letter requesting information from an office-supply company. Nearly everyone who works in the business world acts as an author from time to time.

METHODS OF DOCUMENT CREATION

You will recall that there are five stages in the information processing cycle: input, processing, output, distribution/communication, and storage and retrieval. Word origination is the input stage. During this stage, the author must put his or her ideas into words so that a secretary can process them. The result, or output, is a document.

To communicate her X-ray results to the person who would process the information, Dr. Rodriguez used a dictation system. An author may also create a document with pencil and paper, on a typewriter, by keyboarding on a word processor, or by face-to-face dictation. A secretary may help to create a docu-

Information processing cycle (input).

Input

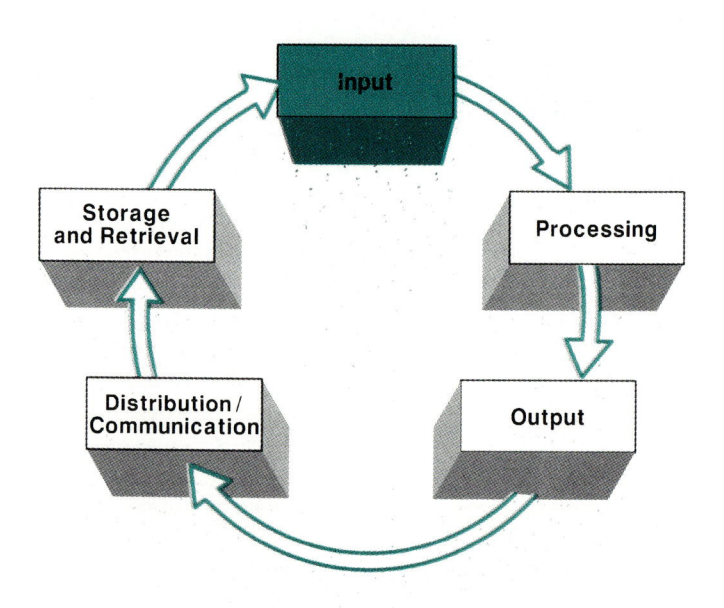

ment by taking an author's dictation in shorthand. Let's take a closer look at some common ways in which authors create documents.

Longhand

Longhand is the most common way of originating documents. It is also the most unproductive way. Most people can write in longhand at less than 20 words a minute. That's slow when compared with the 50 words a minute the average typist and the 100 words a minute the average stenographer can produce. What makes longhand even more inefficient is the time it takes the secretary to read and understand an author's handwriting. Too often illegible handwriting can lead to your spending time questioning the author or fixing mistakes made because you failed to interpret correctly the author's written message.

Despite the inefficiency of the method, many authors prefer to create documents by hand rather than by typewriter, machine recording, or other means. Writing by hand often seems more convenient to an author. It requires no special equipment, so the author can do it anywhere. Even when it isn't more convenient, however, some authors would rather write by hand than use more efficient methods of creating documents. Some say they can't organize their thoughts unless they can see their words on paper. Or they say that talking into recording devices makes them nervous. Dictating a document efficiently or preparing even a rough draft on a typewriter requires skills an author may not have. None of these reasons for using longhand seems justified considering the increased costs and reduced productivity associated with this method of originating documents.

Shorthand

Emily McCarthy, the sales director at Yale Chemical Company, does not like to write in longhand. Instead she prefers to dictate letters and other documents. When she is ready to dictate, she calls her secretary, John Fredericks, who comes into her office and takes down her words in shorthand. If Mrs. McCarthy can't think of exactly the right words to use, she asks Mr. Fredericks. He usually comes up with precisely the words she needs to express her thought. When she has finished dictating, Mr. Fredericks reads back to her what he has written. He may suggest a way of improving the letter. Once revisions have been made, Mr. Fredericks prepares the final document and takes it to Mrs. McCarthy for her signature.

Mrs. McCarthy views face-to-face dictation as the ultimate in convenience. Like most people, she can dictate a letter about six times as fast as she can write it in longhand. Moreover, she

Face-to-face dictation is a common way of creating documents.

knows that her handwriting is hard to read and that Mr. Fredericks can transcribe faster from his own shorthand notes. In addition to viewing face-to-face dictation as a time-saver, Mrs. McCarthy enjoys the feeling of security that comes from having her letters taken down by a private secretary who will keep confidential information confidential.

For the secretary, however, taking face-to-face dictation may not always be convenient. Sometimes when Mrs. McCarthy calls Mr. Fredericks in to take shorthand, he is in the middle of another task. While he is taking dictation, another secretary has to answer his telephone for him, so that the other secretary's work may be interrupted too. Mrs. McCarthy's telephone sometimes rings while she is dictating, and Mr. Fredericks has to wait while she talks to a sales representative or customer. Then he has to read back the last sentence or two that she dictated to remind her of what she was saying when the call came in.

Since not everyone can read shorthand, you can't always ask a co-worker to transcribe a document for you if you have other work you must finish first. And once you have completed the task of transcription, you then have to spend a few minutes getting back into the work you were doing when the author called you in. Time lost during face-to-face dictation, however, is not significant considering the give-and-take nature of dictation. The document can be finalized in one session between the secretary and the author. Together they can efficiently work out any problems, thus ensuring that the message the author wishes to send is clearly communicated in the first draft.

Typed Rough Draft

Andrew Juarez, a vice-president at Texrite Fabric Mills, occasionally writes articles for a decorating trade magazine about the latest textile designs. These articles tend to be much longer than letters, and they sometimes contain sections of previously published documents. Mr. Juarez finds that typing rough drafts is more efficient than writing in longhand or dictating. He sends his rough drafts to the company's public relations department, where editors make revisions that have to do with accuracy and company policy as well as with language and grammar.

Mr. Juarez double-spaces his rough drafts so the editors will have room to make their own handwritten changes, which include editing symbols. Often, many editors go over a rough draft before Mr. Juarez gets it back and gives it to his secretary, Janet Williams. The editors may even have cut the pages with scissors and taped them back together to rearrange the information. In addition to transcribing the words Mr. Juarez typed, his secretary must be able to understand the words and symbols the editors have written. Ms. Williams's task is to produce a neat, letter-perfect document from the typed rough draft, just as she would do from her own shorthand notes. If the editors have made their corrections legible, Ms. Williams's task is easy. If not, she may not look forward to retyping the article.

A typed rough draft can range from almost mailable to almost unintelligible. Its effectiveness as a form of word origination is directly related to each author's definition of the word "rough."

Keyboarding

Greta Mahler is the editor of a popular videocassette publication, *Onscreen Magazine*. The easiest method of input for her when she creates a new document is keyboarding. She learned to type in high school. So when the magazine offered its employees on-the-job training in electronic systems, she enrolled in a course titled "Basic Word Processing."

By now, Ms. Mahler is so comfortable creating at her terminal that hardly a day goes by when she does not keyboard a document of some kind. She keyboards her own memos, letters, notes, editorial comments, and short magazine articles at her desk using her word processor. When she has prepared a rough draft or a document that requires special functions, her secretary keyboards those, and prints out the finished draft for Ms. Mahler.

Ms. Mahler likes word processing because when she gets an idea she does not have to depend on anyone. She can see what it looks like on the screen or in print while it is still fresh in her mind. Not only is Ms. Mahler more productive, but her keyboarding capabilities give her secretary time to handle more creative administrative tasks.

As computer systems are taught and used in more and more schools, even at the elementary level, keyboarding skills will become more common among people who did not previously have them. Over time, keyboarding will likely become a more common method of input. Computerized systems are finding applications in almost every type of business. For example, an operator at an airport enters your plane reservation; a clerk at an auto supply store keyboards into a computer system the serial number of a part you want to order. Increasingly for all of us, keyboarding is becoming a lifelong survival skill.

Machine Dictation

In most situations, the fastest and most efficient means of document creation is by machine dictation. There are several types of equipment for recording dictation. All of them let the author dictate a document when the secretary is not present. If the author is interrupted during dictation, the recording machine is simply turned off for a moment, and the secretary's time is not lost. The secretary transcribes the dictation while listening to a playback of it.

Documents produced by dictation, like any document generated in an office, go through each step of the information processing cycle. The type of equipment that is used for the dictation can be thought of as part of the method of input. The transcribed, finished document is the output in hard copy form.

The recording can be rewound to replay all or part of it. If the telephone rings, the machine can be turned off for a few minutes and turned on again. On some dictation equipment, the author can add words to the middle of a document that has already been created without having to start over again.

Even though working with dictation machines is faster and more efficient than creating documents by writing in longhand, typing or keyboarding rough drafts, or dictating face to face, many companies and managers have been slow to install them. Some companies hesitate to install dictation machines because their managers would rather use more familiar methods.

With some machine-dictation systems, transcription is done by a word processing operator rather than by the author's secretary. Authors may be reluctant to give up the prestige of having their work done by private secretaries. And some authors depend heavily on the help and suggestions they get from their secretaries in face-to-face dictation sessions.

Also, the use of dictation equipment requires skills authors may not have. A manager knows not only how to operate the

This secretary is transcribing machine dictation using a microcomputer.

equipment itself but also how to create a document without a secretary's help. To dictate effectively, authors must be able to organize their thoughts and present them in a manner that will translate well into the written word. Then, too, they must know how to integrate dictation machines into their office systems.

Once authors try dictation machines, most find that their dictation skills improve with practice. As a result, they as well as their secretaries become more productive. Many authors prefer machine dictation to all other means of word origination. They like the convenience of being able to dictate at any time, regardless of what their secretaries are doing.

VOICE STORAGE MEDIA

Whether a dictation machine is a simple portable tape recorder or part of a large central processing system used by hundreds of authors and word processing employees, its job is to store the author's spoken words. The words are stored until a transcriptionist is ready to listen to them and prepare the final document. One way machine-dictation systems differ from each other is in the *media*, or materials, they use for recording the author's voice. There are many kinds of voice storage media. Some of them—for instance, cassette tapes—may be familiar to you from everyday life, while others may be new to you. Let's look at some of them.

Internal Storage Media

In some dictation machines, the author's spoken words are captured on a magnetic recording tape that never leaves the machine except when it wears out and is replaced. These tapes are called *internal storage media* because they are kept inside the machine. You will also hear internal storage media referred to as

Voice Storage Media 53

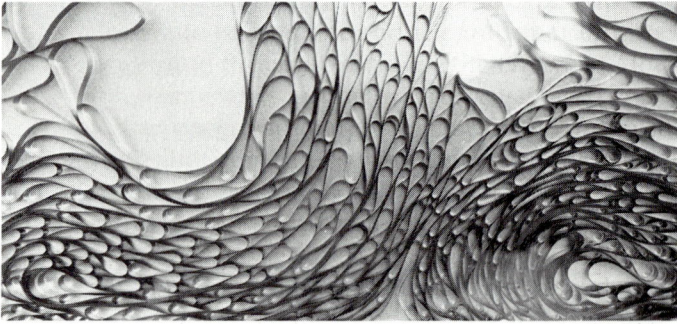

The endless loop travels around inside the tank, between recording and transcribing heads.

endless loops. An endless loop is a long recording tape that has been joined at the ends. It is housed in the tank of the machine and is never touched by the author or the transcriptionist. It travels around inside the tank, recording words as authors dictate and playing them back later for transcriptionists. An endless loop can store dictation for hundreds of documents. As new dictation comes in, the oldest transcribed documents on the tape are erased automatically to make room for the new. A single endless loop may be reserved for priority or confidential dictation or for an author having a great deal of dictation that requires immediate attention.

Internal storage media are used most frequently with central recording systems. A centralized system can record all the machine dictation that originates within an organization, so a single endless loop may hold dictation from dozens of authors. Occasionally, however, internal storage media are used in a machine-dictation system where one author dictates documents that are transcribed by a private secretary, or in a system that is shared by only a few authors.

Discrete Media

Some dictation systems use recording media that can be easily detached from the machines and used on other dictation or transcription equipment. These are called *discrete media*. The

Input

most popular discrete media are cassettes similar to the ones you might use in a tape player at home. One advantage of discrete media is that they can be saved in case anyone needs to listen to them again later. Because they can be detached and used on other machines, discrete media allow secretaries to handle rush transcription jobs with maximum speed.

Let's take the case of a secretary who works for three executives. One day each of them gives the secretary a cassette of dictation that has to be transcribed immediately. If the secretary had to transcribe all three cassettes, working on them alone, it might take too long to finish the documents on time. Cassettes, however, can be distributed to other secretaries. Working simultaneously with co-workers, the secretary can finish the transcription much more quickly.

There are two basic kinds of discrete voice storage media: *magnetic media* and *inscribed media*. Let's look at these two kinds of media and the differences between them.

Magnetic Media.
Magnetic media are usually thin, narrow tapes that record the author's voice by means of electric impulses and magnetism. Since magnetic tapes can be erased, they are quite economical. They are also convenient. On some magnetic media, an author who wants to make a change in a dictated document can rewind the tape, erase the words that should be deleted, and dictate new words in their place. Once the document on a magnetic tape has been transcribed, the tape can be completely erased and reused.

The endless loop discussed earlier is a magnetic medium. The other magnetic medium commonly used in offices is the *cassette*, which has become increasingly popular because of its versatility and convenience. A cassette is a magnetic recording tape that is permanently encased in a small plastic container. You can slip cassettes into and out of dictation and transcription machines easily. Cassettes come in several sizes.

On a *standard cassette*, you can record as much as 180 minutes of dictation—90 minutes on each side of the tape. The tape in standard cassettes is wider than the tape in smaller cassettes, so it can pick up more detail. Some operators prefer standard cassettes for certain uses because of their superior sound quality.

Cassette tapes designed for dictation are better at recording the human voice than are tapes used for entertainment. They are also engineered to eliminate extraneous room noise, and this raises the sound quality.

A *minicassette* is smaller than a standard cassette. You can record about 60 minutes of dictation on a minicassette—30 minutes on each side. The tape in a minicassette is slightly narrower than that in a standard cassette, but the sound quality is nearly as good.

The smallest and least expensive voice storage medium is the *microcassette*, which records 30, 60, or 90 minutes of dictation time. The trend today is to reduce cassette size without greatly diminishing the amount of recording time available to the user. While the sound quality of microcassettes may not be as good as that of larger cassettes, you generally can hear recorded dictation quite clearly.

One advantage of cassettes is that you can file them if you think you might need to listen to them again later. If that is unlikely, you can erase and reuse them. Cassettes are frequently used by authors who spend a lot of time away from the office. They can record dictation anywhere and mail it to the secretary for transcription. Some authors and secretaries also favor cassettes because, unlike internally stored media, cassettes can be marked easily for identification and handling.

Some executives dictate special instructions about a document before they start; others wait until they are finished. Since methods of dictating vary from one person to another, manufacturers' guides for authors often suggest not to rewind the tape cassette if the instructons are at the end, so the operator can easily listen to the last part first.

The same features that give cassettes their advantages, however, can sometimes make them troublesome. While the size of a minicassette or microcassette makes it convenient to use away from the office, a single cassette may not be long enough for the

Microcassettes and minicassettes are smaller than standard cassettes.

document an author needs to dictate. Since a cassette must be handled frequently, it is more likely than internally stored media to be lost or damaged.

Inscribed Media. Although most modern voice storage media are magnetic, you should also be familiar with *inscribed media*. These are media that cannot be erased or reused. Some dictation machines record the author's voice by etching an impression of it on a circular, flexible plastic belt a few inches wide and a foot or two in diameter. These belts are a form of inscribed media. The belts are used mainly by authors who want permanent recordings of their spoken words. Inscribed media also include cassettes, cylinders, and disks. (It is possible to prevent erasures on cassettes, thus making them inscribed media.) Although belts and other inscribed media are no longer being manufactured, they may still be found in some offices.

Media Compatibility. One thing to consider in using dictation systems is *media compatibility*. In order for you to transcribe recorded dictation, it must be recorded on a medium that is compatible with, or matches, your transcription equipment. You can't transcribe dictation that was recorded on a microcassette if your transcription equipment is part of an endless loop system or if it accepts only inscribed belts. Even if your transcription machine accepts cassettes, the cassette must be the right size. For example, a unit that accepts only standard cassettes would be useless in transcribing dictation from a minicassette or microcassette.

Partly because portable dictation machines with microcassettes are becoming so popular, some dictation equipment companies now make adapters. These adapters can be used to play microcassettes or minicassettes on equipment intended for larger cassettes.

DICTATION AND TRANSCRIPTION MACHINES

As the use of dictation machines has increased over the years, manufacturers have developed a variety of machines for dictating and transcribing. An organization with only a few authors who dictate only a few letters a day is likely to have much different equipment from a huge company in which scores of executives are constantly producing documents. Word processing systems run most efficiently and economically when the right kind of dictation and transcription equipment is used for each job. In comparing the different kinds of equipment, you will see that each type has its advantages.

Portable Dictation Units

Small recording devices are especially popular with sales representatives and executives who spend considerable time away from the office. The dictation is recorded on minicassettes or microcassettes. The dictation units are self-contained. They run on batteries, and their microphones are built in. An author can use one on a train, an airplane, or in a car or hotel room without having to deal with a tangle of wires.

These machines can be as small as a calculator, small enough to fit into a pocket and be held and operated with one hand. Some portables are larger, about the size of a hardbound novel, but they still can fit into a briefcase or a large purse. Portable dictation units are easy to use. All an author needs to do is push the correct control button with a finger. The microphones in some units are so sensitive that they can record conferences without missing a whisper, even in a large room.

Some portables have sophisticated features that make dictation and transcription easier and more efficient. One of these, *electronic cueing*, allows the author to play back the dictation and insert special instructions for the transcriptionist at any point in it. *Sonic search*, another option, scans the tape rapidly to find beginnings and endings of dictated documents.

Most portable dictation units allow for *indexing*, which lets the transcriptionist know where a document ends and where any special instructions are located on the tape. On some models indexing can be done electronically. On others the author must note on a piece of paper the number that appears on the recorder's indexing meter at the end of the dictation and the points where instructions have been inserted.

Portable dictation equipment allows dictation by people on the move.

Desk-Top Dictation Machines

The three basic types of desk-top machines are (1) those that can be used to dictate but not to transcribe, (2) those used to transcribe but not to dictate, and (3) those that can be used for both tasks. Machines that can be used for transcription as well as dictation are sometimes called *combination units*, and they are the most popular.

Desk-top units are used primarily by executives who do most of their dictating in the office and who dictate at least three pages a day. Generally, desk-top units are bulkier, heavier, and sturdier than portable recorders. Some of the newest models, though, are small enough to be stored easily in desk drawers and may even double as portables.

Like the portables, desk-top units record dictation on discrete media—any size cassette may be used. With an adapter, you will recall, you may be able to play micro- or minicassettes on a machine intended for larger cassettes.

Desk-top units usually offer more automatic controls than portables. One feature found in modern machines lets authors insert words into the middle of sentences they have already dictated, without erasing any of the previous dictation. A machine equipped for *automatic measured review*, sometimes called *automatic text repetition*, allows you to review up to nine words if you have had to stop the machine. This feature makes it easier to resume dictation or transcription if you are interrupted. On some machines all the controls—such as *record, pause, stop,* and *rewind*—are housed on the microphone. The controls may even be operated with a single button, by using varying pressure on it.

Desk-top dictation units are in widespread use.

Other machines allow you to begin transcribing a document before the author has finished dictating it. These machines have the capability of recording and playing at the same time. The extra time gained by this feature could make the difference between meeting a deadline or not.

The most sophisticated desk-top dictation machines also allow you to locate a specific point in the tape faster and more easily than in portable units. Positions on the tape are indicated by indexing numbers. These numbers may appear in an easy-to-read display similar to one on an electronic digital clock. Some machines have rapid search-and-scan devices, which allow you to locate a particular index point or document in seconds just by pushing a button. One of the newer models may give a readout that tells you the length of each document so you know how it should be set up on paper, or formatted.

Desk-top units play back dictation through internal speakers, remote speakers, or earphones. When you are transcribing, you adjust a control mechanism to alter the volume, tone, and speed. If a machine is equipped with a feature called *automatic gain control*, you don't need to adjust the volume to make up for voice fluctuations. With advances in electronic technology, manufacturers of desk-top units are constantly developing new features that can make the secretary's job—and the author's—easier.

Central Recording Systems

For large offices with dozens or hundreds of authors, a *central recording system* may be more economical than separate desk-top units for each executive. In a central recording system, all the authors dictate their documents into a recording device which is located at a single, centralized place. An author makes a phone call to the recording center and dictates into the telephone or speaks into a microphone that is wired directly to the center.

The recording device at the dictation center may be equipped with a feature called *voice-operated relay (VOR)*. If the author stops talking for a few seconds on a VOR machine, the recording stops until dictation resumes. VOR makes transcription go faster, because the secretary hears a continuous flow of dictation, without long pauses.

A central recording system may use an endless loop, which has already been discussed briefly, or it may record dictation on multiple cassettes. Let's take a closer look at the equipment used in these two kinds of central recording systems and how the systems work.

Endless Loop Systems. In some central recording systems, dictation is stored on an endless loop until it is transcribed. Some endless loops contain dual recording tracks. An author dictates the document onto one track, switches to the other track to make insertions or revisions, and goes back to the first track to continue the dictation. When a secretary transcribes, an audio signal indicates that there is additional information on the other track. An endless loop system may also include a privacy lockout to ensure that no one other than the author, the supervisor, and the transcriptionist can hear the dictation.

Endless loops are often more economical and efficient than cassettes, but they do have their drawbacks. One is that you can't remove a recording from the machine and file it, as you can with cassettes. Another is that it is difficult to identify and locate high-priority dictation among all the other documents on a loop, although some new endless loop systems offer options that make it easier. Endless loop systems are now made so that two transcriptionists can work on one document at the same time. On older models, however, only one person could transcribe any single document, which made it difficult to process a long report in a hurry.

Multiple Cassette Systems. In central systems that don't use endless loops, dictation from a number of authors is recorded on a number of cassettes at the same time. Like an endless loop, a *multiple cassette system* receives dictation from authors who gain access to it by telephone or special microphones. The cassettes are stacked on a machine that records them and plays them back for the transcriptionists.

A large organization with a central recording system may have several transcription teams in different locations. Because cassettes are portable and easily distributed, the transcriptionists don't all need to work in the recording center as they do with endless loops.

With a multiple cassette system, authors can dictate by telephone at any hour, whether or not the system supervisor is on duty. The recording device automatically arranges the cassettes in the order in which they are recorded, so that those recorded earliest are the first to be transcribed—unless another document has been designated more urgent.

Multiple cassette systems have easily readable displays that tell whether the cassettes are ready to take dictation, whether they are currently being used to record whether they are full, and whether they contain dictation that should be given high priority. A cassette may contain just a small amount of dictation

A multiple recording system like this one uses stacked cassettes.

Dictation and Transcription Machines

from a single author, or it can be filled to capacity by several authors.

The system can be programmed to relay cassettes to transcriptionists on either of two signals: when a specific proportion of the cassette's dictation capacity has been used, or when a given number of documents have been dictated onto it. *Turnaround time* is the time it takes for dictation to be processed and returned to the author. Both the department's and the individual's effectiveness are measured to a large extent by how quickly documents are processed. For fast turnaround, a system would be programmed to tape just a small amount of dictation on each cassette. If you were working under such a system, your supervisor wouldn't need to wait until a cassette was filled before giving it to you to work on.

Supervisor's Control. Regardless of whether a central dictation system uses an endless loop or cassettes, a supervisor is needed to keep tabs on the workload and turnaround times, assign the dictation to transcriptionists in sequence or by special priority, and check their work for accuracy.

At many companies, the supervisor of an information processing center uses a computer to keep track of the work. Just as a word processor can store a document in its memory or on disk, supervisors keep a document log stored in the memory of a computer so they can know at all times what work has been assigned, how much has been completed already, turnaround times, and so forth. Supervisors, and in many cases operators, keyboard information about documents at every stage of the information processing cycle. This information is stored in the memory of the word processor or computer and available for viewing on a video display terminal, also referred to as a *display terminal* or *video screen.*

The supervisor can call for status reports on any documents processed by the dictation center. The video screen can show if a document has been finished, is still being transcribed, or is awaiting revision or approval from the author. The computer may contain information about thousands of documents from many authors. The supervisor, however, may want information about only a few specific documents, about the day's work load, or about the jobs that were processed within a given time. The supervisor can use the keyboard to tell the computer which information to retrieve from its memory. The computer will quickly sort through its memory and display only the information the supervisor has requested. The supervisor also can direct the computer to print a copy of the information just as it appears on the video screen.

Computer-Aided Transcription

As the use of computers with keyboards and video screens has spread through the business world, a method of document origination has been developed. It is called *computer-aided transcription*, and is used in situations where longhand, typed drafts, shorthand, and machine dictation might be nearly impossible.

Actually, computer-aided transcription relies on a combination of computer technology and an older, mechanical piece of equipment, the *shorthand machine*. The operator of a shorthand machine, which is portable, presses the keys on it to create letter symbols. The operator uses the keys in combinations to produce several letters of each word rather than the entire word.

A shorthand machine operator can record speech at up to 250 words a minute, which is faster than many experts at handwritten shorthand. While conventional shorthand is more than adequate to record the speech of one person talking or dictating, it may not be efficient in a meeting where several people may be talking in rapid sequence. Shorthand machines are used primarily in courtrooms, public hearings, pretrial examination of witnesses in lawyers' offices, and other settings where a number of people may be speaking, perhaps spontaneously and excitedly, and an accurate record of the proceedings is required.

Older shorthand machines record the symbols on paper read by the transcriptionist. On the newer machines, pressing the symbol keys creates sound impulses that are recorded on magnetic tape cassettes. Instead of transcribing the shorthand manually, the transcriptionist inserts the cassettes into a computer. The computer translates the recorded sounds into words and displays them on a video screen. Reading the words on the screen and using a word processing keyboard, the operator formats the transcript, makes corrections and revisions, then orders the computer to print copies of it. Because the operator doesn't have to keyboard the entire document, computer-aided transcription greatly reduces the time needed to produce the final copies.

Optical Character Reader

Another method of inputting information into an electronic system is the *optical character reader* (OCR). The OCR process scans a typewritten or printed page and converts the characters on it into signals that are recorded on a magnetic medium, usually a floppy diskette. Some OCRs scan documents and convert them into a soft copy on the display screen for editing and proofreading purposes. The OCR provides an interface by putting a printed document into a form that allows it to go on an elec-

Computer-aided transcription is good for large volumes of work (left). Optical character reader (right).

tronic system not otherwise set up to receive it (except through rekeyboarding).

There are two basic kinds of OCRs. One of them, the less expensive kind, requires that the original document be prepared on a typewriter with specific kinds of characters. The other kind of OCR, called an *omnifont reader*, can deal with almost any standard type style.

Some vendors claim their OCRs can scan up to 240 pages an hour, with less than one error for every 100,000 characters. Many OCRs are equipped with feeders that can hold up to 200 pages at one time, so you don't have to feed the sheets in one at a time. Some OCRs can transmit directly to your video screen; you can start working on a document even before the OCR has finished recording it onto the magnetic medium.

Image Processing

So far we have talked only about *alphanumeric* information—letters and numbers—that you can enter into a word or data processing system by keyboarding. However, not all information is alphanumeric. Information can also be visual, such as pictures, charts, diagrams, architects' blueprints, and maps. Images cannot be entered into a computer in the same way as alphanumeric characters. But by linking a camera to a computer, it is possible to process images just as we process words and data.

This image processor takes a picture of the hard copy (on the left) and digitizes it, so it appears on the screen (on the right).

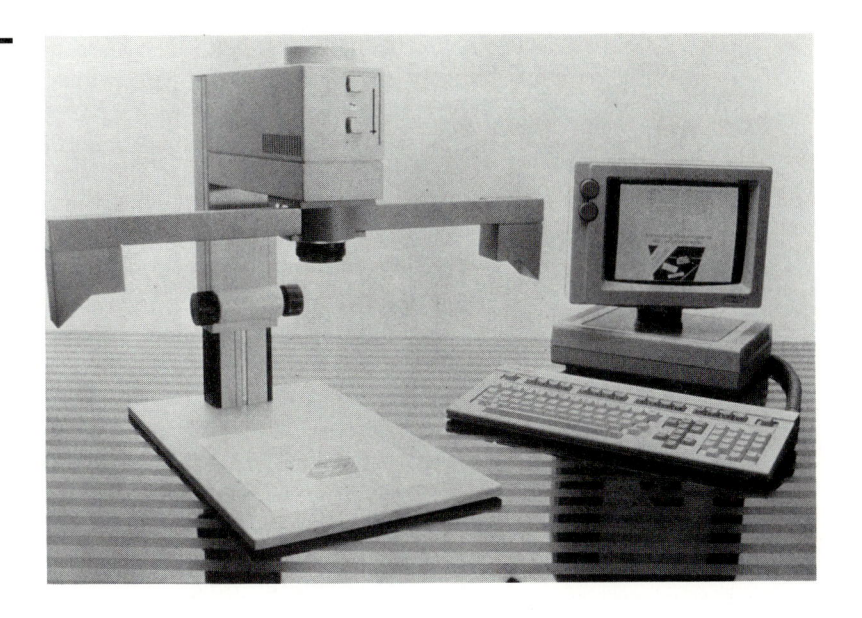

Like the optical character reader, image processors use a scanning device to capture graphic images on a flat surface and *digitize* it, that is, change it into signals that a computer can understand. Then an operator can display the image on the screen and, by keyboarding, manipulate it visually in some ways. It is possible to reposition the elements of a picture, change their size and color, or to use only part of a picture rather than all of it. Once an image is processed, it can be stored in the computer, and sent over telephone lines or by satellite to another location, where an operator can then display the image on the screen or print a hard copy.

Image processing technology will also develop in other ways. Picture yourself one day sitting down with your dentist at a video terminal that looks like a word processor. The dentist keyboards a few letters and numbers to identify your file, and your dental record appears on the screen. It tells the date of your most recent appointment, when your teeth were last cleaned by the dental hygienist, and which teeth were filled. The dentist does not need to hold your X rays up to a light to show them to you. The computer can display a soft copy of the X rays on the display.

Voice Processing

Each of us uses voice processing technology nearly every day of our lives—by using the telephone. But how many of us have spoken to a computer? Voice, like image, is another form of information that cannot be entered into a computer by keyboarding. Voice recognition equipment changes human speech into signals that a computer can change into words and display on the screen just as if they had been keyboarded, letter for letter, on a word processor.

Voice recognition technology is still in its earliest stages of development. The biggest problem is that our voices are like fingerprints. No two people sound or speak alike. Not only do dialects vary from one place to the next, but even in one locality everyone has a distinct style of expression, emphasis, and pronunciation. Moreover, each of us sounds different at different times of the day. We also sound different when we have a cold. Then there is the problem of grammar and punctuation. If a person says ". . . to the ski resort," the computer may hear the words ". . . too, the ski resort," or ". . . two. The ski resort," and so on. Background noise can also throw a computer off. When you think about all these obstacles, it is remarkable that people are able to understand each other let alone expect a machine to.

There are companies that are working on voice recognition. Speakers will need to identify themselves before they can begin communication. This is accomplished either by voice or by inserting a plastic card encoded with magnetic signals that identify the voice for the computer.

For voice processing systems to work, everyone has to know how to talk to the computer, and what it can and cannot understand. The U.S. Postal Service has experimented with a voice processing system for routing the mail. A postal worker might

Voice processing equipment.

read the address on a package or a batch of mail and simply call out a ZIP Code, a city, or a mail route. Then a conveyer belt or other system would direct packages to the correct loading dock.

AT&T's Bell Labs is working on a simulated airline reservation system. You could use it to call and ask, for example, "What flights leave for Chicago today?" A computerized voice would tell you the flight schedule for Chicago. Actually making your reservation by computer may be possible in the future. At that point you could easily press a button on your Touch-Tone phone for the computer to switch you to an operator at the reservation desk.

As we continue exploring the field of information processing, we will encounter other input devices used in conjunction with computer systems, such as light pens, joy sticks, mouse control, and so on.

CHAPTER SUMMARY

- An author is any person who originates information that passes through a word processing system.
- In a business office, nearly everyone acts as an author from time to time.
- Word origination is the input stage of information processing. It is the means by which the author puts ideas into words.
- Kinds of word origination include longhand, shorthand, typed rough drafts, keyboarding, machine dictation, and computer-aided transcription.
- In most situations the fastest and most efficient means of document creation is by machine dictation.
- Machines for dictation use either internal storage media or discrete media.
- Internal storage media, which are kept inside a machine, are also referred to as endless loops. An endless loop is a long recording tape that has been joined at the ends.
- Discrete media are recording media that can be detached from the machines and used on other equipment. They can be further classified as magnetic media or inscribed media.
- Magnetic media are tapes that record the author's voice by means of electrical impulses and magnetism.
- A cassette is a magnetic recording tape that is encased in a small plastic container. Cassettes come in three sizes: standard cassettes, minicassettes, and microcassettes.
- Inscribed media cannot be erased or reused. They include plastic belts, cylinders, disks, and cassettes.

- In order for recorded dictation to be transcribed, it must be recorded on a medium that is compatible with the transcription equipment. Some equipment now includes adapters that can be used to play minicassettes and microcassettes on equipment intended for larger cassettes.
- Three types of machine dictation equipment are portable units, desk-top units, and central recording systems.
- Modern dictation machine features such as electronic indexing, measured review, automatic gain control, and voice-operated relay make it easy to dictate and transcribe documents.
- In a central recording system, all authors dictate their documents to a recording device at a single, centralized location. An author gains access to a central recording system by calling it on the telephone or by using a special microphone.
- A central recording system may use an endless loop or multiple cassettes.
- A major goal of any word processing system is to achieve fast turnaround from transcriptionist to author.
- In a modern word processing center, a supervisor keeps tabs on the work load and turnaround times, assigns dictation, and checks work for accuracy.
- Many supervisors use computers with video display terminals (VDTs) to monitor when work comes in, its priority, length, the keyboard operator assigned, and turnaround time.
- Computer-aided transcription combines the use of the shorthand machine with computer technology. Sound impulses are recorded by the machine onto cassettes that are then inserted into a computer. The computer translates the recorded sounds into words and displays them on a screen.
- Other methods of input include the optical character reader, image processing, and voice processing.

INFORMATION PROCESSING VOCABULARY

author
central recording
　system
computer-aided
　transcription
discrete media
endless loop
image processing
inscribed media
internal storage media

magnetic media
media compatibility
microcassette
minicassette
multiple cassette
　system
optical character
　reader (OCR)
principal
standard cassette

Input

turnaround time
video display terminal (VDT)
voice-operated relay (VOR)
voice processing
word originator

CHAPTER QUESTIONS

1. Which specific kinds of employees in a company might act as authors?
2. There are a number of different methods of creating documents. Name four of these methods and give some of the advantages of each.
3. How can machine dictation help managers as well as secretaries work more efficiently?
4. Why do some authors resist using dictation machines? Give at least three reasons. Which do you consider the most valid and the least valid reasons?
5. What is an endless loop? What are its advantages and disadvantages?
6. What kind of equipment should be used for transcribing dictation recorded on microcassettes? Why is your choice of transcription equipment limited?
7. What is turnaround time and why do you think it is a key criterion in evaluating a word processing department?
8. What is the role of a supervisor in tracing the progress of a document through a centralized word processing system? In what ways can a computer help the supervisor?
9. What technologies are linked in image processing? What industries can you think of that would find image processing most advantageous? Why?
10. Why do you think voice processing would be a most revolutionary computer tool? What changes might it bring about in the way we work in offices?

CASE STUDY

The Universal Calendar Corporation, which has grown dramatically in the last few years, is considering the purchase of word processing equipment. The company has some two dozen executives and scores of other employees now, but its methods of creating documents have not changed much since it was a much smaller operation run entirely by two brothers and a sister.

The executives, who spend most of their working time in the company's headquarters, usually dictate documents to their secretaries. The secretaries take their bosses' words down in shorthand and later give them typed copies of the documents. Sometimes, however, the executives give the secretaries rough drafts of the documents that are typed crudely or written in longhand, and the secretaries transcribe them.

Universal also employs about 25 sales representatives. Each representative is responsible for calling on office supply stores within a large territory. The representatives seldom visit the home office. When they are in the office, they generally spend most of their time writing follow-up letters to customers and prospects, using sketchy notes they jotted down after calling on the stores.

The company's 12 secretaries do virtually all the typing generated by the managers and salespeople. Each of the top 4 executives has a private secretary. The other 8 secretaries each work for two or three lower-level managers. All 12 pitch in to do the sales representatives' typing, since these people do not have personal secretaries.

Using what you have learned in this chapter, what kinds of dictation and transcription equipment would you recommend that Universal Calendar purchase for its new word processing system? Explain your recommendations.

CHAPTER 4

Word Processing Equipment

John Chevalier mentioned to a friend, Alice Blakeston, that he wanted to learn word processing. Ms. Blakeston, who owns a résumé-writing service, invited him to come to her office after business hours to practice on her word processing equipment. In a few months Mr. Chevalier had acquired enough skill to seek a job in word processing. He found, however, that most prospective employers had word processors that differed from his friend's. At first he feared that his recently acquired skill would be useless in another office. A little research, though, showed him that word processors share the same essential functions and procedures. He soon realized that he could easily learn to use new equipment because he knew the basics.

Word processing is a system for producing finished documents from input originated by authors. A word processing system uses trained personnel and automated equipment to do this job efficiently. You have learned how a document is originated during the input phase of information processing. Now let's look at the automated equipment used to turn this raw material into printed documents during the processing phase.

WHAT IS A WORD PROCESSOR?

The most important difference between a word processor and a typewriter is *memory*. Because it has memory, a word processor can record and recall keystrokes electronically. Keystrokes can be kept in a short-term memory or stored on some sort of magnetic medium and then played back later, printing as many "original" copies as needed without requiring any more keyboarding. The first word processors were modified typewriters that could do little more than type form letters automatically. Since then word processors have evolved into complex computerized systems, often with screens, that are used to produce all kinds of documents.

In tracing the development of word processors, you will begin to acquire a new language. Just as the invention of high-fidelity recording and playback equipment added new terms to the language—such as woofer, tweeter, stereophonic, and cassette—the development of computerized word processing has given us many new terms: input, CPU, disk drive, ROM, RAM, and others.

Information processing cycle (processing).

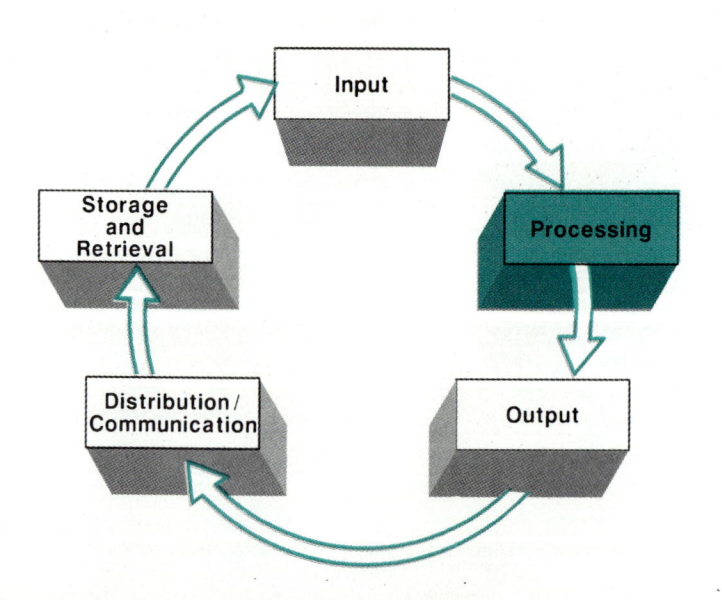

72 Word Processing Equipment

Year	Technology
1868	Manual Typewriter
1876	Telephone
1887	"Census Machine"
1930s	Auto-Typist
1933	Electric Typewriter
1946	ENIAC
1960s	Administrative Terminal System (ATS)
1961	Selectric Typewriter
1964	MT/ST
1969	MC/ST
1971	Lexitron Display Word Processor
1972	Mag Card II
1973	CPT and Redactron Cassette Tape Text Editors
1974	Vydec Display Floppy Disk System
1975	Memory Typewriter
1976	Personal Computer
1978	Wang Cluster System
1980	Electronic/Intelligent Typewriter
1981	Electronic Mail
1981	Voice Mail (Store and Forward)
1981	Teleconferences
1981	Local Area Networks
1981	Multifunction/Managerial Workstations
1983	Voice Recognition Systems

The evolution of information processing.

COMPONENTS OF A WORD PROCESSOR

Many kinds of word processors are being sold today. Their capabilities vary enormously, and some are much more complex than others. However, all word processors have four basic components: (1) keyboard, (2) central processing unit, (3) storage, and (4) printer. Many word processors also include another component: (5) display. Before comparing the various word processing systems, you must become familiar with the components they have in common.

keyboard Much like a standard typewriter keyboard but with additional keys for special word processing functions.

central processing unit (CPU) The "logic" of a word processor; actually a computer, sometimes called an *internal processor*.

storage The part of the machine that holds the storage media (for example, magnetic card, magnetic tape, or floppy diskette).

printer The device that produces the copy on paper (hard copy).

display A screen that allows the operator to verify text content and format before it is printed. It is similar in appearance to a television screen.

Keyboard

The part of a word processor that you are likely to find most familiar is its keyboard. A word processor keyboard is very much like a typewriter keyboard, with the same QWERTY arrangement of letters as well as number keys, a space bar, shift keys, and so forth. These standard keys generally occupy the part of the keyboard closest to you, where you can reach them most easily.

In addition to these keys, a word processor keyboard has *function keys* for communicating instructions to the central processing unit. The function key labeled "delete," for example, is used to tell the processor to do just that—to remove from the text the character or word you have indicated. The function keys help you perform automatically many tasks that would be tedious and time-consuming on an ordinary typewriter.

Function keys may be arranged in different ways. They are usually grouped on the keyboard according to the type of functions they control. Keys that control the cursor's position (see page 75) may be on one side of the QWERTY keys (usually the right), while keys that perform other functions are on the left side or above the QWERTY keys. In most cases the function keys you use the most will be the easiest to reach. Keyboards from one type of word processor to another differ because their function keys vary. Each manufacturer has its own basic keyboard design.

The labels on function keys are sometimes only vague descriptions of what the keys do, and few people remember the locations of function keys they seldom use. For this reason most operators keep keyboard maps and operator instruction manu-

Keyboard.

Word Processing Equipment

als at their workstations. Of course, the function keys you use most often will soon become as familiar to you as typewriter keys. And in some systems, often-used functions are clearly labeled—the centering key, for example, may be labeled "center."

In addition, manufacturers may modify their keyboards to suit the needs of their customers and to reflect the capabilities of the customers' systems. Some keyboards, for example, have function "communications" keys for instructing the machine to send documents to other word processors within the same system. In an office with only one word processor, however, the keyboard does not need a "communications" key and may not have one.

These variations mean, of course, that being an expert on the keyboard of one system won't make you an instant expert on another system. Keyboards are more alike than they are different, however, and transferring from one kind of equipment to another will present little difficulty once you have become accustomed to electronic keyboarding in general.

The more functions a word processor can perform automatically, the more function keys it is likely to have. Word processors with screens generally have more elaborate keyboards than word processors without screens, simply because they perform more functions. Discussed below and on page 76 are some of the different kinds of function keys you will encounter.

Cursor Keys. A *cursor* is a spot of light that indicates the point in the text at which you are working. Keys used to move the cursor up, down, and to the right or left are called *cursor keys*. Most word processors have keys that automatically send the cursor to the next word or the beginning of the document. Some of them also have keys that send the cursor to the end or beginning of the line, to the next paragraph, or to the end of the document.

When you first use a word processor with a screen, you may find yourself using the space bar when you should be using the cursor keys. Because you are accustomed to using the space bar on a typewriter to move the typing element from one space to the next or several spaces along, you may instinctively press the space bar on a word processor and expect the same thing to happen. But when you press the space bar on a word processor with a screen, it creates just that—a space—on the screen, replacing any character that was there before with a blank space. You cannot retrieve these characters; they have to be rekeyboarded.

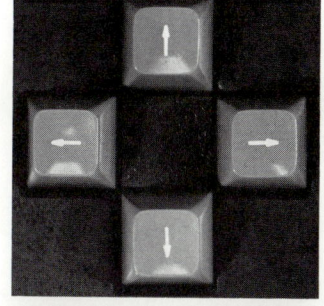

The cursor on the screen is controlled by cursor keys (with arrows) on the keyboard.

Components of a Word Processor

Operation Keys. The keyboard of a word processor with a screen also includes a few keys that control other components in the word processing system. You use these keys to send keyboarded documents to the storage unit or to retrieve them from storage for viewing on the terminal. You may also use operation keys to order printed copies of documents or to send your keyboarded work to another terminal.

Function Keys. Function keys tell the word processor what functions to perform automatically, such as insert, delete, and so on. There are many functions that word processors can perform. The function keys eliminate the repetitive, tedious, and time-consuming tasks performed on a typewriter and help the secretary become more efficient and productive.

Format Keys. Some function keys control the *format* of the document. Format is the page margin, vertical line spacing, printing requirements, and so on, of a document. Format keys may call for tabs, indentions, centering, underlining, or page breaks—in short, factors that affect the placement of type.

Statistical Keys. A keyboard that is frequently used for statistical work may include a special set of function keys for that purpose. These keys control such things as decimal tabs, superscripts, subscripts, (if they are not a part of the function keys), and other alignment or spacing adjustments often used in preparing tables or lists of figures. To enter numbers easily, a ten-key numeric pad similar to a calculator's keys may be used along with the keyboard. The pad is usually positioned to the right of the keyboard.

Central Processing Unit (CPU)

You might think of the central processing unit as the brain of the word processor. If a friend tells you a good joke, signals from your eyes and ears cause your brain to send messages to other parts of your body. Your brain may tell your facial muscles, your diaphragm, and your throat to perform the motions that go into a hearty laugh. The central processing unit of a word processor is mechanical and nowhere nearly as complex as a human brain, but it acts in somewhat similar ways. In fact, the central processing unit is often referred to as the logic or intelligence of the word processor.

The central processing unit, or CPU, receives instructions through one component—the keyboard—and relays instructions to other components. By pressing a particular function key, for example, you might tell the central processing unit that you want the title of a document to be centered. The CPU stores this keystroke in its memory. If the word processor has a video

Central processing unit.

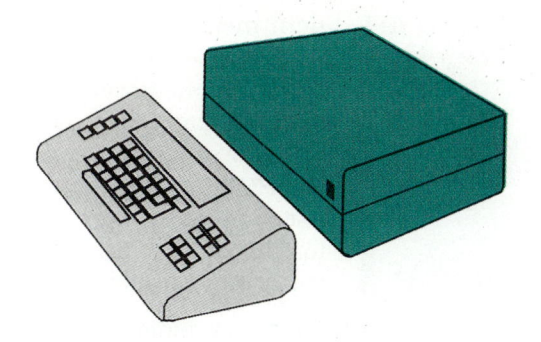

display, the CPU usually sends an instruction to display the title centered, so you can see exactly how it will look before it is printed. When you print the document, the CPU sends an instruction to the printer to center the title on the hard copy.

Although the central processing unit is a very important component of the word processor, it is the one you will notice least as you work. You can see the keyboard, but—unless you take the word processor apart—you can't see the component that receives the instructions from the keyboard.

When you use the function keys, you are communicating with the central processing unit. The central processing unit of a word processor with a display is a computer. Fortunately, word processors are *user-friendly*. This means they are designed so that you do not have to know how a computer works in order to use a word processor. But since there are differences from one manufacturer to another in the way machines operate, it is important to understand what happens in the central processing unit.

There are two sections inside the central processing unit of a word processor—the permanent memory and the temporary memory. Let's compare them.

Permanent Memory. The set of instructions (or the *program*) given to a word processor by its manufacturer is kept in the *permanent memory* of the central processing unit. The user cannot change what is contained in the permanent memory; this is the set of instructions that enables the word processor to act on the information entered from the keyboard. When a central processing unit takes instructions from the permanent memory, the process is called "reading." The permanent memory is thus called *ROM*, which stands for *read-only memory*. The larger the capacity of the ROM section of the memory, the more special and automatic functions the word processor can be instructed (or "programmed") to perform. And it is permanent; if the machine is turned off, the contents of the perma-

Components of a Word Processor

EPROM chip.

nent memory will be there when it is turned on again. ROM is unalterable once programmed. Recently, *PROM* (programmable read-only memory) and *EPROM* (erasable programmable read-only memory) chips were developed so program changes could be made easily and frequently. PROM allows the user to program the ROM for applications used frequently. EPROM allows the user to erase programs and program the system to be specific for the user. Until these developments were introduced, ROM could only be altered by the manufacturer.

Temporary Memory. The temporary memory, also called the *buffer* memory, is quite different from the permanent memory. In its temporary memory the word processor holds the instructions and characters you give it via the keyboard. The temporary memory contains not just the page or part of a page that you see at any one time on the screen, but everything that would appear on the screen if you moved from the beginning to the end of the document.

The temporary memory is just that—temporary. The central processing unit will not remember what was on the screen after you turn off the equipment. To retain your work, you must use your function keys to send it to the storage unit. Otherwise, your work will be lost from the temporary memory and will disappear forever.

When the central processing unit takes electrical information from the keyboard into its temporary memory, the process is called "writing." The temporary memory section is also called *RAM*, which stands for *random access memory*. This term is used because the central processing unit can add to, take from, or change information in its temporary memory "randomly."

The permanent ROM section may be compared to a textbook and the temporary RAM section to a notebook. You can read and reread a textbook, but you cannot change what is printed there. In your notebook, on the other hand, you can write down your

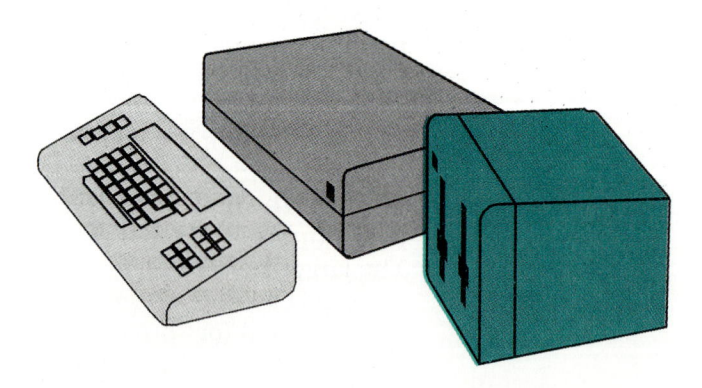

Storage.

thoughts, change what you have written, read your notes, and go back and read them again at any time.

Like permanent memories, RAM sections vary in size. Some word processors have such large temporary memories that you may never fill the RAM section to capacity with a document you are keyboarding. Other systems have memories so small you may have to work on a long document in sections, keeping all the sections in storage except for the one you are keyboarding or printing.

Storage

The storage component houses the document when you have finished keyboarding it and want to save it for future use. If the document is to be worked on again, you retrieve it from storage, then send it back when you have finished. If you make changes in the document, they are automatically included and recorded on the storage unit.

In some systems each word processor has its own storage unit. In others all word processors share a storage unit at a central location. (Note the similarity here to machine-dictation systems, where centralized storage is also common.) Word processors that share a central storage unit may also have individual storage as a way of expanding the storage of the whole system. An optional storage unit is one kind of *peripheral*, a term that refers to any device that extends the capabilities of equipment but is not necessary to its operation.

Memory is sometimes called *internal storage*. There is also external storage. The purpose of external storage is to retain your keyboarding—the document as well as your instructions to the word processor on how the document should look in print—after you have turned off the equipment. External storage lets you put a document aside and retrieve it when you want to work with it again later. The external storage unit keeps you from having to keyboard a document again when you want it to reappear on your terminal.

The storage media often used with word processors are floppy diskettes and hard disks. Both floppy diskettes and hard disks are magnetic—that is, they have a coating of magnetic material on which recordings can be made. As you will see, however, hard disks are capable of storing much more information than floppy diskettes.

Floppy Diskettes. The most common storage medium is the *floppy diskette*. To visualize a floppy diskette, think of a 45-rpm phonograph record in its protective jacket. A floppy diskette looks like a phonograph record, although it is much thinner—which makes it flexible, or "floppy." Floppy diskettes for word

Components of a Word Processor

processors come in two sizes: 8 inches and 5¼ inches. They differ from records in one obvious way: Rather than having grooves, they have a magnetic coating. The delicate Mylar (a kind of plastic) is permanently encased in a stiff paper or plastic jacket, which not only protects it but also makes it easier to handle. This jacket has a few openings, and these permit the storage unit to "read" the contents of the diskette to find the documents you want.

Care and Handling of Floppy Diskettes

1. Never touch the diskette surface.
2. Never remove the diskette from the sealed protective jacket. When the diskette is not in the machine, keep it in its protective envelope or plastic jacket.
3. Handle the diskette only near the label on the top.
4. Do not fold, bend, or crease the diskette.
5. Do not write on the surface of a diskette. Write identification labels separately, then place them on diskettes. Remove old labels before placing new ones on the diskettes. Never put the labels on in layers.
6. Diskettes have a life expectancy of between one to two years; always have a backup diskette ready just in case.
7. Never leave diskettes in direct sunlight or near any source of heat.
8. Diskettes should be stored upright—never stacked—when not in use.
9. Because of the magnetic coating on the diskette, never place a magnet on it or near it.
10. Never try to clean a diskette with alcohol, cleaning fluid, paint thinner, or any other kind of commercial cleaner.
11. Never put a heavy object on a diskette.
12. Never use rubber bands or paper clips on a diskette.
13. Never try to erase with an eraser any writing on a disk.

A floppy diskette can store much more information than a card, cassette, or tape. Most floppy diskettes also offer *random access*—which means that you don't need to go through the entire contents to find the document you want. Using function keys or a document directory displayed on the screen, you simply identify the document and it is automatically retrieved from the diskette and displayed on your screen.

An 8-inch diskette can store up to 200 pages of text, and a 5¼-inch diskette can hold about 75 pages. The capacity of a diskette depends on its density and whether both sides of it can be used to store information. There are four basic diskette sizes:

single side, single density; single side, double density; double side, single density; and double side, double density. Single-sided, single-density diskettes have the least capacity. Double-sided, double-density diskettes can store the most information. The storage capacities given on page 80 are for single-side, double-density diskettes. The storage capacity of a diskette can vary depending on the word processing equipment. If both the diskette and the word processing system in which it is used are maintained properly, the data stored on the diskette can last several years.

Some systems use tape cartridges to back up keyboarded information stored on disk. The cartridges can be compared to tape cassettes but store far more information.

Manufacturers are conducting research into media more advanced than those in use now. It is almost certain that disks in ten years will be made from different materials than the disks used today. The trend is to smaller size and greater memory capacity. The 3M Corporation is currently evaluating a stretched disk it expects to introduce in 1986. Its new disk will have a storage capacity about 12 times greater than floppy diskettes in use today.

Hard Disks. Large companies often need to store a great many documents. These companies may use a *hard disk* rather than a floppy as their word processing storage medium, because of the disk's large capacity—it can store upwards of 5,000 pages of text. Most hard disks are about the size of a $33\frac{1}{3}$-rpm phonograph record and are housed in a rigid, protective plastic casing.

Hard disks are about the size of 33⅓-rpm records, while floppy diskettes resemble 45-rpm records in protective jackets.

Winchester Disks. The type of hard disk most often used with word processing systems is called a *Winchester disk*. These disks come in four sizes: 5¼, 8, 10½, and 14 inches. The magnetic storage is permanently sealed inside a casing, which protects the disks, thus making them extremely reliable; floppies can be affected by static electricity and dust, but Winchester disks in their protective casing cannot. They also have far greater capacity than floppies—in the millions of characters—allowing for storage of a large number of documents.

The disadvantage of Winchester disks is that they are not removable. Once the capacity of a disk has been filled, you must erase (or "purge") some copy to record more. However, since their capacity is so large and their storage so reliable, Winchester disks are increasingly popular in word processing sytems.

Disk Drives. A word processor that uses disk storage has a component called a *disk drive*. The disk drive works something like a tape recorder. For example, you insert diskettes into the drive in much the same way that you insert cassettes into a recorder. Inside the drive, the floppy diskette spins at a high speed under a device called a head, which "reads" already recorded text to find the information you want. In recording new text, the head transfers information from the keyboard by "writing" it onto the disk. (The terms "read" and "write" as used here are derived from the read/write heads on cassette tape recorders.)

A floppy diskette drive may be in the same housing as the terminal, or it may be in a separate console. A word processor is often built with a single disk drive, but sometimes as many as

A floppy diskette fits in a disk drive.

Courtesy of IBM Corporation.

Word Processing Equipment

three additional drives can be added to it as peripherals. The additional disk drives let you work with more information at one time, since each additional diskette increases storage capacity.

Multiple disk drives also allow you to copy your work onto separate floppies so that you have a backup in case one is damaged. *Backup* is the term used to describe duplicate text that is magnetically stored. The backup diskette becomes part of an archive. An *archive* is a collection of stored backup diskettes.

Printer

The printer is the device that produces the finished document after it has been keyboarded and after any corrections and revisions have been made. The paper copy of a document, which is the output of a word processor, is referred to as either *hard copy* or a *printout*. Printers are available in a variety of speeds and with different printing mechanisms to suit various office needs. (Printers and their peripherals are discussed in greater depth in Chapter 6.)

Printer.

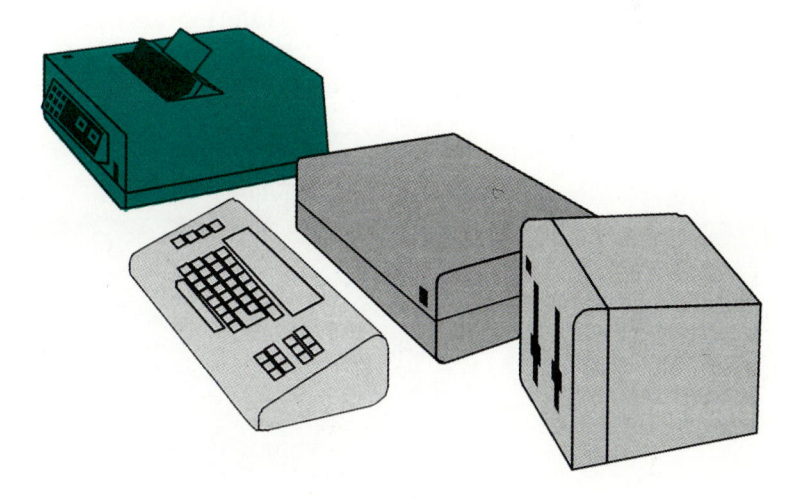

Display (Monitor)

A fifth component of many word processors is the *video display terminal*, or *VDT*. As a document is keyboarded, this television-like screen displays the characters either in a light color against a dark background or vice versa. The operator can read the characters on the display, sometimes called a monitor, and make changes or corrections before the printer produces a hard copy. VDT, terminal, monitor, cathode-ray tube, CRT, video display, display screen, and display terminal are all terms word pro-

Components of a Word Processor

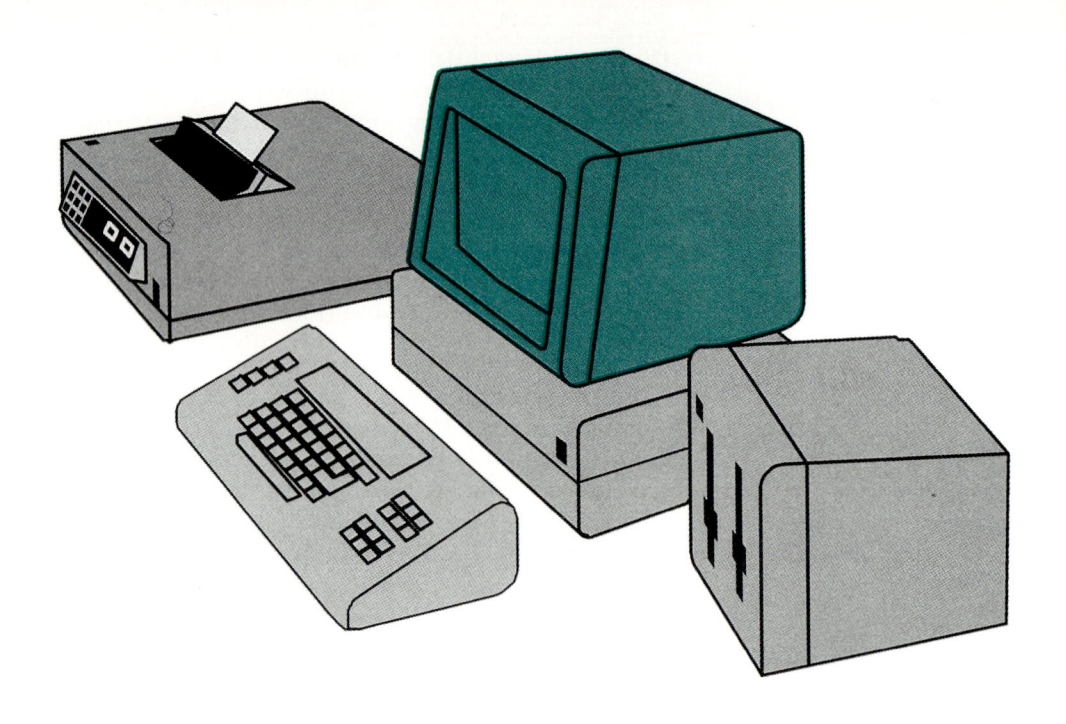

The five components of a
word processor.

84 Word Processing Equipment

cessing people use for the same thing—a video display terminal.

Although any equipment that provides automatic editing and typing of documents is considered a word processor, it is display word processors that have brought about the revolution in office procedures. Display screens have expanded word processor capabilities significantly. Today word processors are generally divided into two categories: display (those with VDTs) and nondisplay, or "blind" (those without VDTs).

The display screen brought with it a number of changes in word processing. For one thing, keyboarding now produced documents not in typewritten pages but as *soft copy*—that is, images in light on a screen. As a result, the printer became a separate machine. One great advantage of this separation is that it allows you to view an entire keyboarded document before ordering the printer to produce a hard copy of it. With equipment that does not have a screen, it is necessary to make rough draft copies to "see" what has been done. The separation of keyboarding from printing means that you can proofread and edit more thoroughly and efficiently than you can using equipment without a screen.

Herb Glatzer, a manager at the engineering firm of Barstow and Dunn, studies the waste-disposal problems of the firm's clients and writes reports on how those problems can be solved. Mr. Glatzer is highly respected because of his technical background and problem-solving skills, but he doesn't express himself well. He admits that his reports tend to be wordy and difficult to understand. In the past, his secretary, Jane Sarton, would transcribe a report Mr. Glatzer dictated on an electronic typewriter and then review the typed draft. She would often notice sentences and paragraphs that needed revision. Due to the limited memory of her machine, however, it was impossible for her to make changes without completely rekeyboarding the report.

The office traded in the electronic typewriters for word processors with display screens. At first Ms. Sarton was intimidated by the new equipment, and it took her a week or two to become accustomed to using it. The turning point came one morning as she was keyboarding a report. When she came to paragraphs on the display screen that she thought were awkward, she corrected them.

When she had gone over the report thoroughly, she directed the printer to prepare a printout. Then she wrote Mr. Glatzer a note describing her changes. He welcomed her suggestions, and he agreed with almost all of them. Ms. Sarton then went back to her workstation, where she could move words, sentences, and

Text changes can be made without rekeyboarding the whole document.

paragraphs around on the screen with just a couple of keystrokes. It took a few minutes to make the revisions Mr. Glatzer had requested. The final printed copy of the report was on his desk before lunch.

Within a month, Ms. Sarton was so accustomed to her word processor with the display that she could hardly imagine ever working on a typewriter again—or even on a word processor without a screen. Her only complaint about the screen was that it sometimes was hard on her eyes, a concern voiced by many people who work with display equipment. (See Chapter 7 for a full discussion of this.)

Like television sets, terminals sometimes need adjustments to stop the images on them from blurring or wavering. You can make some of these adjustments yourself, using knobs on the terminal. You can also usually adjust the contrast and the brightness of the image on the screen.

Displays differ from one another in various ways: configuration, screen size, and type of display. Let's look at some of these differences.

Configuration. On Ms. Sarton's word processor, the screen and the keyboard are housed in the same console. However, some word processors combine storage and display in a single console, with separate keyboard and printing consoles connected to it by cables. On many others, each component is in its own console. When the components are in separate consoles, you can arrange them in ways that are comfortable and convenient for you. Consoles that contain more than one component may take up less space, but they don't allow as much flexibility.

Screen Size. Screens differ from one another in the size of their display areas. The amount of text that can be viewed on a

Use vertical scrolling to see keyboarded text that precedes or follows a screenload.

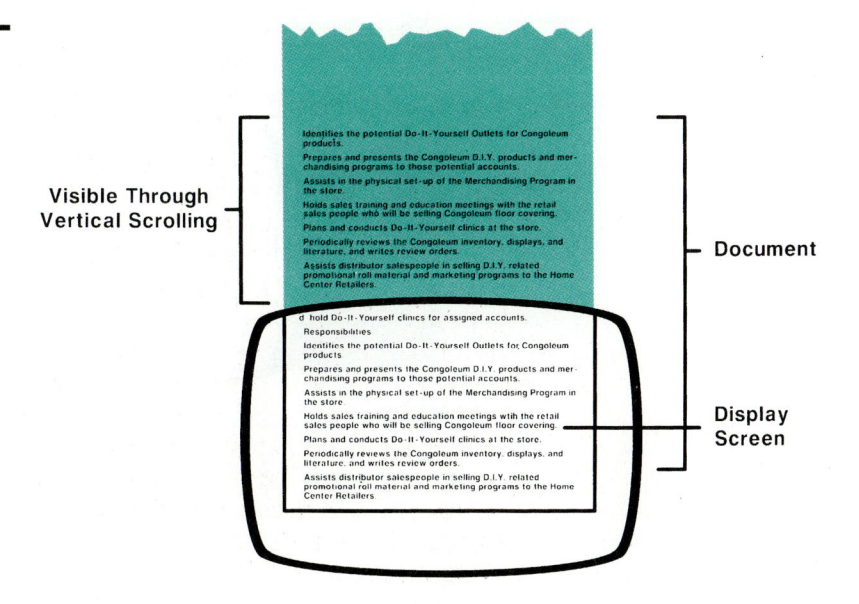

Visible Through Vertical Scrolling

Document

Display Screen

terminal at one time is called a *screenload*. You see a document one screenload at a time. When the screenload in front of you doesn't contain the part of the document you want to see, you press function keys to *scroll* the document, which means to move it backward or forward on the screen. You might think of scrolling as the electronic way of turning the pages. With the function keys, you can move instantly to the screenload immediately preceding or following the one you are looking at, or you can scroll the document continuously backward or forward until you find the part of the text you need. You can use the cursor keys to scroll on a number of systems.

Full Page. On some terminals a screenload is equal to a full page of an $8\frac{1}{2}$- by 11-inch document, about 66 lines of 80 characters each. Some people prefer working on a word processor with a full-page screen because it lets them see the page just as it will appear in print. This can be very helpful for people who spend most of their time working on documents that are usually just one page long, such as letters and memos.

Partial Page. Screens may display only part of a document page at one time. While it may take some adjustments to work with partial pages, this kind of display is not usually a big drawback, because you can scroll to the rest of the page with just a keystroke. While some partial-page screens display about half a page, others hold only six or eight lines of text. Word processors with partial-page screens are not as expensive as ones with full-

Components of a Word Processor

Use horizontal scrolling to see keyboarded text alongside a screenload.

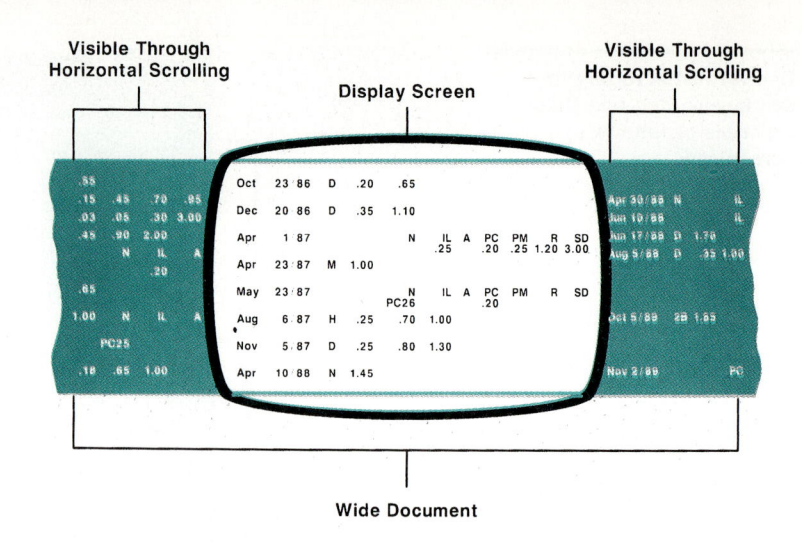

Visible Through Horizontal Scrolling

Display Screen

Visible Through Horizontal Scrolling

Wide Document

page screens. For this reason, partial-page screens far outnumber full-page screens in most offices.

Display screens generally are about as wide as a piece of ordinary typing paper, although some are narrower. Some systems also allow you to scroll horizontally, which is useful if you are working with tables or other unusually wide documents. With horizontal scrolling, you can move the displayed text from side to side on the screen so you can see the right or left side or the middle of the page as it will look when it is printed. While the screen may display only about 80 characters per line at one time, the horizontal scrolling may let you work with documents that have 132, 154, 180, or more characters to the line.

Type of Display. Most word processors have a single-screen display that shows one document at a time. Some systems have a *dual display*, which means that two documents can appear on the screen at the same time. You may hear this feature referred to as a split screen.

Harold Saunders discovered the convenience of using a split screen when he compiled a new price list for Cicchini Tiles, where he works in the Customer Service Department. His manager had given him an old brochure that had the new prices penciled in over the old ones, next to the descriptions and pictures of the company's merchandise. A few new items and their prices were written on the back. Mr. Saunders' job was to pre-

Word Processing Equipment

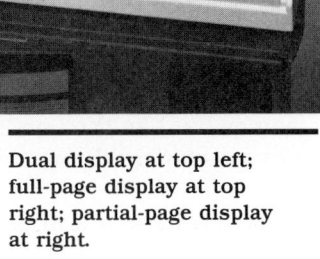

Dual display at top left; full-page display at top right; partial-page display at right.

Components of a Word Processor

pare a revised price list for the new brochure the company was developing.

Mr. Saunders had stored the previous year's list on the word processor. Rather than thumb back and forth through the printed 10-page list, he decided to work with it on the display screen. Using the dual-display feature, he was able to see his new list, with the revisions he was making, on the left side of the screen and the previous price list on the right. Comparing the lists item for item was much easier than constantly looking back and forth between a single screen and the printed page.

The video display is such an integral part of word processing today that it is difficult to think of a word processor without one. But when manufacturers first developed the office equipment that led to word processing, they did not use a TV tube. Let's now go back to that time and take a look at the earliest office automation equipment.

BLIND EQUIPMENT

The concept of word processing has been around since 1918, the year the Hooven Company sold the first automated typewriting system. This system used an Underwood typewriter as both the keyboard and the printer. The storage unit was an embossed cylinder, somewhat like the one in a music box. The power was provided by a noisy mechanical device that needed frequent oiling.

In the 1930s and 1940s, quieter automated typewriters were introduced. These machines recorded keystrokes by punching patterns of holes in paper sheets or strips. This was the same mechanism used in the old player pianos. When the punched paper was inserted in the typewriter, the machine automatically produced error-free typewritten copy.

These early models were used mostly to produce form letters that looked as though they were individually typed. Without an automated typewriter, a typist might have had to retype a letter hundreds of times, changing only the address and salutation. Automated equipment saved employers a great deal of money while freeing typists from repetitive tasks. These early models, however, allowed for no corrections or revisions, because the paper sheets or strips could not be changed once the holes had been punched into them. If you made a mistake, you had to start over.

The Beginning of Modern Word Processing

Word processing as we know it today did not begin until the invention of magnetic storage units—tapes that could be erased and corrected. Magnetic storage gave word processors the text-editing capabilities that make them useful for producing documents of all kinds, not just repetitive letters. Let's examine the

The MT/ST was the first modern word processor.

different kinds of blind equipment, beginning with the first magnetic-storage word processor, to see how the four components—keyboard, CPU, storage, and printer—have changed over the years and what new capabilities have been added.

MT/ST. Introduced by IBM in 1964, the MT/ST (Magnetic Tape Selectric Typewriter) was the first automated typing system to record keystrokes on a magnetic storage medium. It combined an IBM Selectric typewriter with processing and storage components.

The typewriter, which is modified to include a few function keys not found on other Selectrics, serves as both keyboard and printer. If you make a typing error, the MT/ST allows you to correct it by simply backspacing and typing over it. Because the strikeovers are visible on the typewritten page you produce as you keyboard, the original typed copy is not usable. However, the MT/ST can automatically type an unlimited number of flawless copies.

The MT/ST provided new text-editing features not found on earlier automated typing systems. You could use it to delete and insert words automatically. If the revisions did not fit in the space, the MT/ST adjusted line lengths to make room for the changes. It printed about 150 words a minute, about three times as fast as most typists.

The MT/ST stored up to 20 printed pages on a reel of magnetic tape. The reels could be filed, or erased and reused. Access was *serial* rather than random. That is, if you needed the fourth document on a tape, you had to skim through the first three documents before you got to the one you wanted.

IBM made two MT/ST models: one that used a single reel of tape, and one that recorded on two reels. The two-tape model could print one document using information from both reels. You could record a letter on one reel, and the names, addresses, and salutations of the people you were sending the letter to on a second reel. When you printed, the MT/ST merged both tapes to produce original-looking letters for a mass mailing.

MC/ST. The next big advance in word processing was the MC/ST (Magnetic Card Selectric Typewriter), sometimes called the Mag Card, which IBM introduced in 1969. Like the MT/ST, it is built around the Selectric typewriter, which serves as both keyboard and printer. The keyboard includes more function keys, such as automatic centering and underlining, that the MT/ST lacks.

The biggest difference between the MC/ST and its predecessor, though, is its storage unit. The MC/ST stores keystrokes on a magnetic-coated card rather than on a tape. Each card can record one page of keyboarding—up to 75 lines, with 100 characters a line. Like the tapes, the Mag Cards do not permit random access; you can't retrieve just part of the material on a card without manually skimming through unwanted information. Because each card holds only one document page, however, you don't have to go through as much text to get to the part you want. In addition, the storage console of the Mag Card, where you insert the card you are working with, is smaller than that of the MT/ST, and its controls are simpler.

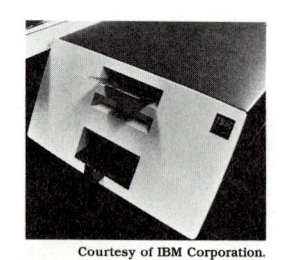

Mag Card II. IBM introduced an advanced version of the MC/ST, called the Mag Card II, in 1973. The Mag Card II was the first automated typewriter with an internal memory apart from the storage unit. Keystrokes are recorded first in the 8000-character internal memory. When you have made corrections and finished keyboarding, you use a function key to transfer the documents from the internal memory to the card, where it is stored. The Mag Card II introduced other features that represented significant advances in word processing. They include:

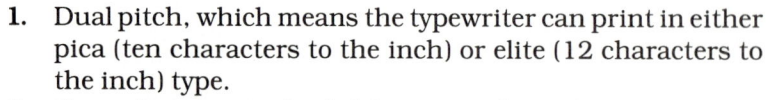

Courtesy of IBM Corporation.

The Mag Card II is an advanced version of the MC/ST.

1. Dual pitch, which means the typewriter can print in either pica (ten characters to the inch) or elite (12 characters to the inch) type.
2. Correcting tape, which lifts errors from the paper when you backspace and type over them. With this feature you produce usable hard copy as you perform your keyboarding.
3. Automatic tab, a function key enabling you to find automatically the part of a form letter where new material (such as the addressee's name) is needed.

Improvements

Over the next few years, several manufacturers introduced blind word processors with greater capabilities. These advanced models include cassette tape text-editing machines and memory typewriters.

Cassette Tape Text Editors. Cassette tape text-editing machines were introduced in 1972 by CPT and Redactron. In these machines storage is on a tape cassette that holds up to 60 pages of documents. Tape cassettes have greater capacity than MT/ST tapes or magnetic cards, and they are also less costly. Other components of cassette tape text editors are similar to those of the MT/ST.

Memory Typewriter. Introduced by IBM in 1974, Memory Typewriters offer many of the same capabilities as the Mag Card II but cost less. The component parts are all housed in the typewriter unit; there is no separate storage console. The storage capacity is about 50 to 100 printed pages, depending on the machine model—enough capacity for correspondence but not enough for long documents.

Blind Word Processing Today

Two types of blind equipment—mechanical and electronic—are being manufactured today. Although they resemble each other in many ways, their capabilities differ.

Mechanical Word Processor. A mechanical word processor is any "blind" unit that has the keyboard and a printer in one console, and a primary storage medium—tapes or cards—in another. This equipment includes the Mag Card and other models already discussed.

Mechanical blind word processors are used for automatic letter typing and other tasks that do not require more sophisticated functions.

Electronic Typewriter (ET). By the end of 1984 it became apparent that *electronic typewriters* (also called ETs) were edging out and would eventually replace the Mag Card and other electromechanical typing equipment. Currently, about a quarter of all office typewriters are electronic. Venture Development Corporation, an office automation consulting company, expects that by 1990 more than a third of all office typewriters will be ETs.

What is the ET and why is it so desirable? Although an electronic typewriter has the same basic components as a blind

An electronic typewriter is a blind word processor.

word processor—keyboard, CPU, printer, and storage unit—the ET also has many of the advantages of a word processor with a screen. ETs can print in a wide range of type styles, in regular or boldface type, at speeds of from 12 to 22 characters per second (cps).

When you type on a regular typewriter, every line begins at the same place on the left side of the page. This is called *left justification*. An ET can print a document with both left *and* right justification, so that every line also ends at the same point on the right side of the page. To do this, an electronic typewriter prints with proportional spacing—some characters are closer together, others are farther apart, so that every line is the same length—like the type on this page.

Automatic features of an ET include:

automatic end-of-line carriage return	**statistical functions: arranging columns**
centering	**aligning decimals**
erasing	**superscript and**
formatting	**subscript**
setting margins	**underlining**

Some electronic typewriters offer still more advanced features that include:

1. A memory that will store for 72 to 500 hours any text you have keyboarded in case you shut off the ET by mistake, or have a power failure.
2. Additional memory that can store up to 300,000 characters on double-sided diskettes.
3. A video display screen you can add onto the unit.
4. Exchanging information with other ETs, word processors, and computers by networking.
5. An electronic dictionary that automatically checks spelling.
6. Word processing functions that can search through a document for any character; delete, insert, or copy text anywhere in a document; and automatically correct over 4000 characters.
7. Computer software programs that further increase the information processing capabilities of the ET.

Electronic typewriters are ideal for handling letters, memos, reports, proposals, invoices, and other short documents in offices where quick turnaround and revisions are required. ETs are also being used increasingly for envelope addressing.

Electronic typewriters are designed so that they can be *up-*

graded. This means that the basic capabilities of the ET are enhanced. Adding peripherals is one way of upgrading equipment. One such peripheral, for example, is a disk drive.

Electronic typewriters are faster, easier to use, and cost less than word processors with screens for many office applications. For this reason, some office management experts agree with surveys that show that the ET will tend to dominate and then take over the office as electric typewriters currently in use grow obsolete. Other experts predict that the more sophisticated word processing systems will predominate, even though they are more expensive. Still others who study the office environment think the personal computer will become as indispensable in the office as the typewriter.

There are now portable word processors (also called *paperless typewriters*) which are small enough to fit in an attaché case. These run on batteries and make it possible for someone to produce a document anywhere.

Linear Display Word Processors

Most electronic typewriters have a special feature called a *linear display*—sometimes referred to as a "thin screen" or a "window into memory." With other ETs, this feature can be added on to upgrade the equipment. Most linear displays can show from 20 to 40 characters, not quite a full line of copy. They show enough, however, to allow operator verification of input—and they are thus classified between blind and display types of word processing systems.

A linear display is often called a "window into memory."

Blind Equipment

DISPLAY WORD PROCESSORS

In 1971 Lexitron introduced the first display word processor. This machine had all the capabilities of earlier equipment—with one important addition. The Lexitron had a VDT that looked very much like a television screen. The display screen did not bring you *General Hospital*, however. It brought you a picture of the document you were working on. That single feature has had a great impact on the processing of documents, on the later development of word processing equipment, and on office work in general.

Because it displays illuminated text during keyboarding, the display word processor allows the operator to make much more extensive revisions—and to make them more easily—than can be done on blind equipment.

The key to using a display word processor is the *cursor*. Most commonly, the cursor simply shows where the next letter, number, or mark of punctuation will appear when a character key is pressed. Various function keys can make the cursor move up, down, left, or right. Wherever you stop the cursor, you can keyboard something with the help of additional function keys—add new material in the usual way, correct errors many lines back, or even insert whole sentences or paragraphs into text you have already keyboarded. The cursor works almost like an editor's pencil.

Since the first display word processing system was introduced, scores of other manufacturers have begun producing them. Each manufacturer's equipment is slightly different.

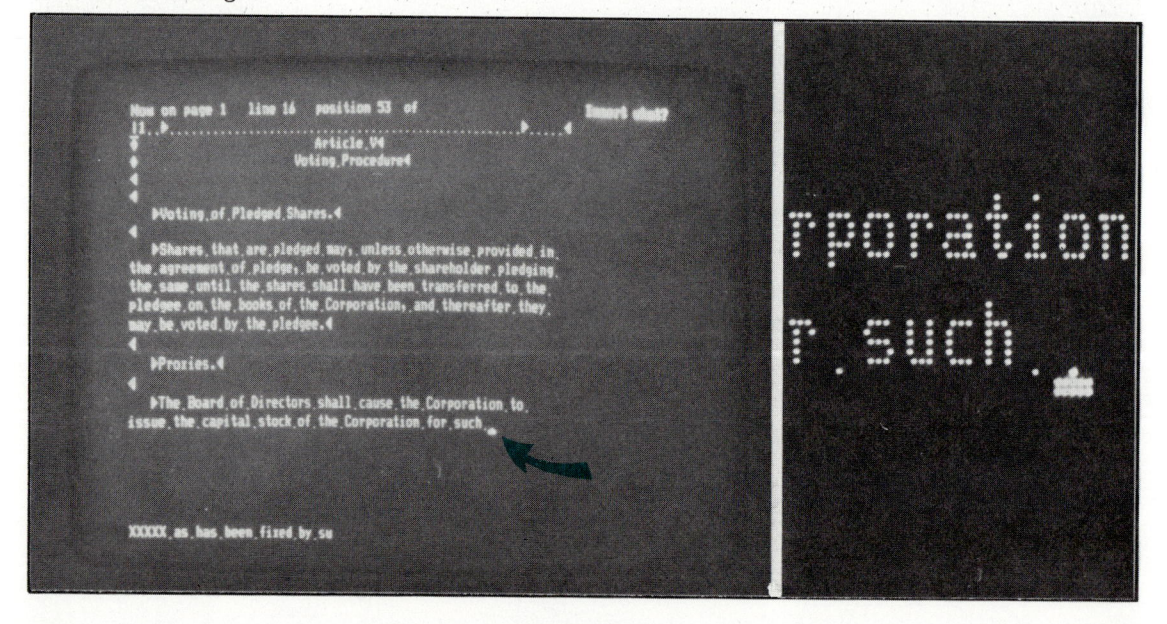

The cursor indicates the place in the text where the user is working.

Word Processing Equipment

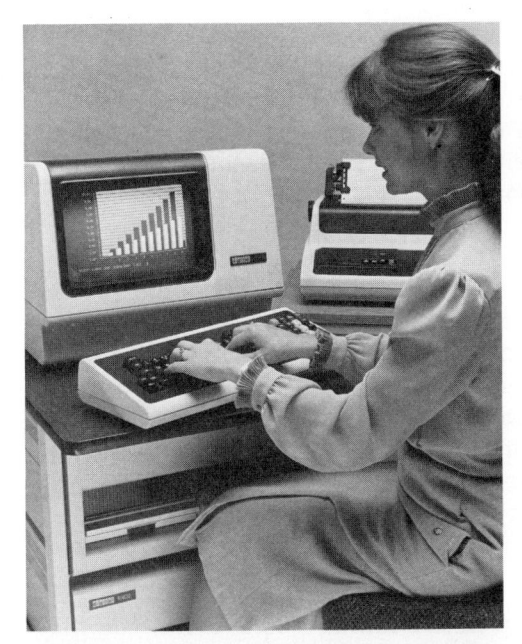

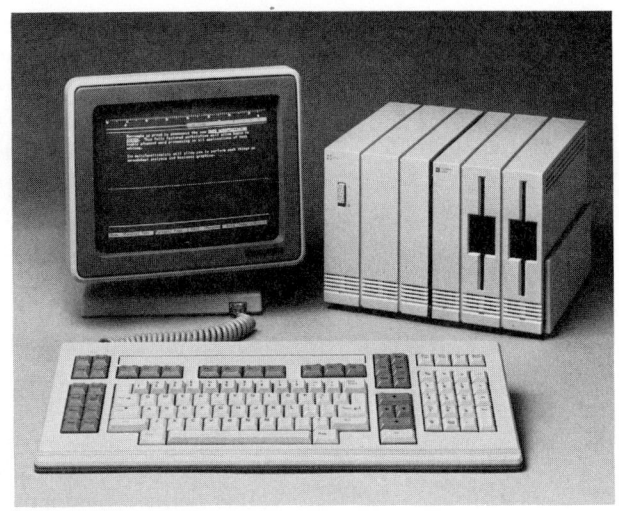

Display word processors are available in many different configurations.

Display Word Processors

Usually, though, when a display screen is part of the system, the five components are housed in two or more separate pieces of equipment. In some systems, components, such as the printer, can be shared by more than one word processor. Some systems include special peripherals to further increase their capabilities. The specific components and peripherals that make up a system are called the *configuration* of the system.

As manufacturers have competed vigorously for sales in this multibillion-dollar market, rapid advances in technology have not only expanded the capabilities of word processors but have also reduced their prices. When word processors first came on the market, only a few large organizations could afford them. Yet by the early 1980s word processor prices had decreased so drastically that many small companies could afford them, and some people—writers, for example—have them in their homes. Today some types of display word processors cost far less than a new car.

How to Use Display Word Processors

When you consult a map before taking a long drive, you may discover that several routes will get you to the same destination in a reasonable time. Still, one route may be faster because it bypasses towns with heavy traffic, even though you must travel more miles. The route that takes longer might be more economical, though—and you might prefer it because it takes you through towns you want to visit. With word processing, too, there are different ways to reach the same goal. Even among word processors with similar capabilities, there are differences in the steps required to perform the same task.

There are three basic styles of word processor operations: menu, functon menu, and coded. Now that you know about the basic components of a word processor and the variations you may find in them, it's time to discuss the differences in how the systems operate.

Menu. When you turn on the power, some word processors will display on the screen a list of the tasks you can perform. Such a list, or *menu*, may offer you choices that include creating a document, editing a document that you have already stored, printing a stored document, or looking up information about existing documents. Using your keyboard and the cursor, you indicate which task you want to perform.

Let's say you're going to print. Once you have made that choice from the menu and identified the document—for example, a form letter requesting payment of a bill—a secondary menu will appear on the display screen. It lists questions about how you want to format and print the letter. From the keyboard,

98 Word Processing Equipment

This shows the main menu for a Wang Alliance system. The list of choices at the right of the screen represents the system's word processing features.

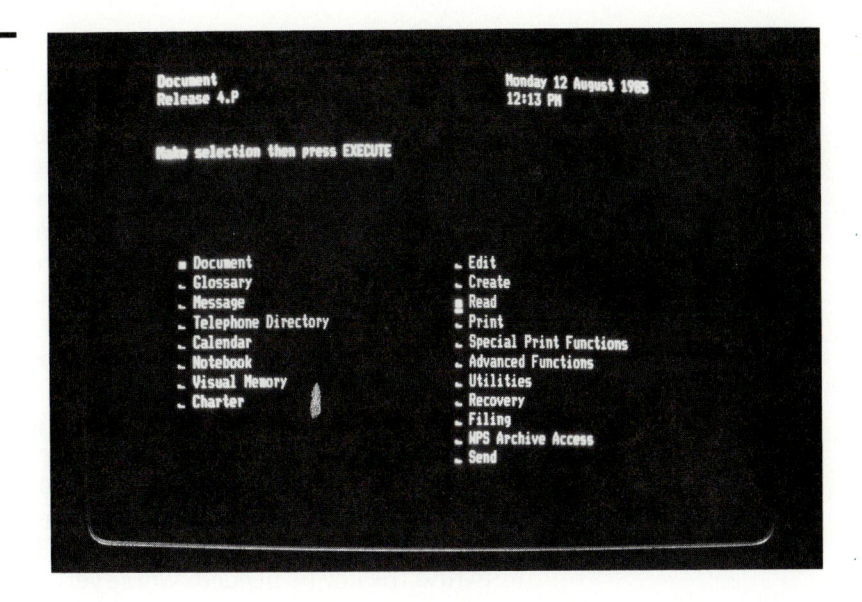

you give the word processor your instructions: how many copies you want; single or double spacing; pica, elite, or micro type; margin width; and so on. Some systems also use a secondary menu to display information about the document, such as the number of keystrokes in it, which operator created it, and when it was last revised or printed.

Function Menu. In a word processing system with a *function menu*, you must follow a selection procedure even to perform relatively simple tasks such as centering a line or inserting a word. Here are the steps you would follow to insert text on a Wang word processor, which uses a function menu.

1. Push the function key marked "Insert." The system responds with a prompt displaying the question "Insert What?"
2. Keyboard the material you want to insert.
3. Press the function key labeled "Execute."
4. The system will respond by inserting the new material and automatically adjusting the text lines to make room for it.

Beginners often find it easy to work with a function menu system because it guides them through the text-editing steps. Many experienced users, however, find function menu systems too time-consuming because the operator must take many steps to perform even a simple task. On some systems it is possible, however, for a user to bypass these steps.

Display Word Processors

Coded. A *coded* word processing system has no menu to guide you through its operation. Instead it requires you to keyboard your commands with a "code"—either with function keys or with combinations of function and character keys. As a result, it may take longer to learn to operate a coded word processing system than either the menu or function menu system. Besides learning the positions of the function keys, you must memorize the codes for many functions, such as retrieving documents from storage, changing the margins on a page printout, or combining two documents into one file. In the long run, however, this kind of system is faster to operate than a menu system once you memorize the codes.

Here's a case in point. When Joel Marin started his new job in an office that used coded word processors, he worried because his work went too slowly. The keyboard contained more function keys than the keyboard on the menu word processor at his last job, and he often had to scan the keyboard for a few seconds to find the key he needed. Worse yet, text-editing functions such as copying a paragraph from one document to another required that he use special codes. Each time he performed one of those functions, he had to look up its code in the word processor's operating manual. At first Mr. Marin was afraid he would never be able to memorize the codes and key positions. He thought he would never be able to work as fast as he did at his old job.

He was wrong. He learned rapidly and a few weeks later, he had changed his mind about the coded system. By then he had become familiar with the function key positions, and he found

The top row of keys in this photograph are the function keys for a coded system.

Word Processing Equipment

that he remembered most of the codes after he used them a few times. Already he was finding the coded equipment faster and easier to use than the menu system, mainly because fewer steps were involved in performing each function.

What Display Word Processors Can Do

Display word processors offer many more automatic text-editing functions than blind equipment, because you can see an entire document on the display screen before it is printed and because their CPUs are more advanced. Here is a chart showing some of the capabilities of display word processors.

Some Capabilities of Display Word Processors

Feature	Function
Status line	The status line shows the name of the document you are working on that identifies it for the CPU. It also shows the position of the cursor in relation to the rest of the document. The status line appears on the screen just above or below the document. It tells the secretary that, for example, the cursor is positioned in the twenty-third character for a forty-seventh line of a document named Collins Letter. The status line is not printed with the document.
Format line	The format line indicates where the margins and tabs are set and whether the document is single- or double-spaced. Format lines appear on the screen just above or below the document, but not on the printed page.
Automatic word wraparound	At the end of a line of keyboarding, the cursor automatically drops down to the next line without the use of the carriage return. If the last word won't fit on a line, that word is automatically "wrapped around" and entered as the first word on the next line.
Search	To find the spot where a particular word (or any series of characters) appears in a document, the word processor will scan the text until it locates the given word. The text will scroll until the cursor lands on the word—or until it has searched the whole document without finding it.

Global search and replace	If a word or phrase recurs throughout a document and needs to be changed, the word processor can find each place where the word or phrase appears and automatically replace it with a correction.
Move	An unlimited sequence of characters can be moved automatically to any other spot within a document.
Super move	An unlimited sequence of characters can be moved automatically from one document to another.
Copy	An unlimited sequence of characters can be copied so that the same text appears in two places in a document.
Super copy	An unlimited sequence of characters can be copied from one document to another.
Right-margin justification	The right margin of a document can be aligned automatically as it is printed.
Pagination	A document can be separated automatically into pages containing the number of lines specified. Pages are numbered automatically on the screen. The numbers appear at the top or bottom of the printed pages, or not at all, according to the operator's instructions.
Undo	A special feature that allows you to "undo" any text you have keyboarded. For example, if you have just moved a paragraph and then realize you moved the wrong paragraph, this function would return the document to its original form.
Columnar wrap	A feature you can use to keyboard columns on a page. This feature lets you insert, delete, move, and copy text in one column without disturbing any of the other columns. The text will automatically wrap around and stay in its column.
Text shelving	This feature allows the secretary to move a part of the text to a "shelf" (rather than to another position in the document) just as you move books from one shelf in the library

HELP   The HELP function key is growing in popularity and can be found on almost all systems today. By pressing the HELP key during editing, the system displays a series of screens that define the function the user is performing, the proper keystroke sequence to complete the function, and additional keys relevant to the function. After viewing the HELP screen, the user can go back to the document and complete the function.

to another shelf. The text moved is held on the shelf until the user decides where to place the information. At that point, the information is removed from the "shelf" and placed in the document.

WORD PROCESSING SYSTEMS CONFIGURATIONS

An employee's *workstation*—the place he or she performs most work functions—is no longer just a desk and chair. Today's idea of a workstation includes all the equipment, furnishings, and accessories a person requires to perform the work.

Some workstation specifications are of a technical nature—providing special electrical outlets to accommodate word processing equipment, for instance—or are simply general layout guidelines, such as allocating 88 square feet per workstation. What these ideas and specifications share in common is a key underlying principle: To maximize both productivity and job satisfaction, workstations should suit the needs of the people who work with them. Suiting the needs of the workers is, similarly, the guiding principle in deciding how word processing systems can best be arranged to fit an office's organizational structure and work flow. Let's look at some of the most common word processing system configurations.

Standalones

A word processing workstation used as a self-contained system—with its own keyboard, CPU, storage, printer, and perhaps display screen—is commonly called a *standalone*. Up until the mid-1970s, all word processing equipment was standalone. Technically speaking, standalones are designed and built without the capability to communicate with other machines through a cable connection (the same type of cable used to bring cable television into your home). However, since even equipment that does have this communication capability is often used in offices as a self-contained system, the way in which it is used provides the better definition.

Display standalone word processor.

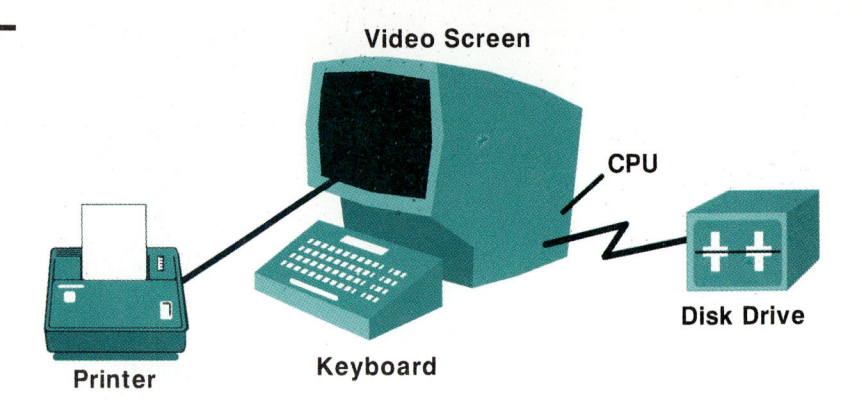

Clustered Systems

Rather than being self-contained, *clustered* systems are arrangements of word processors that share one or more components. The ability to share brings down the cost of the overall installation and offers companies needing large systems various options in matching equipment to their work needs. Because of these advantages, clustered systems are becoming more and more popular. There are two basic types of clustered systems.

Shared Logic. A *shared logic* system houses its "intelligence" in one central place. In this type of system, the word processors do not have their own CPUs (or they may have CPUs with very limited capabilities). Instead they are hooked up to and share a central processing unit.

For organizations with many word processors, shared logic configurations may be more economical than other systems, because their individual workstations cost less if they don't have their own internal processors. In addition, CPUs for shared logic systems generally are more sophisticated and more powerful than individual internal processing units, so shared logic systems have bigger memories and more capabilities.

However, one drawback is that if the central processing unit breaks down for any reason—and they do—all the workstations that share it are out of commission. A CPU failure can even erase documents from the memory or scramble documents with others.

It is also common for shared logic configurations to share a central external storage unit. Such a storage center receives documents from many workstations and generally stores them on hard disks. Hard disks offer much greater capacity and faster retrieval than floppy diskettes. The volume of a storage center is the total amount of text in storage. To make retrieval easier, the volume is divided into libraries. There may be differ-

Shared logic word processing system.

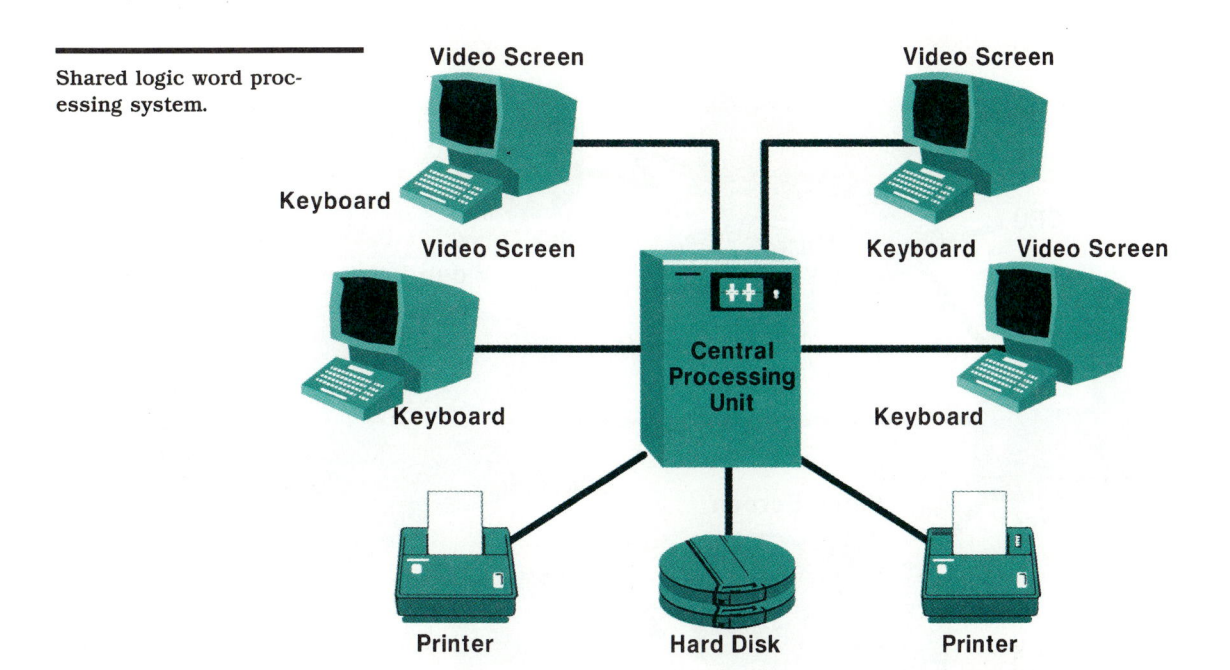

ent libraries for various kinds of documents: Library A for reports, Library B for interoffice memos, and so forth. Or the storage center might instead designate a library for each author or each department. Libraries, in turn, are divided into files, which represent individual documents.

In a shared logic system word processors can communicate with each other. Utilizing this feature increases productivity in offices where many people may work on a single document. After you have keyboarded or edited a document, you send it electronically to the workstation of the person who sees it next. This saves the steps involved in printing out a copy of the document for each person who works on it and then keyboarding each person's revisions. Shared logic systems generally require users to key in passwords or identification numbers to prevent unauthorized people access to confidential documents.

As a safeguard against CPU malfunctions and to add storage capacity, workstations in some shared logic systems are equipped with their own central processing units, as well as with self-contained storage. Some people refer to these as *smart* or *intelligent workstations*. (Workstations not so equipped that are entirely dependent on the CPU for memory and operating instructions are sometimes called *dumb workstations*.) A sys-

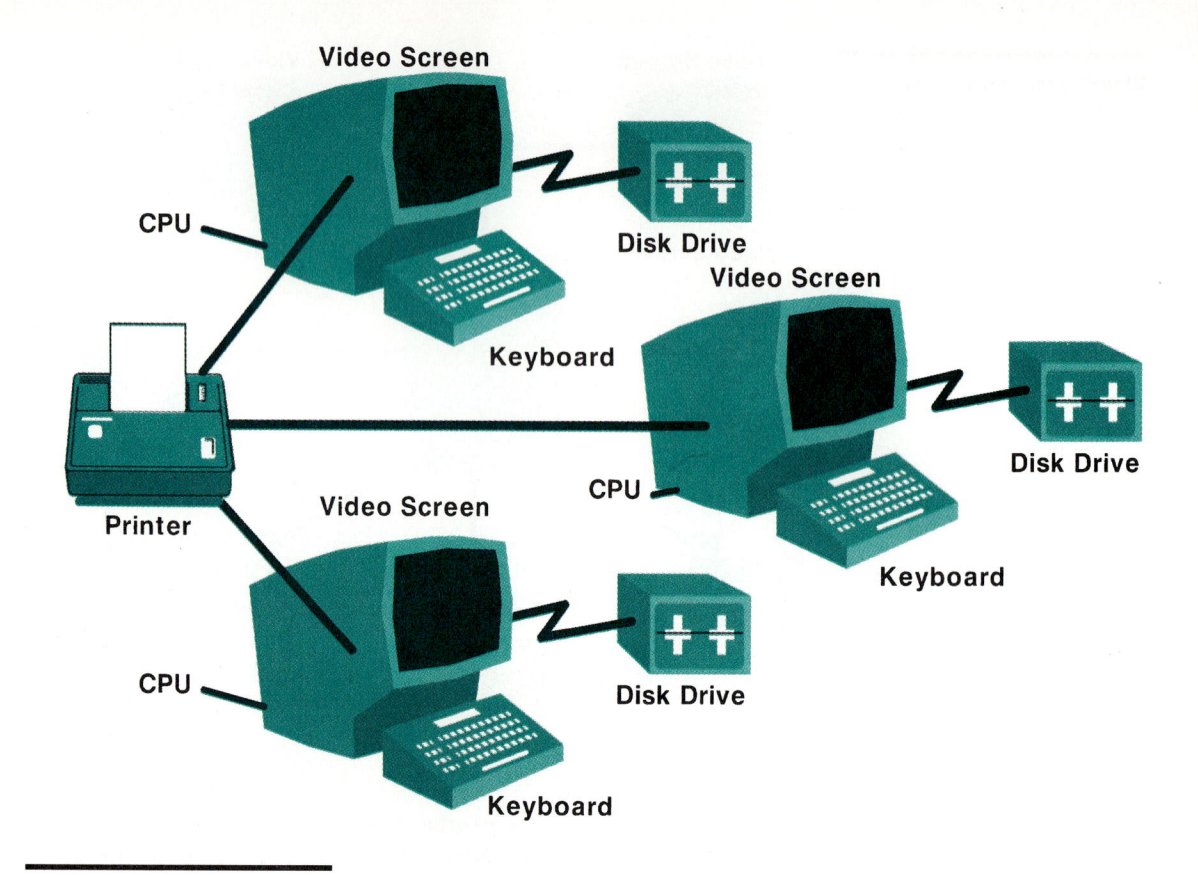

Shared resource word processing system.

tem configuration using intelligent workstations is sometimes called a *distributed logic system* or *distributed processing*.

Shared Resource. Another kind of clustered system is the *shared resource* system, in which workstations with their own floppy disk drives share resources such as printers and central storage. Some systems can also share hard disks for document storage. Security measures are built in to protect confidential documents. Because they have central processing units, the workstations in shared resource systems cost more than the dumb workstations usually found in shared logic systems. They save money in other ways, though. Equipping each workstation with its own printer, which probably would be idle much of the time while the operator was busy with other tasks, is obviously more costly than allowing several workstations to share a printer. Thus in a shared resource system the company saves money on printers.

Time-Sharing Systems

If an organization does not wish to purchase a computer big enough to provide the speed, storage, and capabilities it needs for word processing, it may instead subscribe to a time-sharing system. Subscribers may pay fees for using time accessed from a computer owned by another organization.

Because the subscribers are physically removed from the computer, telephone lines are used to gain access to it. The computer keeps track of how much time each keyboard operator spends using the system, and the subscriber receives a bill, usually monthly, for the total time its operators have spent on-line, or connected to the computer and for the amount of storage used.

Time-sharing systems are used by many organizations with branches scattered around the country. When the branches and the home office are sharing the same computer, their word processing workstations can communicate with each other.

For example, when George Avery, an economist at the San Francisco branch of Willison Brothers Securities Brokerage firm, found that he needed a copy of a report for an important meeting the next day, he panicked. The report had just been prepared in the New York home office, and Mr. Avery was afraid he wouldn't receive a copy in time, even if an express courier were used. From Sandy Silverman, a secretary in the New York office, he learned that the report had been prepared on word processing equipment and was stored in the time-sharing system used by both offices. By pushing a few buttons on her keyboard, Ms. Silverman sent the report electronically to Mr. Avery's office. Within two minutes, a printer in the San Francisco office was printing out a copy of the report that had been keyboarded 3000 miles away!

Sometimes the sponsor of a time-sharing system oversells it, which creates one of the biggest drawbacks of time-sharing. If too many keyboard operators are using the system, you may get busy signals when trying to reach the computer. Another drawback is the fact that time-sharing systems are less "user-friendly" for the operator; for example, special instructions must be followed to "log on" and "log off" the system. Otherwise, from the operator's point of view, a time-sharing system operates in much the same way as a shared-logic system, except that it has more capacity and capabilities.

As you can see from this overview, there is a tremendous variety in the ways word processing equipment can be arranged within a system. The range of word processing capabilities is becoming greater as advances of technology make new kinds of equipment available and as new arrangements become possible.

CHAPTER SUMMARY

- All word processors have four components: keyboard, central processing unit, storage, and printer.
- Today many word processors also have a fifth component, video display.
- In addition to the character keys and space bar found on a typewriter, a word processor keyboard has function keys, which are used to communicate instructions to the CPU.
- The central processing unit acts as the "intelligence" or "logic" of a word processor. It receives instructions from the keyboard and conveys them to the other components.
- The storage unit houses magnetically recorded documents for future use.
- The printer produces the output of a word processing system. On nondisplay word processors, such as electronic typewriters, the printer is part of a single machine; on display models it is separate.
- The display screen shows what characters are being input as a document is keyboarded, which allows the operator to review and revise them before producing printed copy.
- Modern word processing began with the invention of magnetic storage media. These media record keystrokes, which can be easily erased and corrected.
- Two types of blind, or nondisplay, word processors are used in today's office: electronic units and mechanical units.
- A mechanical word processor has a keyboard, central processing unit, and printer in one console and a storage unit in another. Mechanical units are used for form letters and other uncomplicated writing tasks.
- An electronic typewriter has all its components in a single console. It has a number of automatic formatting capabilities, and some are modular so that their features can be upgraded.
- Linear display word processors are electronic typewriters that display almost a line of copy on a thin screen.
- Display word processors permit extensive revisions and format changes before a document is printed, and offer more automatic features than blind equipment.
- Some display word processors display menus that tell the operator what tasks can be performed on them. These menus guide the operator through the steps of the tasks. Other display word processors require the operator to use codes to tell them what to do.
- An employee's workstation—the place where she or he performs most job functions—is no longer regarded as just a

desk and a chair. In the modern office the workstation includes all equipment, furnishings, and accessories a person requires to perform job tasks.
- Standalone word processing equipment consists of a self-contained workstation that does not share components with other workstations.
- There are two kinds of clustered systems: shared logic and shared resources.
- In a shared logic system, all workstations are linked to a powerful central processing unit (CPU).
- In a shared resource system, workstations may have individual internal processors but share other components such as printers.
- In a time-sharing system, organizations share in the use of a powerful, remote computer to which they gain access by using telephone lines.
- As computerized information processing becomes more sophisticated, word processing and data processing are increasingly integrated to make more efficient use of equipment, employees' abilities, and other resources.

INFORMATION PROCESSING VOCABULARY

archive
backup
buffer
clustered system
configuration
CPU (central processing unit)
CRT (cathode-ray tube)
cursor
disk drive
distributed logic
electronic typewriter (ET)
EPROM (erasable programmable read-only memory)
floppy diskette
format
function key
hardware
hard disk
intelligent workstation

mechanical typewriter
memory
menu
peripheral
program
PROM (programmable read-only memory)
RAM (random access memory)
ROM (read-only memory)
screenload
scroll
shared logic
shared resource
standalone
time-sharing
upgrade
user-friendly
Winchester disk
workstation

Information Processing Vocabulary

CHAPTER QUESTIONS

1. What are the five components of a display word processor? How does the keyboard of a display word processor resemble that of an ordinary typewriter? How does it differ?
2. Which component makes display word processing systems so much more versatile than blind systems? How does it do this?
3. People talk about the "logic" of a word processor. What is this logic? What is the difference between temporary and permanent memory?
4. When was the first word processor introduced? What was it called? What special capability did it have that put it far ahead of earlier equipment?
5. What kinds of storage media are used on word processors today? Which kind is most appropriate when great storage capacity is required?
6. Where is the printer located on blind equipment? Where is it located on a display word processor? Which location is most advantageous, and why?
7. What is a screenload? What is scrolling? Why is it helpful to be able to scroll?
8. Compare and contrast menu and coded systems of operating a display word processor.
9. Identify and explain at least ten capabilities of display word processors.
10. What are some of the advantages and some of the disadvantages of a shared logic system? Of a shared resource system?

CASE STUDY

Jordan Husk, Jr., is president of Metropole Communications, Inc., a small advertising and public relations firm. The company employs about 20 people who produce advertising and market research reports for a number of clients. In addition, the company also has a typing and photocopying service for local clients.

Mr. Husk is seriously considering installing word processing equipment in his company. He has assigned his administrative assistant, Alice Gomez, to obtain information from several vendors about their equipment. Ms. Gomez is familiar with all the operations of Metropole Communications, has obtained brochures on equipment from various manufacturers, and has completed an evening course in word processing and information systems at the local college.

Ms. Gomez has organized the brochures into categories of equipment, such as display equipment, printers, blind processors, storage units, and so on. The next phase of her investigation will include meetings with sales representatives from the vendors.

Based on the information presented in this chapter about the types and equipment capabilities of word processing systems, make a list of questions that Ms. Gomez might ask when she talks with sales representatives. Keep in mind that Ms. Gomez will want to find out how easily and efficiently equipment can be installed at Metropole and how well it can do several kinds of tasks, such as reports, form letters, and proposals, to meet the company's current and future needs.

CHAPTER 5

Microcomputers and Software

One afternoon Rosalie Maddalena, the new manager of the Public Relations Department of Chiudioni Advertising Agency, conducted an informal survey of her staff to find out what kinds of tasks and office duties they performed most frequently. She found that Mary Lou Hofmann was responsible for processing all the incoming and outgoing correspondence; Dick Callahan handled budgets, departmental accounts, and cash flow analysis; and Bridget Ragan designed and created charts, graphs, and other visuals. Ms. Maddalena had read about microcomputers and software programs that could help in processing words, numbers, and graphs. She decided to investigate different microcomputers and software programs that could best handle the needs of her department.

The computer is the basic element, or hub, of any electronic office system. Computer technology allows the combining of word processing and data processing systems. When the power and storage capacity of computers are joined with the user-friendly, text-editing capabilities of word processors, the result can be a highly efficient office information system. Let's look at the variety of computers on the market today and the variety of functions they perform.

COMPUTERS

When computers were first being used in business, they were seen as gigantic and enormously expensive metal boxes with flashing lights and reels of tape that would put people out of work and otherwise make a mess of things. Now many computers cost less than new cars, and we can use them to balance checkbooks, store favorite recipes, and play video games. And while some jobs may have been eliminated because of computers, the computer industry has created many more jobs than it has done away with. Since computer use is increasing, it is vital that we learn more about computers, software, and the use of computers for information processing.

Although the first computers were big enough to fill several rooms, today's computers are more powerful than those early ones and yet small enough to fit easily onto desk tops. People in the computer industry divide computers into categories according to their processing power, their information storage capacity, and their cost. The industry is expanding fast, and some new computers don't fit clearly into any one category. But, generally speaking, computers are categorized as mainframes, minicomputers, or microcomputers.

Mainframe

The biggest computers, called *mainframes*, can process the most information at the highest speeds. Mainframes can also accommodate a wide variety of optional equipment to increase their usefulness. They may accept additional storage and many additional terminals.

Mainframes can cost millions of dollars each. They require highly trained operators and their own special programs in order to run efficiently. But because of their speed and vast storage capacity, big business is likely to be using them for many years, despite the development of smaller and easier-to-use equipment. For some tasks, such as processing a payroll for a company with tens of thousands of employees, a mainframe is the best computer for the job.

Minicomputer

Many of the medium-sized computers now in use can do jobs that would have required a mainframe ten years ago. The *minicomputers*, or *minis*, have less storage capacity than mainframes; however, they also cost less. Minis sometimes are used as the central processing units (CPUs) of shared logic word processing systems. Some users prefer to have several minicomputers rather than a mainframe—or in addition to a mainframe—so that a single computer failure won't disrupt the whole organization.

Microcomputer

The smallest computer is a *microcomputer*. It is also called a *micro*, and sometimes a *personal computer*, or *professional computer*, or *PC*. Micros are relatively inexpensive and yet versatile enough for word processing, data processing, and many types of software programs.

Some *small business systems*, which are a step above personal computers, can process information with speed and efficiency rivaling a minicomputer's performance. We use the terms microcomputers and personal computers interchangeably.

Not since television swept the land in the 1950s have we seen anything like the personal computer phenomenon. In 1984, worldwide personal computer shipments surpassed those of minicomputers. Industry experts predict that by 1987 they will be even with mainframe shipments. In the decade from 1977 to 1987, the worldwide installed base of personal computers will have grown from 200,000 to over 80 million. Annual shipments in 1987 will be over 20 million.

According to a recent survey conducted by Future Computing, a McGraw-Hill market research firm, by the mid-1990s 75 percent of business employees will have PCs, and by 1995 an estimated 54 million employees will be using personal computers—a fivefold increase from a 1985 projection.

Micros can be used by small, medium, and large companies in every type of industry. They can also be used in homes, schools, government offices, and other institutions. Imagine living in the modern world without cars or telephones. In a few years life without microcomputers may seem just as unimaginable.

Micros have the same components and the same operating steps as larger computers. The operator uses a keyboard to send instructions to the central processing unit. Regardless of whether the micro is processing words or numbers, output can be captured in hard copy by a printer. Some micros store information on small $3\frac{1}{2}$-inch or $5\frac{1}{4}$-inch floppy diskettes. Others store information on hard disks or tape cassettes.

A microcomputer is very versatile. It can be used for word processing and data processing.

Microcomputers and Software

There are now *portable microcomputers* (also called *transportables* or lap-size computers). They can range in size from pocket-size computers to those that can fit in an attaché case. The larger versions of these may have pop-up display screens. These smaller computers have many of the same capabilities as their larger cousins, personal computers.

Components of a Microcomputer. The components of a microcomputer are the same as those of a word processor: keyboard, CPU, storage, printer, and display. Let's examine some of the similarities and differences between the components of a word processor and a microcomputer.

Keyboard. The keyboard layout of a personal computer is in most cases similar to that of a word processor. The keyboard includes the standard QWERTY keys, cursor keys, function keys, operation keys, format keys, statistical keys and/or a numeric keypad, and code keys if necessary. Many personal computer manufacturers and a few word processor manufacturers offer a feature called *programmable/special function keys.* Since personal computers are used for a variety of applications rather than being dedicated to only word processing functions, certain keys can be "programmed" to have special functions, depending on the application being used. Many of these programs come with a template or "function strip." Some templates have openings cut out so they can fit over the keyboard; others are cards intended for use at the operator's desk next to the keyboard. A template tells you the letter, number, or special function each key represents in the selected application such as accounting. New templates or strips are usually provided for a wide range of applications. We will learn more about these functions when we study software applications later in this chapter.

When typewriters were first invented, the keyboard was designed differently from the QWERTY keyboard. It was found that as typists gained speed, they went too fast for these early typewriters and the keys would jam. As a result, about a hundred years ago the QWERTY keyboard was designed. The QWERTY system was developed to deliberately slow down the typist. For example, the most commonly used keys were placed on the left side of the keyboard. It also required the typist to reach for often-used keys. These keyboard developments slowed typists down and lessened the problem of the keys jamming.

In 1932 August Dvorak, a professor of education at Washington State University, invented a keyboard designed to reduce fatigue, cut down on errors, and increase typing productivity. Dvorak identified the most commonly used letters. He relocated those keys on the middle, or "home" row, where the fingers rest

This template defines the uses of the function keys.

Computers

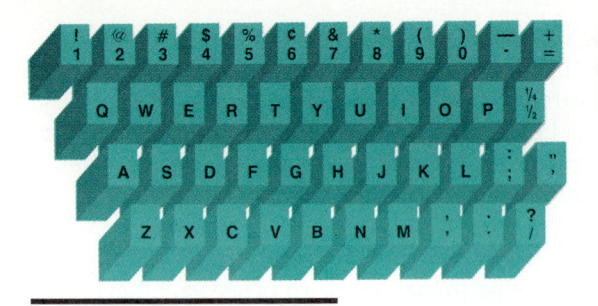

A QWERTY keyboard at left. A Dvorak keyboard at right.

between keystrokes. This put all the vowels and five of the most frequently used consonants where typists could reach them with the least finger movement.

You cannot jam the keys on an electric typewriter that uses a typing element, on a word processor, or on a computer the way you can on a manual typewriter. Today's technology thus has eliminated the need for the QWERTY keyboard's built-in inefficiency. Spurred by research evidence that the Dvorak keyboard can increase a typist's productivity by more than 20 percent, several manufacturers are already offering a keyboard option referred to as the "flick of a switch." For example, Apple Computer, Inc., has developed a system for instantly switching its QWERTY keyboard to the Dvorak and back. The company believes, as do several other manufacturers, that the dual-function keyboard is the ideal way to introduce the Dvorak keyboard because it gives the users a choice without forcing them to make a major commitment to either keyboard.

Many types of input devices have been created for use on today's microcomputers—designed for the individual who wishes to minimize the amount of keyboarding. These devices replace the use of function keys. Some of these have been used on mainframe and minicomputers, especially on graphics terminals. Most of us are familiar with the *joystick*. Joysticks are handheld devices that let the user manipulate the cursor on the display and are most frequently used with video games.

From left to right: a joystick, a light pen, and a touch-sensitive screen.

116   Microcomputers and Software

Like the joystick, the mouse moves the cursor on the screen.

Light pens resemble a standard writing pen, except that the end of the pen has a light-sensitive cell. When the tip of the pen comes in contact with the display terminal, a point on the display is identified. In this way data and graphic illustrations can be entered or "created."

With a few of today's personal computers, the user has the option of a *touch-sensitive* display as the input device. Instead of memorizing commands or typing in menu-selection numbers, you simply touch a point on the menu displayed on the screen to operate the system and its application programs.

The *mouse* is an input device a few inches long and an inch or so high, which is small enough to fit in the hand. It has a "tail"— an electrical cord that connects to the PC. Apple's mouse has a magnetic ball on it's bottom, which allows it to roll around on a desk. When you roll the mouse, the cursor moves on the screen. By pressing a button you can open and close files, and display menus on the screen.

CPU.   You can think of the central processing unit (CPU) as the headquarters for all the computer's operations. The CPU is where data is manipulated—added, subtracted, multiplied, divided, and sorted in other logical ways. The software programs that give the computer the electronic instructions to do the work you want it to do are also executed in the CPU.

The CPU is made up of *microprocessors* wired together in an electronic circuit on a plastic board. A microprocessor is sometimes referred to as a *microchip* or *chip*. Each microprocessor is a small chip of silicon that, in turn, contains its own electronic circuit. As technology advances, manufacturers are finding ways to fit more electronic circuitry into less space. Some microprocessors made today are no bigger than a baby's fingernail. Their circuitry is too small to assemble by hand—nearly too small to see with the eye alone.

If we think of an electric light, we can see that the light is either on or off. The circuitry of a computer is vastly more complex than that of a light bulb, but it works the same way. The only thing the computer really "understands" is whether it's on or off. Computer scientists and programmers use the number one to mean "on" and zero to mean "off." The number one then means that the electricity can go through the circuit; zero means the circuit is broken and electricity cannot get past. By sending electricity through the circuit, and then switching it on and off with great speed, information can be processed.

A single one or a single zero represents the smallest unit of information a computer can understand. This unit is called a *bit*. *Bit* stands for *binary digit*. Binary means made up of two parts. Computers use this binary logic to process information.

Programmers put the bits together in groups. For example, a group of 8 bits is called a *byte*. One byte is equal to one alphanumeric character. Computer programmers write in bytes the way the rest of us write using letters and numbers. If we consider a byte to consist of 8 bits, then there are 256 possible ways to arrange combinations of ones and zeros in groups of eight; for example, 11001110; or 10010001; and so on.

In a sense, the bytes can represent letters, numbers, and punctuation marks—all the things we use when we write. With 256 byte combinations for one 8-bit byte, there are more than enough bytes in an 8-bit system to represent all 26 letters of the alphabet, numbers 0–9, and every mark of punctuation. The remaining bytes are often used for instructions to the computer. Each byte has a location. A *location*, called an *address*, is the place where information can be stored. The computer's storage capacity is its memory.

Two 8-bit bytes would yield 65,536 (256 × 256) possible byte locations. A computer's memory is usually discussed in terms of kilobytes (kilo stands for 1000). A memory capacity of 65,536 is referred to as 64K bytes, (K stands for kilo), 64KB (B stands for bytes), or, most commonly, just 64K. The more memory a computer has, the more informaton it can process. For example, if you are using a microcomputer with 64K, you could not run a software program on it that required 128K.

Today's microcomputers are designed with the user in mind. For example, the office automation director may have allocated only enough money to purchase a microcomputer for your office with 64K of memory. As time goes by, you become more proficient with the system and find your work load increasing to the point that to run new programs you need more memory, let's say 256K. By purchasing and installing an *expandable memory board* you would have upgraded the memory capacity of your system without buying new hardware.

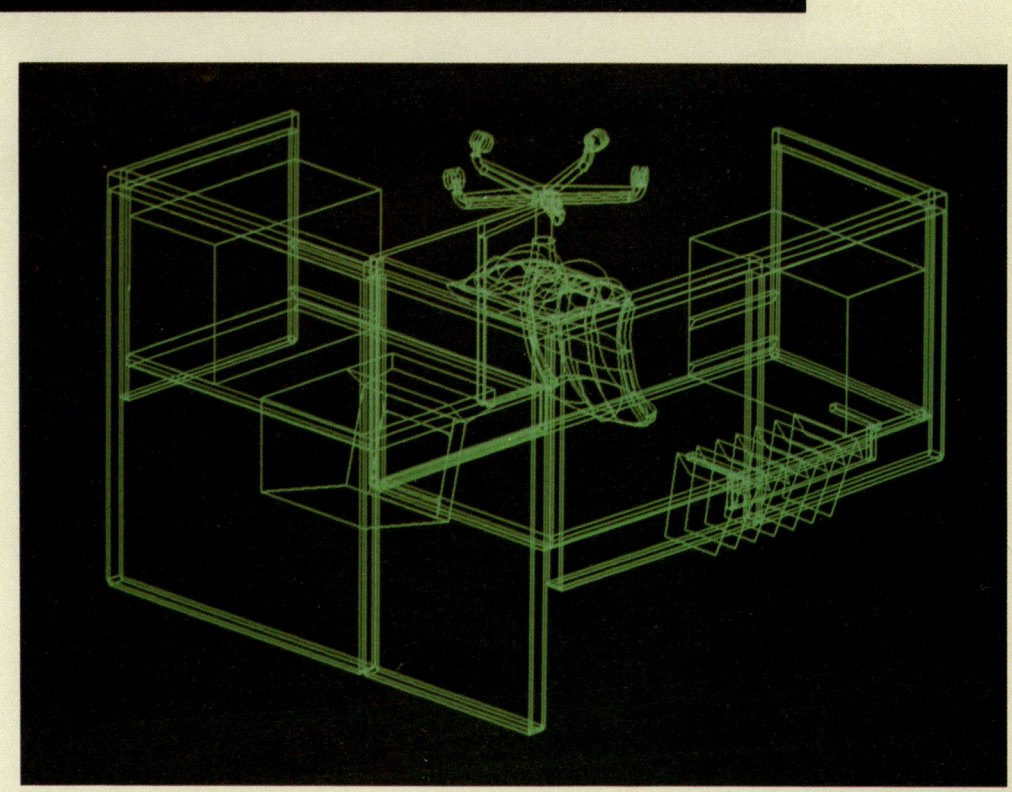

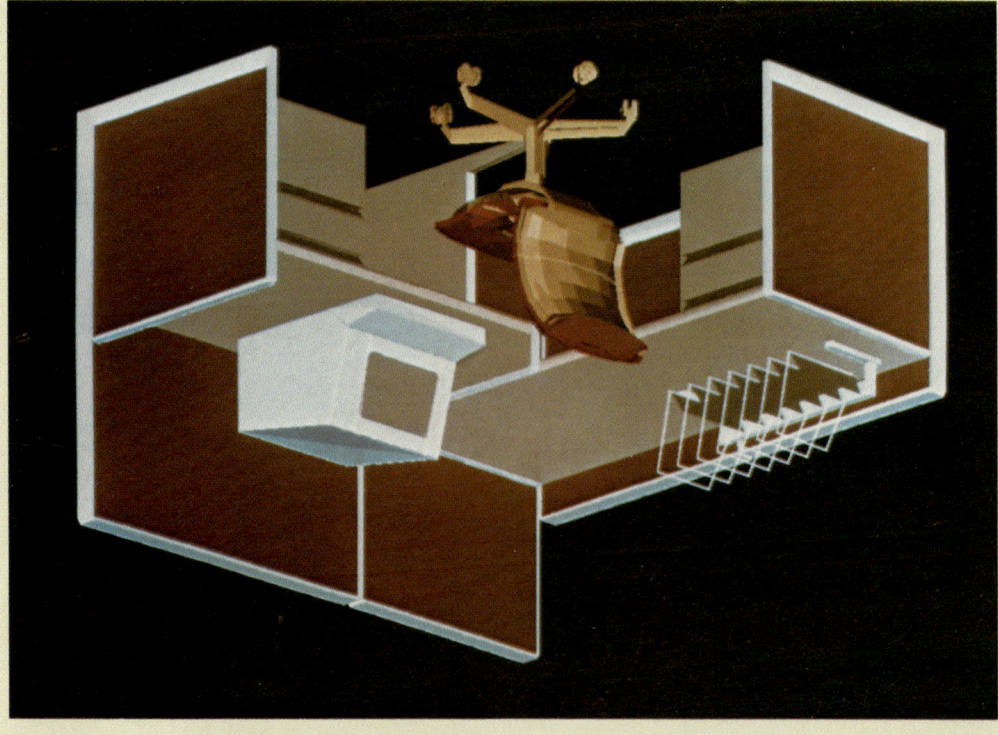

Line drawings can become three-dimensional with the touch of a few keys.

A color plotter is used to create a hard copy of the graphic image on the display screen.

II B

A color palette provides a variety of colors from which you can select the one you want to use. You make your selection by touching the appropriate box with the light pen.

It is possible to draw directly on a display screen by using a light pen.

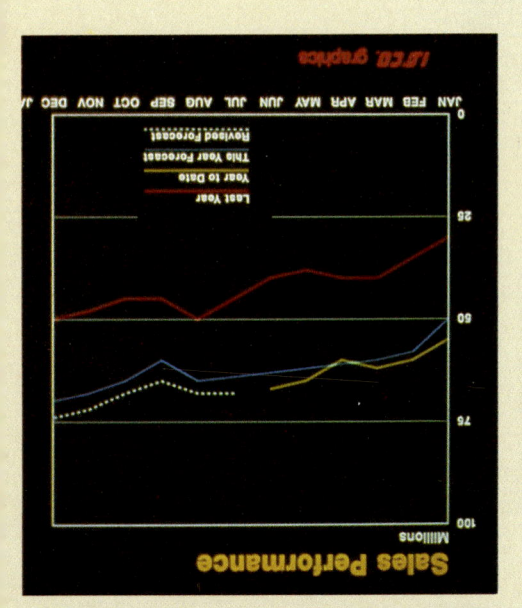

These four illustrations show how numeric information can be converted into graphic images on a screen. Top left, pie chart; top right, vertical bar chart; bottom left, horizontal bar chart; bottom right, line graph.

Computer graphics programs have a wide range of applications. Some create pictorial representations of numeric data; others can be used for drawing or for drafting.

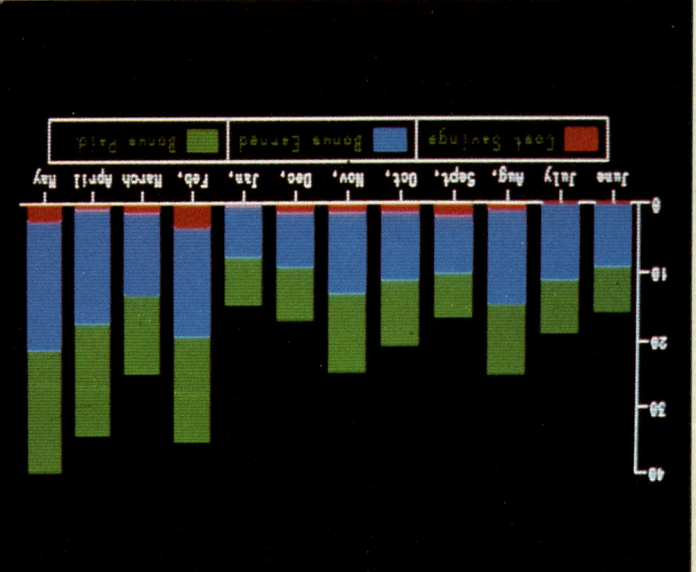

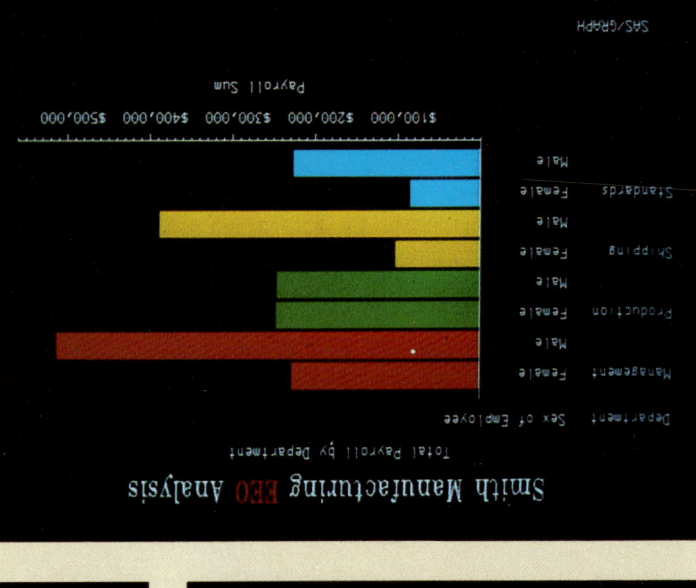

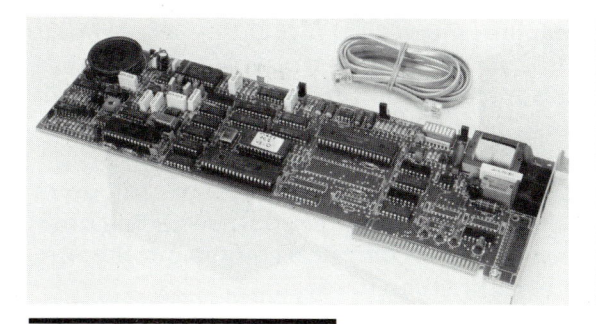

An expandable memory board (at left) fits neatly into the back of the microcomputer.

In addition to memory capacity, a computer's performance is also affected by its *cycle time*—the time it takes to perform one instruction. The speed of a computer's CPU is considered to be the number of cycles performed in one second. The cycle time for computers varies very greatly; it can range from 2 million instructions per second (mips) to 12 million instructions per second. A *cycle per second (cps)* is called a *hertz (Hz)*. A million hertz equal a *megahertz (MHz)*. A computer's cycle time is often referred to in megahertz, so you can see the enormous speed of computers. When you combine bit size, memory capacity, and cycle time, you can evaluate the overall efficiency of any computer.

Storage.   Like word processors, microcomputers store information on diskettes. Depending on the model, word processors use 8- and $5\frac{1}{4}$-inch floppy diskettes; microcomputers use $5\frac{1}{4}$- and $3\frac{1}{2}$-inch floppies. A $3\frac{1}{2}$-inch diskette has a memory capacity of 125 to 250 pages. It is because of improvements in the technology of storage devices that the $3\frac{1}{2}$-inch diskette can hold as much as, if not more than, the $5\frac{1}{4}$-inch diskette.

Printers.   Many types of printers are available for use with today's personal computers. The quality and speed of the printer are, as usual, dependent upon the price the user can pay. Information on printers is in Chapter 6.

Video Screen.   Although word processors come in a variety of screen sizes, most microcomputers have partial page displays consisting of 8 to 24 lines per screenload. Just like dedicated word processors, displays come in a variety of colors, including green on black, amber on black, and white on black.

SOFTWARE

Some equipment has special capabilities that enable you to produce documents more easily and quickly because its operation is based in part on software as well as hardware.

Hardware, as we said earlier, is the physical equipment of a system. On mechanical word processors such as the Mag Card

II, the operating capabilities are called *firmware*—a basic part of the hardware—just as they are on a typewriter. Firmware is the set of permanently installed instructions that tell the hardware how to function. The only way to change what a mechanical word processor can do is to rebuild it.

On the other hand, the operating capabilities of computers are, in part, stored electronically in the central processing unit. Because they are not a part of the physical equipment, they are referred to as *software* rather than hardware.

Computers of all sizes, whether they process data or words, rely on *software*, or programs, for their operating instructions. You do not need to know how a computer works to use it. You only need to learn how to use the software, the programmed instructions that tell the computer what to do.

As recently as 1984 the interest in the office was on computer hardware, for technology was changing at an alarming rate. Many systems were being thrust upon the marketplace without proper planning strategies for their implementation. Now that the computer hardware industry has stabilized, the software industry is growing at an ever-increasing pace. Today a user can find a software package for almost any purpose. An estimated 20,000 to 34,000 software packages are available to meet the business needs of personal computer users.

Expenditures for software already exceed those for hardware in many companies. With a calculated annual growth rate of about 29 percent from 1984 to 1989, software will outpace hardware's 25.5 percent increase. Since total personal computer expenditures are expanding each year, sales for both hardware and software may reach nearly $40 billion by 1989.

Software can be divided into three categories: systems software, development software, and applications software. Each works with and supports the others like building blocks. Let's examine each of the various levels of software.

Disk Operating Systems

If computer software were a building, its foundation would be the system software. The system software coordinates all the other software. For most word processors and all microcomputers, system software is called the *disk operating system (DOS)*, pronounced "doss." DOS manages the resources of the system. It handles all the functions of the computer including the keyboard and printer, transferring information from soft copy to diskette. DOS enables all computer components to interface.

Currently, there is no standard operating system in the personal computer environment. There are, however, many operating systems in use today—CP/M (control program/microproces-

System software.

sor), MS/DOS (MicroSoft/Disk Operating System), PC-DOS (the IBM PC operating system), and the UNIX system originally developed by Bell Laboratories.

There are two types of word processors: the dedicated word processor designed mainly for processing words—or text editing; and the microcomputer that you can use as a word processor, but which can also perform a number of other computer functions. Both systems are *software-based*. But each receives its instructions—the program—in a different way.

In a dedicated word processor, the program is housed in the computer's permanent memory. That is, the instructions are built into its circuitry as ROM (read-only memory). The CPU can read and execute the instructions but cannot change them. A dedicated word processor has the DOS and the word processing software *bundled* together in the ROM. Bundled software works automatically. When you turn the machine on, it is ready for keyboarding. When you turn the machine off, the word processing program remains in the ROM.

With a microcomputer, the operating system software and the word processing software are on external storage media. To use this kind of software, you "load" the DOS program and the word processing program before you begin keyboarding. Loading a program means to store it in the computer's *temporary memory*, called RAM, or random access memory. You do this by inserting a diskette that contains the program in the disk drive and keyboarding a few instructions. Temporary memory is lost when you turn the machine off. You need to repeat this procedure—inserting a disk and loading a program—every time you use a microcomputer.

It might seem like an extra step, designing a central processing unit without the operating system and the word processing instructions built in, but this gives the machine one important advantage. You can change it and use it not just for word processing but for hundreds of different applications. DOS and the word processing software on a microcomputer are usually separate. Every time you want to use a PC as a word processor, you

Development Software

need to load both the DOS program and the word processing program. In some offices, however, both programs are stored on the same floppy diskette to simplify this procedure.

Software is written in *programming language*. But computers do not "understand" programming language. In order for a computer to perform its operations, programming language has to be translated into a different language that the machine understands, called *machine language*.

Machine language is written in the combinations of ones and zeros that we defined before as bytes. It is a painstaking job to write or read row after row of ones and zeros. Also, it is easy to make errors and difficult to find them. Fortunately, this task is no longer necessary, as development software automatically converts programming language into machine language. Development software helps programmers create programs. Every program you are likely to work with will already have been compiled in machine language. Unless you go on to learn programming or computer science, you will probably never use development software.

There are more than 200 computer languages. The following are the most common:

> BASIC, the simplest of all computer languages, used for a wide variety of purposes; the easiest language in which to write programs.
> RPG, used most commonly in programs for report writing.
> FORTRAN, primarily for scientific and mathematical use.
> COBOL, mainly for business use.

You may have heard about other programs including PASCAL, SNOBOL, LOGO, LISP, C, and ASSEMBLER.

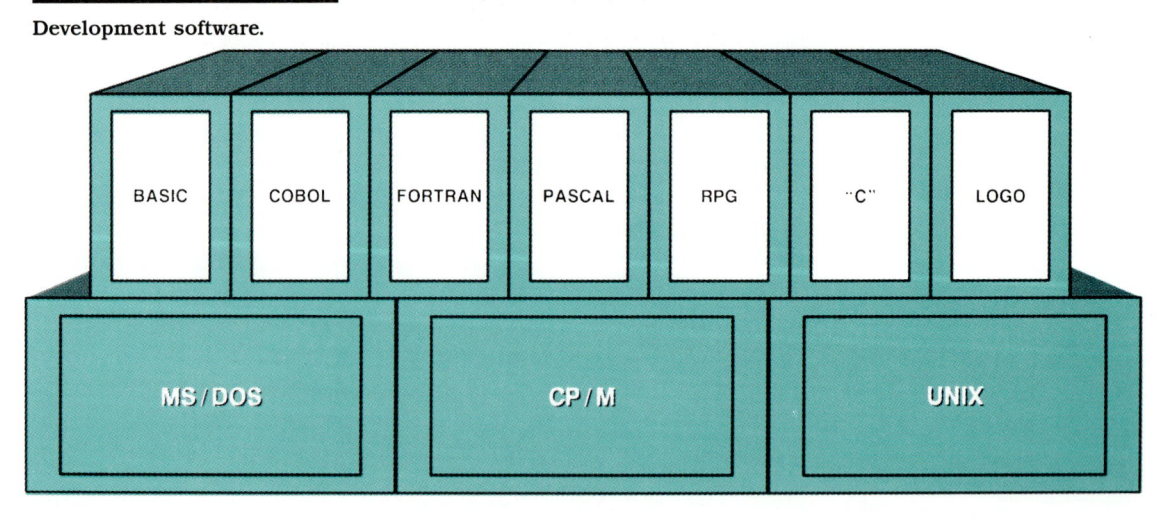

Development software.

Microcomputers and Software

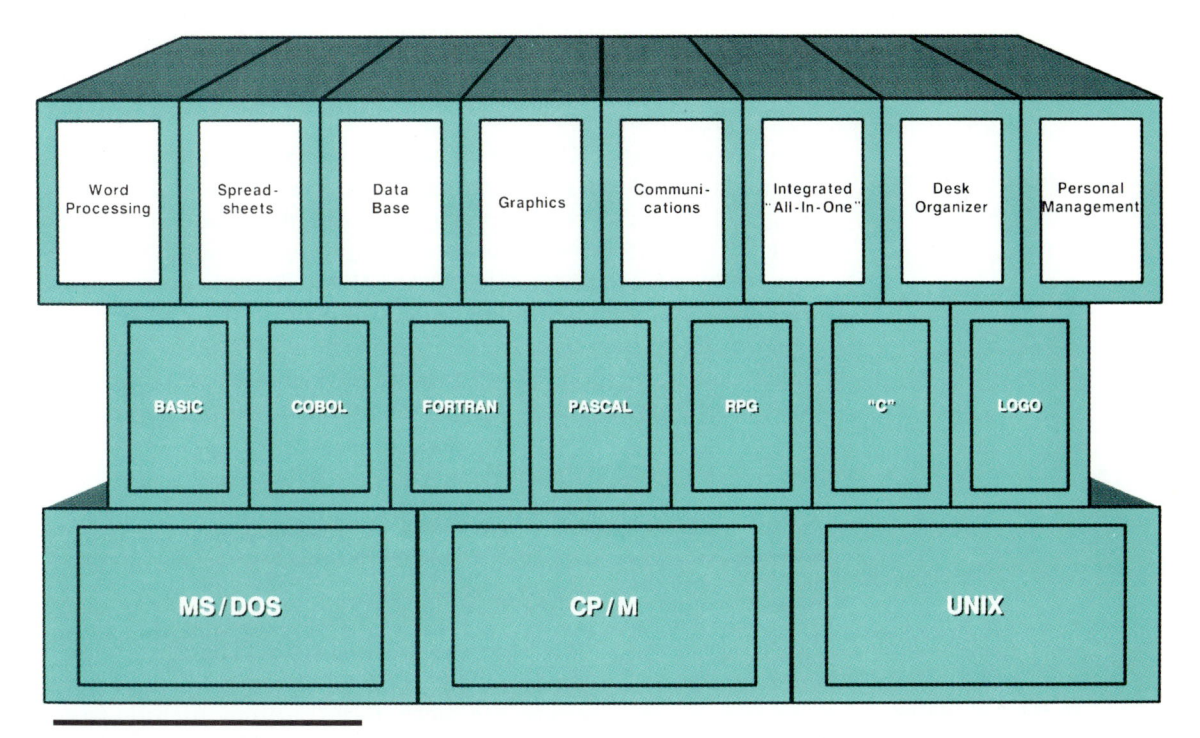

Applications software.

Applications Software

You will probably use the same DOS software every time you operate a micro. But you may use any number of different applications programs. Applications software, as we said earlier, is used for a specific purpose—business, personal, recreation, or education. A microcomputer can handle alphanumeric or graphic information for either word or data processing, depending on the kind of applications program that you run on it. Thousands of prepackaged applications programs are available for personal computers to help office employees:

- Draw up budgets, forecast sales, project labor and materials requirements.
- Analyze cash flows or prospective mergers and acquisitions, plan products, develop performance requirements.
- Determine the best sources and prices for raw materials, as well as amounts needed.
- Monitor production processes, oversee delivery of finished products.
- Handle accounting and inventory control, electronic mail, and other telecommunications.

Applications programs are what give your personal computer personality. Because of their flexibility, microcomputers with applications programs are used increasingly now in systems designed for more than just word processing. In the following section, we look at some of the applications software that is available for today's personal computers.

Word Processing. Dozens of word processing software programs are available for personal computers. Some of the popular general word processing programs are MultiMate and WordStar. Word processing programs for microcomputers are becoming more sophisticated all the time. There is no question that personal computers increase the productivity of authors who use them to create documents on their keyboards. In addition to many or all of the functions of dedicated word processors, there are software programs that can do the following:

Some Common Word Processing Software

Program	Function
Spelling verification	The spelling verification program, sometimes called "spelling checker," provides an electronic dictionary that may include from 50,000 to 100,000 words. The word processor scans a keyboarded document, checking against all the words in its "dictionary." Misspelled or unfamiliar words are highlighted. With many programs, you can keyboard and store words that are not included in the software program. Some programs will automatically insert the correctly spelled word in place of the misspelled one. The user must determine the correct spelling of unfamiliar words.
Math	Most math programs perform addition, subtraction, multiplication, and division. They will also subtotal columns, add horizontal rows of figures, calculate percentages, and calculate grand totals. In many cases, the user can specify simple equations; for example, the machine can total a column and divide the total by the number of items to find an average total.
Sophisticated math	Sophisticated math is a program for processing accounts receivable, accounts payable, general ledgers, payrolls, and for per-

Microcomputers and Software

forming other recordkeeping functions requiring greater mathematical capabilities than basic math programs offer.

Sorting — Sorting is arranging. The program puts columns or lists of information into alphabetical or numerical order, in ascending or descending order. Some sort programs include a search feature that allows you to search, for example, a mailing list and select only addresses in a particular ZIP Code area.

Communications — Communications programs allow compatible but independent word processors and computers to exchange information.

List processing — Sometimes called electronic filing systems, the purpose of list processing is to create and maintain files; retrieve information from them; and create letters, memos, and reports from the information obtained. List processing is used with personnel records, mailing lists, and membership rosters.

Write — Write software allows a programmer who is familiar with computer language to create new programs.

Foreign language — As its name suggests, the foreign language program allows the word processor to function in any of several foreign languages.

Forms (fill-ins) — The forms program displays purchase requisitions, invoices, and other commonly used forms so that the secretary can keyboard information into the blanks, then order printed copies. Other fill-ins include travel requests and expense reports. Some forms software packages are capable of picking up information from one form and using it as input for another.

Graphics — The graphics program enables an author to enhance reports by including charts and graphs. Some programs offer color graphs. (These can only be printed in color on appropriate printers.)

Selective search — Selective search programs offer the capability of searching through large libraries of

	stored documents for information. Law offices use these programs to search for stored reports of court decisions on specific subjects.
Glossary	A glossary stores frequently used formats, paragraphs, and long words so that they can be retrieved and inserted into documents.

Word processing software programs continue to be developed to a level of sophistication that automates the writing process and aids the author in creating the document. Many of these programs are used on word processing equipment and several are adaptable to the personal computer. Some of the most recent developments include those discussed in the table below.

Word Processing Software Developments

Advanced spelling checker	This program may run through your document twice: on the first pass it will list on the screen any words it cannot find in its unabridged dictionary. On the second pass it will see if those words are listed in your personal dictionary of frequently used words. Any word not found in either reference could be misspelled, or it could be a special spelling, in which case you may want to add it to your list of frequently used words.
Readability index	A readability index is a system that measures the "readability level" or grade level of understanding. This automated text analysis system scores the author's documents and assigns a grade-level index using both the Flesch and Kincaid indexes in 10 to 15 seconds a page on some systems.
Definition special function	The option of viewing rarely used words; striking any key will cause the computer to display the meaning of the word so the user can decide if the word is really appropriate.
Style book	Similar to the *Chicago Manual of Style*—electronically. For example, the program can

recognize the titles of address. The title would be capitalized if it preceded the proper noun (Secretary of State George P. Shultz) but lowercase when following a name (George P. Shultz, secretary of state).

Grammar checkers — This program helps you with grammar and syntax. It will point out such common errors as matching subjects and verbs. It can also help you with your own style idiosyncracies. For example, if you find yourself using one particular cliché too often, you can enter that in the program memory, and it will be pointed out each time it is used.

Thesaurus — The program hunts through the electronic thesaurus and provides synonyms for any word the user chooses to enter.

Hyphenation — Correct hyphenation of a word is merely an extension of its proper spelling. Some packages automatically access hyphenation during reformatting or printing functions.

Standardized abbreviations — Determines when to use standardized abbreviations (Mass./MA), commas around dates, and many other stylistic and grammatical requirements.

Electronic Spreadsheets. One of the most popular computer applications available is the *electronic spreadsheet*. The spreadsheet is basically a series of *cells*, made up of rows and columns. You use these programs by "programming" the meaning of each of the rows and columns.

For example, in some spreadsheet programs the cell where Column A and Row 36 intersect is Cell A36. There can be thousands of these cells. You can enter whatever alphanumeric information you want in a cell, such as your electric bill, phone bill, and so on. After you make your entries, you can keyboard instructions for the program to perform mathematical calculations with any numbers you have entered. For example, you can add up your bills and ask the program to put the total in another cell, or perform any other calculation in any combination, using simple arithmetic, trigonometry, algebra, or logarithms. When you finish creating a spreadsheet, you can print the results in hard copy or store them on a disk.

Software

At the left is a paper spreadsheet. The illustration at the right shows how a paper spreadsheet relates to the video screen.

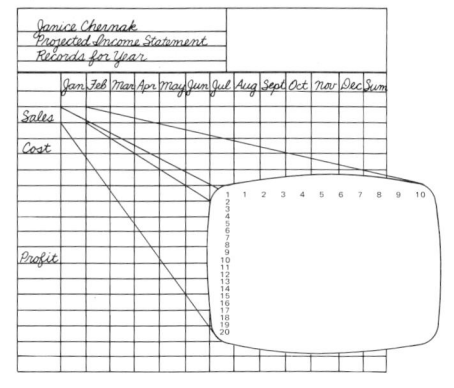

An electronic spreadsheet.

In addition, once you have programmed a spreadsheet, you can change any number in any cell, and the entries in the other cells related to that entry are automatically recalculated to conform to the new information.

Here is how *automatic recalculation* works. Assume that you want to figure out the payments on a bank loan. You enter the amount of the loan, the interest rate, and the length of time you want to take to pay back the loan. The spreadsheet program will calculate the amount of each monthly payment. Now you can change the original amount of the loan, the interest rate, and the number of monthly payments. When you do, the program will automatically recalculate each amount. The more popular spreadsheet packages used by businesses today include Super-Calc and Multiplan.

Data Bases. As computers have become more and more widespread, vast amounts of information have been stored in them. This information has many applications. But to be useful to everyone in an information processing system, the data must be arranged and stored in a way that gives users fast and easy access to it. The concept of the data base arose out of this need. A *data base* is a collection of related information stored so that it is available to many users for different purposes. It is an electronic filing system with many cross-references that give you a tremendous number of ways to reorganize and retrieve data. To be more precise, it is an electronic representation of a filing system such as you might find in any business. What is unique about a data base is the way it is organized to allow users to search for information.

A data base can represent the electronic equivalent of ordinary 3-by-5 index cards, or it might contain every bit of information concerning a business or organization. It can also calculate "unknowns" from the data stored in the files. A data base can handle all the details of a business inventory, such as accounting and filing. It can be used to prepare summaries, estimates, and other reports drawing on the information in its files. It can store newspaper articles, magazines and books, games, and even digitized pictures (photographs). In fact, a data base is whatever the last programmer to write one says it is.

Businesses and individuals have found that the more effectively they can collect, file, sort, and reproduce information, the more productive and successful they will be. In addition, with the proliferation of personal computers in offices around the country, data base applications have become more popular than ever. With the personal computer bringing information manipulation closer to the end user, the important thing to bear in mind is that if the information is stored in a general-access data base, it can probably be transferred into your personal computer for use at your convenience. More information on data bases is in Chapter 6.

Graphics. Once information is processed, the form in which it is presented is also important. A graph can picture information in a way that often reveals more than tables with columns of statistical data. Computer graphics programs help people understand ideas and solve problems more quickly and easily.

Today's computers can do more than just process words and numbers and graph the results. They can store and transmit graphic information. They can integrate graphic material with

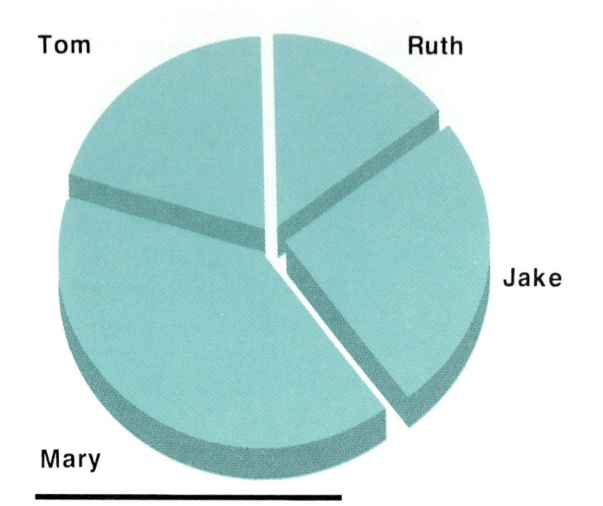

Computer graphics can range from simple bar graphs and pie charts (left) to complex engineering drawings.

the text, and can help create the graphics. Some graphics software prepares not only charts and graphs but also drawings—even ones that look three-dimensional.

The widest use of personal computer graphics has been in the production of charts and graphs for business analyses and presentations. The ability to convert data from a spreadsheet or other report into an easily comprehensible chart lends more power to a presentation. Standalone business graphics packages compete to offer the widest variety of fonts (type faces), colors, scaling (size) options, and chart types.

Despite the increasing graphics power of software, computer graphics are only as good as the output devices that present them. There are several special kinds of printers that print in color and are used in computer graphics. These are discussed in Chapter 6.

While it is easy to overlook a single figure in a sea of numbers, you can hardly miss the orange wedge in a colorful pie chart—the wedge that shows what proportion of a department's budget is spent on salaries. Rather than list page after page of numbers, managers increasingly are using computer graphics to show important relationships between such numbers. This trend should also have the effect of reducing the amount of paper used for printing long, hard-to-read statistical reports.

Communications. On August 3, 1984, the New York Stock Exchange enjoyed the heaviest day of trading in its history. Over 70 million shares changed hands in a single hour. Many factors were responsible for this, but one of the most significant was the increased use of data communications. Now that brokers and investors can receive the latest market information over telephone lines and quickly analyze stocks on their PCs, they can respond to tips and trends instantly. So much information and the chance to act on it so quickly can, in itself, turn a snowball into an avalanche in a single day.

Stock trading is only one communications application. You can use a computer to send information to, and receive it from, someone using a computer at another location. You can also work with a computer that has no operator but is programmed for communication. For example, not only can you use a microcomputer to search great libraries, but you can also use it to shop through electronic catalogs, play games, contact special interest groups, and exchange information on *bulletin board services (BBS)*. A bulletin board service displays on your micro screen the same kind of information that you would expect to find tacked up on a community or school bulletin board.

Integrated Software. All the software packages we have discussed so far run independently of one another. That is, you use a word processing software program to keyboard text and a spreadsheet program to prepare a budget. Unfortunately, with this kind of software, transferring data—for example, from a spreadsheet to a word processing document—can be time-consuming. *Integrated software* eliminates this problem. Its goal is to interface or link more than one program so you can: perform a variety of tasks uniformly (often referred to as *multitasking*); pass information freely between tasks (called *information sharing*); enter figures onto your spreadsheet; insert text into your word processor; update your data base; and use the same commands to perform all tasks in a similar way (known as a *unified command structure*).

In 1982 the Lotus Development Corporation announced the first integrated software package called *Lotus 1-2-3*. It integrated three fundamental software applications: spreadsheets, graphics, and simple data base management. It is possible with integrated software to store the programs for all three functions in the temporary memory of a personal computer. Once the software is loaded, you can move freely from one function to the next—retrieve data from a database, calculate it on a spreadsheet, and graph the results—without changing programs. For example, transferring data from one program to another using a conventional spreadsheet and graphics program is an involved process. First you must change disks, then load the graphics program, reenter the spreadsheet data, and then run the graphics program. Integrated software reduces this operation to a handful of keystrokes. If you decide to change an item of data on the spreadsheet and make a new graph on a conventional program, the same thing happens in reverse. You need to remove

A windowed screen allows the user to see several items at once.

the graphics disk, change the data, remove the spreadsheet disk, reinsert the graphics disk, and so on. With integrated software these changes can be made immediately.

Integrated packages introduced more recently by Lotus and other software companies have added capabilities. They include spreadsheets, graphics, data base management, word processing, communications, appointment schedulers, and a cross-indexed electronic file that will dial phone numbers.

Windows. Integrated software packages have "windows" that let you see various functions simultaneously. Each window is a separate area or box on the screen which can display a different aspect of your work. For example, if you are preparing this year's financial report, you can display a word processing window to prepare the text, a spreadsheet window for your year-end balance sheet, and a graphics window for a pie chart depicting the year's expenses. The windowing system makes it easy to refer to the spreadsheet for statistics while writing the report, to create the pie chart by transferring figures from the spreadsheet and, finally, to move the graph into the word processing document. Windowing tasks are made even simpler because many of the systems perform these functions with a *mouse* instead of keyboard commands.

Two techniques are used in windowing. In the first, several windows overlap on the screen, similar to the way you might overlap sheets of paper on a desk, keeping the one you are working with on top. The other windows are each partially covered. But you can uncover them with a mouse as easily as if they were real sheets of paper.

The second technique, called *tiling*, limits the size of each overlapping window in proportion to the total number of windows on the screen—the more screens, the smaller each window is and the less of its contents you can see. If you delete a window, the remaining windows expand to fill up the screen. You can do this by keyboarding or with the mouse. Some 15 windows can fit on the screen and in the temporary memory of the micro. Four or five windows are usually all you need.

THE COMPUTER CONNECTION

The number of microcomputers in offices all around the country is expected to keep on growing for years to come. This change in the office environment creates a need to interface or link PCs with mainframe and minicomputer systems already in place. We have explained that microcomputers can be connected to external CPUs in a shared logic system. These systems can be programmed to create a word processing, data processing, minicomputer, or mainframe terminal out of any terminal. Programming a terminal to carry out instructions from another computer is called *emulation*. In this kind of system, micros are used to supplement medium- and large-sized computers.

The Personal Computer Link

Executives and secretaries today are working with a greater volume of information than ever in preparing spreadsheet budgets, financial plans, and company personnel records. This has placed increased demands on the systems which process the information. In response, some corporations have linked personal computers to mainframes so users can access and maintain corporate data bases. Other companies have installed minicomputers whose primary function is to connect with and serve the company's microcomputers. Large corporations often use all three systems—making information from mainframes, minis, and PCs available interchangeably to all users.

There are several ways to connect personal computers with mainframes, minicomputers, or each other. One way is to link the PC and mainframe directly. The user who needs information from the mainframe keyboards in the request. The mainframe software finds the information from its data base. The information is put in an intermediate file, called a *clipboard*. The program reformats the clipboard file so it is compatible with the personal computer software. At that point, any secretary or executive can *download* or transfer the information and use it with a PC spreadsheet, data base, word processing, or other applications program.

A *transparent* link between a microcomputer and a mainframe will do all this automatically. "Transparent" means that the software and hardware are meshing so well you do not even notice that it is happening—it is invisible. For example, a secretary using a spreadsheet program can specify that one of the cells should contain data from the mainframe data base. Once the instruction is keyboarded, the mainframe will send new data to the personal computer whenever it is available to update the spreadsheet automatically. For example, a PC user can define the cell of a spreadsheet program as mainframe data. Then the user can retrieve from the mainframe the most current data for that item and insert it in the cell of the spreadsheet.

As the demand for information continues and as the transfer of that information between systems—mainframe, mini, and micro—becomes more important, technological advances will lead to easier, faster, and more cost-effective methods of transferring files and data.

PC Networks

So far we have seen how a personal computer can be used as a self-contained standalone unit, or to exchange information with a mainframe or a minicomputer. But just like word processors, personal computers can also share information with each other. In many offices, PC networks make it possible for users to work from a common data base, exchange information, and use hardware such as a printer or other peripheral device. If you recall, word processors linked to a common CPU in a shared logic configuration can also perform these sharing functions. The storage for a microcomputer office information network is a hard disk, or Winchester disk. The hard disk acts as:

- A post office with a "mailbox" for each microcomputer workstation in the network.
- Storage space for individual files and files everyone shares.
- A reservoir of applications software that can be downloaded to any workstation.
- A buffer space that holds material waiting to be printed until the printer is ready for it.

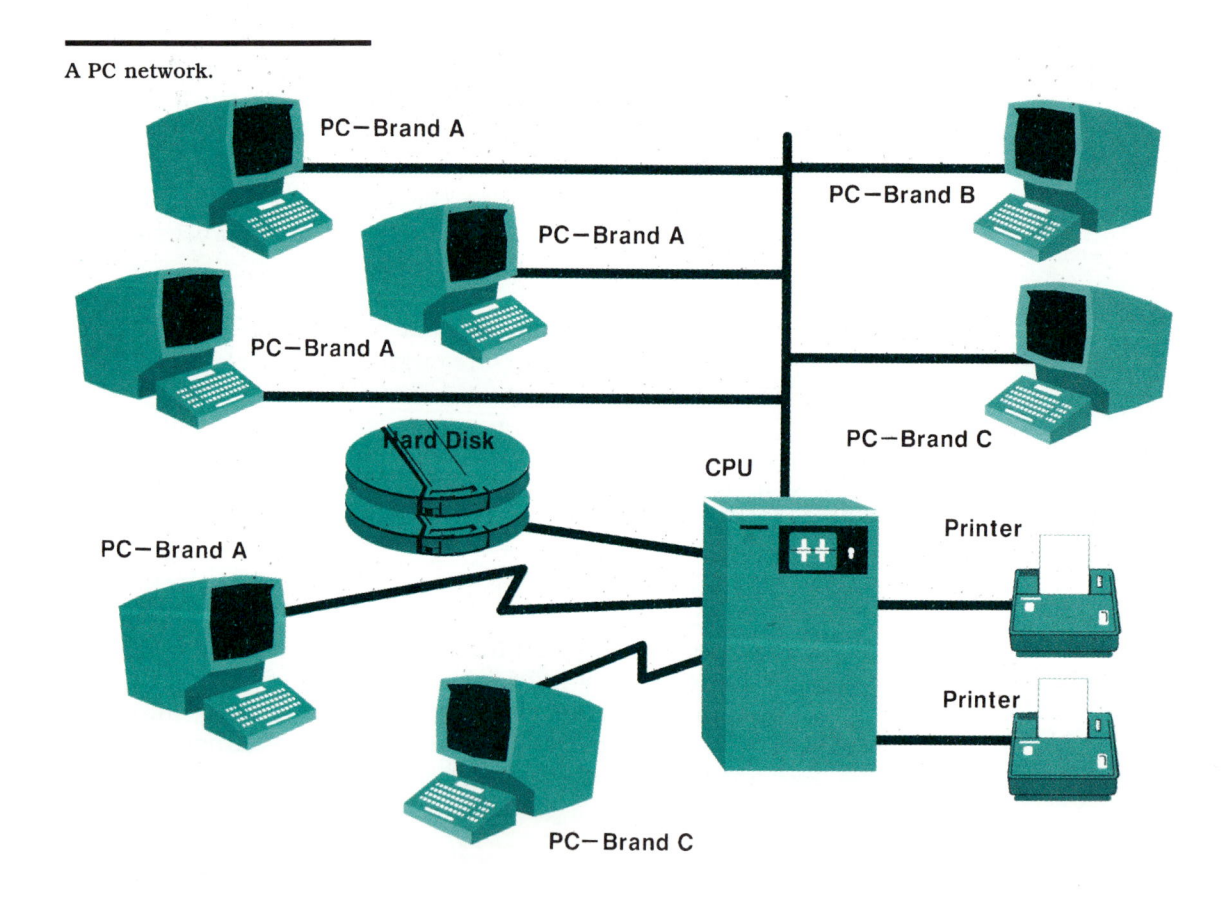

A PC network.

Microcomputers and Software

Linking PCs in a local area to a hard disk makes it possible to form a network for cooperative information processing. Such *local area networks,* or *LANs* as they are called, can connect PCs up to three to five miles from each other. Hard-disk-based networks are an alternative to companies that cannot afford a larger computer.

Only a few years ago networking had its limits, and technology impeded the office automation marketplace. Today, technology is the driving force behind companies that want to pool their resources with greater efficiency. Both the hardware and software for local area and other multiuser networks are still in development. This is a strong growth area of information technology, and we will continue to see changes and new systems in the future.

CHAPTER SUMMARY

- Computers can be classified as mainframes (large), minicomputers (medium-sized), and microcomputers (small).
- Personal computers are microcomputers. They are increasingly being integrated with other electronic equipment to enhance the information processing capabilities of offices.
- Many input devices can be used with personal computers: joysticks, light pens, touching the screen with your finger, and the mouse.
- Microcomputer software is available that switches back and forth easily from the QWERTY to the Dvorak keyboard.
- Microcomputer CPUs (8, 16, and 32 bits)—are evaluated in terms of speed and volume of data.
- Software is divided into three categories: system, development, and applications.
- Software programs are written in special computer languages. Some of the better-known languages are BASIC, RPG, FORTRAN, and COBOL.
- Bundled software means that both the disk operating instructions and the word processing functions are built into the hardware and begin working automatically whenever you turn on the computer.
- Software-based display word processors can be given additional capabilities because their internal processing is based on software (programs) rather than on hardware (the machine itself).
- Some software packages let computers convert numeric and other data into graphic form, making the information easier to comprehend.

- In both large and small computer systems, related information can be organized into data bases so that many users can retrieve it from the system's storage for a variety of purposes.
- Applications software is what gives a microcomputer personality and is created to solve a particular problem, whether it be business, recreational, personal, or educational.
- Some of the applications software packages include word processing, spreadsheets, data base management, graphics, communications, and integrated all-in-one programs.
- Some integrated software programs use a feature called "windows," which display various functions on the screen at the same time.
- With different prepackaged programs, a single microcomputer can be used for either word processing or data processing. The user can turn a micro from a word processor into a data processor by inserting a new diskette into the disk drive or, with some programs, by giving the computer a keyboard command.
- Executives and secretaries are demanding more information and ways to process it. As a result, corporations are using minicomputers whose sole function is to serve a PC network, linking PCs to large corporate mainframes and data bases.
- Just like word processors, personal computers can be clustered rather than self-contained to share one or more components.
- Personal computers in an office environment, when properly networked, can work from a common data base, exchange information, and use the same printer as well as other connected peripherals.
- As companies seek new ways to pool their information, we can expect technological advances in multiuser applications.

INFORMATION PROCESSING VOCABULARY

applications software	download
automatic recalculation	Dvorak keyboard
bit	firmware
bundled software	integrated software
byte	joystick
chip	light pen
cycle time	mainframe
data base	microcomputer
development software	minicomputer
disk operating system (DOS)	mouse

multitasking
personal computer (PC)
programmable
 function keys
software
spreadsheet
tiling
windows

CHAPTER QUESTIONS

1. Do you think you would have a difficult time learning both the QWERTY and Dvorak keyboards? Explain your answer.
2. What are the three basic categories of computers? How is each different from the other?
3. The number of microcomputers is increasing very rapidly. Why do you think this is happening?
4. Do microcomputers have word processing capabilities? Explain.
5. Define software. What are the three levels of software? How many different software applications packages can you name?
6. Suggest a possible data base and discuss two ways in which it might be used.
7. What are the advantages of using a computer to illustrate information in a report?
8. What is an alternate input device? Briefly describe two or three.
9. Explain the term *binary logic*. Define a *bit* and a *byte*. What is machine language?
10. What are the advantages of integrated software? Define *cell, automatic recalculation, windowing, tiling*.

CASE STUDY

M. A. Orban, Inc. is a Charlevoix, Michigan, mail-order house that markets camping goods. It markets everything from tweed shirts to fishing lures to corduroy knickers. Orban, Inc. attributes much of its success to a personal computer network system installed two years ago. Many of the operations that once took days, if not weeks, to accomplish are now completed within a matter of hours. For each of the applications listed below, identify which software package would be required. Explain your reasons for selecting that specific program.

1. Automatically typed response letters to customers.

2. An up-to-the-minute inventory list which allows the company to control its inventory rather than over-concentrate on merchandise.
3. A quarterly report of itemized income and expenses.
4. A pie chart, created in conjunction with the quarterly report, depicting each of the expense areas.
5. The sending of internal documents to the branch office in Seattle, Washington.
6. An in-depth list of all preferred customers indicating the customer's size, color preference, and hobby or interest.
7. The catalog customers' file which enables the company to track customers. The file includes ZIP Codes for establishing target markets.
8. Individual customer accounts indicating dates of purchases; items ordered, including catalog number, quantity, and a brief description; amounts received and outstanding; and balance due.
9. The company annual report to be sent to all stockholders. The report includes the president's annual message, reports from department managers, financial statements, and multicolor charts and graphs.
10. A printout of a customer's final order, including a mailing label and the amount of postage required.

CHAPTER 6

Information Systems

Nicole Edwards is in the middle of a busy day at the executive offices of Rearden's, a nationwide mail-order firm. Ms. Edwards has spent most of the morning planning the buying strategy for next year's catalog. Before going to lunch, she checks her computer terminal. On the screen she sees a blinking light, indicating that she has a message. She keys in her identification code and requests the machine to identify the caller. The machine responds by printing "Margaret Padilla." Ms. Edwards keys in a command to view the message from Ms. Padilla, her boss, who is visiting a plant in Boise, Idaho. Ms. Padilla's message reads, "Cancel order from Hilton Fashions. Manufacturer unable to deliver on time." Ms. Edwards acts immediately on the instruction.

OUTPUT

The continuing explosion in electronic processing, distribution/communications, and storage and retrieval capabilities have created major changes in the way modern companies get these jobs done.

Before high-speed output equipment was developed, many companies used outside companies to handle their high-volume reprographics needs. In recent years, however, many of these companies have purchased printing and reprographics equipment that interfaces with word and data processors for greater production and cost efficiency. The new equipment is capable of handling a wide variety of projects. In today's office, you will need to be aware of the rapidly expanding capabilities of this output equipment and its relationship to information processing.

Soft Copy

The video display terminal brought with it the single most important advance in output to date—soft copy. Text displayed on a screen does not require paper, printing, or reprographics. In offices where every person who needs a terminal has one, many letters and memos are never printed in hard copy.

Printers

Soft copy may have changed the office dramatically, but the printed word still is irreplaceable. Typewriters and blind word processors combine keyboarding and printing in the same unit. On display word processors and microcomputers, the printer is a separate component. Many systems are designed so that you can keyboard, edit, or revise one document while another docu-

Information processing cycle (output).

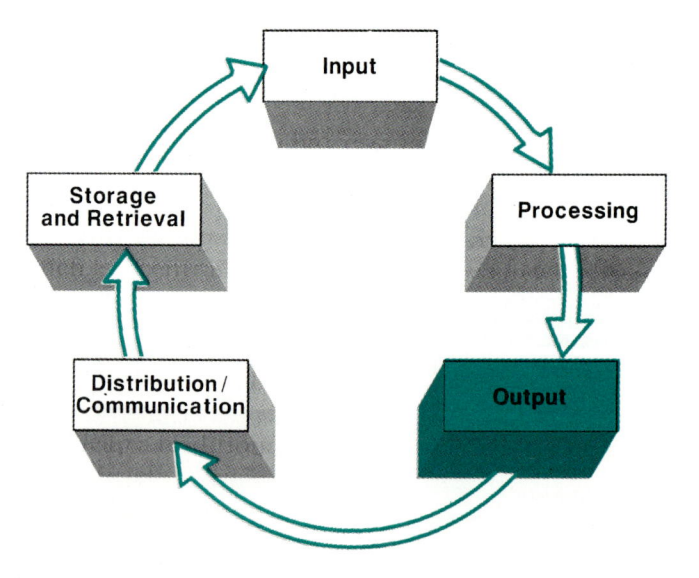

Information Systems

This impact printer uses a daisy wheel type element.

The daisy wheel type element takes its name from its shape.

The thimble type element is also named for its appearance.

The words at the top of this illustration were printed by a dot-matrix printer of lesser quality than the words at the bottom.

ment is being printed, a feature called *background printing*. This flexibility enhances your efficiency.

Almost all the printers available for display word processors and PCs are faster than printers for blind systems, and they also offer a wide range of printing quality, speed, and capabilities. There are two basic categories of printers: impact and nonimpact. Within these categories there are several different kinds of printers that you should know about.

Impact Printers. *Impact printers* print by striking the type against a ribbon and the paper, just as a typewriter does, so they can produce carbon copies of documents. On an impact printer, the type element may be *bidirectional*, which means it moves first from left to right and then from right to left, unlike a typewriter. It can do this because the text has already been keyboarded and is in memory.

Impact printers that print one character at a time are called *character printers*. These printers, which may or may not be bidirectional, are used for letters and other kinds of output that must be of high quality. The type element on a character printer includes upper- and lowercase letters. Type elements are available in pica, elite, and micro size (15 characters to an inch) as well as in many typefaces. You can change them just as you change the typing element on any element typewriter.

Daisy Wheel. Most character printers use a *daisy wheel* type element, which gets its name from its shape. Its "petals" are straight bars of type, with the characters at the ends. The type wheels may be metal or plastic. (Metal is more durable.) The wheel spins at high speeds, and, when the correct character is positioned over the ribbon and paper, a tiny hammer strikes it. Daisy wheel printers can print 40 to 50 characters a second.

Thimble. A *thimble* element also has bars arranged in a circle and extending from a center, with alphanumeric characters at the tip. But because of how the bars are shaped, instead of a daisy it resembles a thimble. Thimbles are made of plastic, and the quality of their output is not as high as that of a metal daisy wheel. A thimble spins constantly as it travels back and forth across the page, something like a "golf ball" element on an electric typewriter.

Dot Matrix. As you can see from the illustration shown in the margin, characters produced on *dot-matrix* printers are made up of many closely spaced dots. There are several methods of printing a dot-matrix character, both impact and nonimpact. One approach uses a printhead with tiny wire bristles. As the printhead shuttles back and forth, the wires change position and form the characters before they strike the ribbon and

Output

Thermal printer.

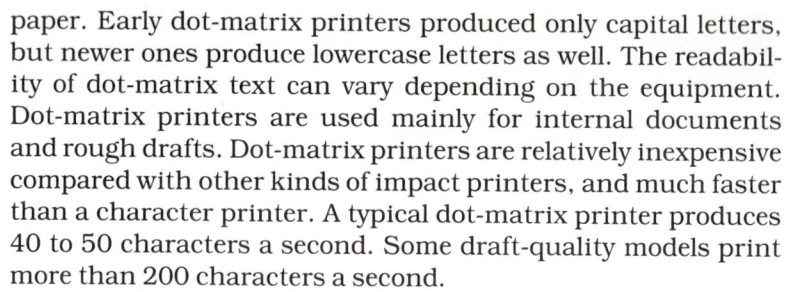

paper. Early dot-matrix printers produced only capital letters, but newer ones produce lowercase letters as well. The readability of dot-matrix text can vary depending on the equipment. Dot-matrix printers are used mainly for internal documents and rough drafts. Dot-matrix printers are relatively inexpensive compared with other kinds of impact printers, and much faster than a character printer. A typical dot-matrix printer produces 40 to 50 characters a second. Some draft-quality models print more than 200 characters a second.

Line Printers. The fastest dot-matrix printers are *line printers*, sometimes called *band printers*. A typical printer produces 300 to 1200 lines a minute. Some models print as many as 3600 lines a minute. The reason for the fantastic speed of the line printer is that in one stroke it produces an entire line rather than an individual character. Line printers generally produce only uppercase letters. The quality of the printing is much too poor for business letters, but many organizations use line printers for internal documents.

Nonimpact Printers. The other types of printers are classified as *nonimpact printers*. They cannot produce carbon copies, as impact printers can, and some require special paper, but they are capable of producing even higher-quality output than character printers with no loss in speed.

Ink-Jet Printers. One kind of nonimpact printer is the *ink-jet printer*, which sprays electrically charged ink onto the paper. Ink-jet printers can shape characters in a variety of type styles and sizes. And like all nonimpact printers, they are practically noiseless.

Thermal Transfer. A method of document printing using an ink, heat, and matrix technique is *thermal transfer*. Thermal transfer printing transfers ink from an ink roll to plain paper. The ink roll passes over a grid of wires called the *thermal printhead*. A microprocessor selectively heats wires within the grid, melting ink on the roll. A rubber roller then presses the ink roll against the paper and the melted ink is transferred onto the paper. The output from a thermal transfer printer is clear and sharp, closely resembling the output from a photocopier.

Laser Printers. By using focused light instead of ink and ribbon, lasers can print high-quality characters faster than any other printer. Although the finest laser printing equipment is only cost-effective for large corporations and other businesses with special printing needs, the newer, inexpensive compact models have placed laser printers within the reach of smaller businesses.

Laser printers are fast and versatile. Shown above is a desk-top model.

Information Systems

A plotter is used for sophisticated graphics.

Sheet feeder.

Tractor.

Laser printing uses a laser—a narrow beam of pure red light—that can carry millions of characters at once. With high-speed photography, the light is shaped into characters and beamed onto light-sensitive paper, making it possible to print whole pages at a time at speeds of more than 100 pages a minute. Like many other printers, you can use more than one type style on a page with a laser, in more than one size, from pica and elite to micro. The quality of laser printing is so good that, besides printing text, you can use it to print company logos and letterheads. A laser printer can print facsimiles of signatures which are virtually indistinguishable from handwriting.

Plotters. Sometimes graphic illustrations require equipment more sophisticated than dot-matrix printers. To highlight data depicted on a graph, such as the red piece of a pie chart, color plotters can be used. Because plotters use pens containing a variety of colored inks, the final graph output is multicolored. Plotters are used not only for illustrating statistical data, but also to design maps, engineering data, weather forecasts, and many other types of art work.

Devices Used With Printers. Several manufacturers offer devices that help printers perform at their maximum speed and efficiency. These devices include automatic sheet and envelope feeders, tractors, and bursters.

Automatic Sheet Feeders. Available in several different models, most *automatic sheet feeders* hold between 50 and 250 sheets of paper in a bin, align the sheets correctly, and insert them one at a time into a printer. Sheet feeders are controlled by built-in microprocessors that can be commanded from the keyboard or set independently from the feeder itself. Controls on the feeder can also be used to feed pages manually into the printer if desired. The feeder automatically signals the operator when paper has run out, if paper is misaligned, or if there is a paper jam. Also available are *dual-sheet feeders* that hold two separate stacks of paper in separate bins.

Envelope Feeders. Functioning like sheet feeders, *envelope feeders* hold a stack of up to 200 envelopes and feed them individually into a printer. They can feed up to 1200 envelopes to the printer in an hour.

Tractors. When you see the word tractor, you probably think of a farm machine. But in information processing, a *tractor* is a device that guides continuous-form paper through the printer. *Continuous-form paper* can be identified by the holes along its outside edges and the perforated horizontal edges that separate the sheets. It may be single ply or multiple ply, having up to six duplicate sheets.

The tractor mechanically moves the paper forward and sometimes backward through the printer by a series of sprockets that stick into the holes along the outside edges of the continuous form. Tractors that move the paper in two directions, called *bidirectional tractors*, make it possible to print charts and graphs as well as subscripts and superscripts.

Bursters. The continuous roll is a convenient and efficient form of paper supply for high-speed printing of large amounts of text or data. However, it is often necessary to separate the continuous form into individual sheets for distribution. A device known as a *burster* cuts continuous-form rolls along perforated lines into individual sheets.

Paper Shredders. Offices generate an enormous amount of printed information. Often this information must be kept confidential. *Paper shredders* are a convenient and foolproof way of destroying large amounts of paper so that the security or confidentiality of information is protected.

Burster.

Reprographics

Take a close look at some of the printed information you see every day—books, magazines, newspapers, announcements, bills, and so on. All these are copies of one kind or another—that is, they are reproduced. Even your telephone bill is a reproduced form, which has been individualized by adding your name, address, phone number, and charges for the month.

The process by which one or more copies of graphic or written material are produced is called *reprographics*. This term covers several different technologies, including photocopying, phototypesetting, offset printing, and duplicating. Strictly speaking, reprographics does not include processes that are only related to the assembly of copies, such as collating, binding, folding, and inserting. However, since these processes complete the total job, it makes sense to examine them as part of the general subject of reprographics.

You will recall that a main function of business is to manage information, a task that includes getting the information to people who want or need it. The number of copies to be made depends on the purpose of the document and how many people are to receive it. Determining the number of copies means investigating the most efficient and economical way in which to produce them. It means choosing the most appropriate kind of reprographics equipment to use.

Methods of Reprographics. Offices may use several methods to produce copies of documents. Some methods use equipment

Information Systems

such as typewriters or printers. Others use equipment that has the sole function of producing multiple copies, such as photocopiers, duplicators, and offset printers.

Repetitive Printing. *Repetitive printing* simply means printing more than one original hard copy. On an electric typewriter, you would have to type the original document over and over. But with automated word processing equipment you can command the printer to print as many hard copies as you need. By combining repetitive printing with a sheet feeder, a secretary's time can be freed to do other things.

Carbon Copies. One of the advantages of using word processsing equipment is that error-free documents can be created and then printed. To create up to five copies of a document that has been keyboarded, proofread, revised, and proofread again while still in soft copy form, you need only insert carbons in the printer and command the printer to print the document. In a few seconds you have one error-free hard copy and several perfect carbon copies.

Most carbon paper today comes in the form of *carbon packs*, or *copysets*. These are commercially prepared sets of about five sheets of carbon paper interleaved between thin tissuelike sheets of plain paper, all of which are attached at the top. After the printing has been done and the pack is removed from the printer, the carbon sheets are removed and the tissue copies can be distributed. NCR copy packs that do not have carbon ("*no carbon required*") may also be used.

Offset. A common method of duplication is *offset duplicating*, or *offset lithography*, which requires the preparation of a *master*—a hard copy of a document typed on paper or textured material that has been treated to absorb ink or dye. The master is placed on a plate or cylinder that receives ink and water from a set of rollers. The typed or drawn images on the master take on the oil-based ink, while the blank areas retain the water. Next the images are transferred, or "offset," to a roller or drum, which in turn transfers the image to blank sheets of paper. Copies produced by offset duplicating are extremely clear—every copy looks like an original.

Photocopying. *Photocopying* is the most common method of reprographics used in offices today. It does not require the preparation of a master, nor does it demand special training. Photocopiers, which come in a wide variety of models, reproduce documents on either plain or coated paper. They use an electrostatic process, originally called *electrophotography*. The name of the process was later changed to *xerography*—or xerox for short—and the rest is history.

Photocopies can be almost equal in quality to copies made by

Offset duplicating gives very clear copies in large numbers.

Photocopiers today can make copies of such high quality that they look like originals.

offset lithography. Some photocopiers print on both sides of the paper, a process known as *duplexing.* Some print copies that have a reduced image of the original document. Some provide copies in color. Large photocopiers collate, staple, and stack copied documents.

Facsimile. In reprographics, *facsimile* refers to a special process by which a copy of a document or graphic illustration is sent electronically from one machine to another via telephone lines or other electronic means. These machines may be in the same building or may be separated by great distances. Facsimile can also be a method of distribution and communication.

Facsimile technology involves changing the visual image of a document into electronic signals. These signals can then be transmitted and reconverted into an exact image of the original document. In *analog facsimiles,* a scanner moves across the document, reading every part of it—characters, spaces between characters, spaces between lines, margins, and other blank spaces. Each scanned element is converted into an electrical signal transmitted over telephone lines to another facsimile machine. These devices produce very good copies at the rate of one every 2 to 6 minutes. In *digital facsimiles,* a scanner "reads" only the part of the document that contains actual information. It does not read blank spaces or margins the way an analog facsimile does. The digital scanner converts images to short binary signals (a series of ones and zeros) that can be easily and quickly transmitted over telephone lines. Digital facsim-

146   Information Systems

A facsimile machine transmits and receives exact copies anywhere in the world.

iles transmit copies at a much faster rate (60 to 90 seconds per page), but they may not be as clear as those produced by analog machines.

Image Scanners. In 1985 Federal Express, a private overnight mail carrier service, announced an alternative to facsimile systems. ZapMail, an electronic express document service, is the linking of state-of-the-art reprographics technology with satellite and telecommunication equipment. This gives you a unique combination of speed, convenience, range, and quality of electronic document reproduction and delivery. ZapMail uses technology for image processing—the scanning of images—for electronic reproduction and transmission. The scanner in ZapMail is a reprographics equipment terminal.

Electronic Copier/Printers. Electronic copier/printers are an important kind of reprographics equipment. These machines combine the technologies of data processing printer, office copier, and facsimile machine. They are being used more and more with word and data processing equipment. The difference between *electronic copier/printers* and other kinds of copiers lies in their ability to accept input from either word or data processing equipment and to convert this input into high-quality hard copies.

There are two kinds of electronic copier/printers—those that are "intelligent" and those that are "dumb." *Intelligent copiers* are designed to accept many kinds of data, manipulate it, and convert it to output in another form. For example, they can com-

Output

Photocomposition offers high-quality printing for office documents.

bine two kinds of data, such as graphics and text, in the same report. Intelligent copiers can also transmit data over telephone lines in much the same way as facsimile machines.

Phototypesetting or Photocomposition. The type in a paperback or hardcover book is of a different kind from that produced by a typewriter. This is because the type in a book has been typeset. The most noticeable difference between typeset text and typewritten text is the spacing between characters. The space around typed characters is uniform. In typesetting, less space is allowed for characters that take up less space—such as i, l, and t—and more space for letters that take up more space, such as M and W. Most typewriters give the same amount of space to each letter, whatever its width, and therefore spacing between letters varies.

The most common method of typesetting is *photocomposition* or *phototypesetting*. In photocomposition, a light source exposes an image of a character on film, producing a photographic positive. The film positive can then be proofread, corrected, and converted to a master that is reproduced, usually by offset printing.

In phototypesetters that have a CRT light source, instructions for forming the characters are contained on a disk or on film. The characters are beamed one at a time on the cathoderay tube and projected to a film, which is then developed. The speed at which characters are beamed and photographed is extremely fast, with some phototypesetters reaching over 25,000 characters a minute.

The speed and storage capacity of phototypesetting units make them an ideal choice for the production of various kinds of books, including catalogs, directories, dictionaries, and indexes. Phototypesetters are also widely used in newspaper and magazine printing. Businesses that have a large volume of printing, such as supermarket chains, department stores, and insurance companies, have found it worthwhile to set up their own in-house phototypesetting facilities rather than use an outside service.

Many businesses use phototypesetting in conjunction with word processing. A floppy diskette from a word processor can be fed directly to the phototypesetting unit, which then translates the text on the diskette into clear, distinctive, professional-looking print.

Methods of Assembly

You have seen how information that has been keyboarded, edited, proofread, and stored can be printed and reproduced in any number of ways. Once hard copies are produced, several additional processes may be needed to complete the job. These include collating, sorting, binding, and folding and inserting copies. Most often these tasks are performed by separate pieces of equipment; however, a photocopier may have a built-in sorter, and an automatic collator may include "finishing" units that fold, trim, stitch, and staple copies.

Reprographics Office Systems

In planning printing and reprographics operations, the people in an office must determine the best location for the equipment to be used. This decision is affected by the size of the office, the frequency with which the equipment is used, the number of people who will need to use the equipment, the amount of space the equipment will take up, and the volume of work generated on it.

Printers Are a Shared Resource. Although some word processors and personal computers may have their own printers, it is common that printers are shared. Occasionally, one word processor may be linked to two kinds of printers to fill different needs.

Centralized Reprographics Systems. Large offices producing a heavy volume of copies usually set up some form of *centralized reprographics* area. The centralized operation—sometimes called the "copy center"—serves the entire company or office and may even serve branch offices in other buildings. A heavy volume of copies requires large-size copiers or duplicators, which in turn require a good deal of space.

In a centralized system, original documents, masters, and requests for copies are picked up and delivered to the reprographics area through the company's internal mail system. Copies of documents are distributed by the same means.

A modern reprographics center.

An alternative is a system of minicenters in which a few reprographics areas serve the needs of a large office. Masters and copies may be picked up and delivered by the office mail system, or employees may have access to the distant equipment.

Decentralized Reprographics Systems. In a *decentralized reprographics system*, copiers are conveniently located throughout the company. This kind of system works well in smaller offices with a fairly low volume of copies. Many companies have a combined centralized and decentralized system. For example, if an office routinely produces a large volume of copies, but employees in certain divisions also need a small number of copies, the company may have one centralized copy area as well as one or two local machines.

DISTRIBUTION/ COMMUNICATION

Information is useful only when it reaches the people who need it and want it. Distribution/communication is therefore an important phase of the information processing cycle. Business information can be communicated and distributed among offices and individuals by several means, including the telephone, the regular U.S. Postal Service, and, increasingly, a variety of electronic devices. The following pages examine various methods of distributing information in and beyond the office.

The U.S. Postal Service

It will come as no surprise to you that the oldest and most widespread method of distributing information outside the office is the U.S. Postal Service. To meet a steadily increasing demand

Information processing cycle (distribution/communication).

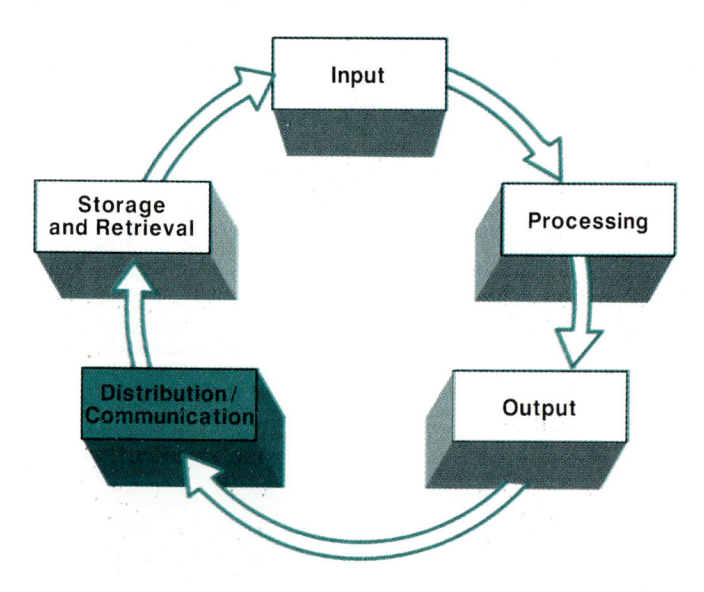

150   Information Systems

INTELPOST messages are transmitted electronically around the world.

for speedier service, the postal system introduced *Express Mail*. Express Mail guarantees overnight delivery of mail to many cities within the continental United States.

To further accelerate communications, the U.S. Postal Service, like other businesses, has begun to use computers in its operations. *INTELPOST*, an acronym for *International Electronic Postal Service*, is designed for the high-speed, computer-assisted transmission of information. INTELPOST messages are transmitted by means of communications satellites—space vehicles that relay information electronically.

Almost any kind of document can be transmitted by INTELPOST, including photographs, graphs, and charts, as well as text. INTELPOST is especially useful for transmitting shipping documents, purchase orders, customs documents, invoices, and legal and financial statements.

Electronic Data Communications

As you have seen, the U.S. Postal Service makes some use of electronic equipment. Using electronic equipment, great quantities of information can be transmitted at very high speeds over communications lines. This method of transmitting information is sometimes referred to as *electronic mail* or *electronic data communication*. More generally, electronic data communication can be defined as the movement of any encoded information from one point to another by means of electrical transmission systems. It is becoming an increasingly important tool for businesses that need to distribute large amounts of information quickly.

There are two points to remember about data communications: First, different pieces of electronic equipment can communicate with each other through *telecommunication lines*, such as telephone and telegraph lines, and via satellites. Second, the information between communicating machines is in the form of electronic signals, not paper.

Telex, TWX, and Mailgrams. The two oldest and most widely used systems for transmitting text messages are Western Union's Telex and TWX. In both the *Telex* system and *TWX*, information is transmitted over telecommunications lines between two terminals. The terminals have keyboards, like typewriters, with rows of keys, and are called *teletypewriters*. The message is sent over telephone or telegraph lines to the receiving teletypewriter, which prints out the message automatically.

Mailgram is another form of electronic mail. A Western Union Mailgram uses the capabilities of the telephone, the telegraph,

The Model 5200 Telex Editor resembles a word processor and increases the amount of text that can be transmitted at one time from one terminal to another.

Distribution/Communication   151

and the U.S. Postal Service to send a text message. To send a Mailgram, you may phone the Western Union office nearest you and dictate your message. An operator keyboards it into a video terminal, and it is transmitted via Western Union telecommunications equipment to a major U.S. post office near the destination of the message.

Communicating Word Processors. You may not think of word processors as being in the same category as Western Union telecommunications equipment, but some have the same basic capabilities. Consider what word processing equipment can do. In a shared logic system, for example, documents can be sent electronically from one workstation to another. These workstations are *communicating word processors*. Using communicating word processors, two people can exchange more than a hundred pages of information in 10 minutes.

The ability of word processing equipment to communicate—to transfer information from one terminal to another—is one of the most important developments in information processing. Experiments have been conducted on transferring text electronically from one word processor to another. The success of these experiments has enabled manufacturers to develop equipment that could be linked through communicating networks including not only word processors but also mainframes, minicomputers, and microcomputers; Telex terminals; intelligent copiers; and phototypesetters. The communicating machines may be located in the same building or may be separated by many miles. They may be across the aisle or around the world.

Computer-Based Message Systems. Computers as well as word processing equipment can send electronic messages that are received instantly. When a company already has a computer system and many employees have display terminals at their workstations, a message system is easy to implement. Basically, the system consists of a simple data processing program that introduces a message blank on the terminal screen. To send a message to another terminal, you simply fill in the blank on your display terminal, using the keyboard. You then keyboard the address of the person who is to receive the message, and the computer instantly routes the message.

You can categorize messages according to priority and privacy. For example, a message labeled URGENT is positioned ahead of all others. Messages labeled PRIVATE require that the recipient use a special password code to access them. If you send a registered message, you will be notified when it is accepted. You can also designate a message to be delivered at a

Computer-based message systems use a message blank on the screen to be filled in by the user, as shown.

specific time of day—a useful advantage when sending messages across time zones.

Public Computer Networks. If a company does not have its own computers or does not wish to use them to relay messages, it can establish a message system by buying into the services of a public computer network. There are several such networks; one is GTE Telenet's Telemail service. Telenet serves over 200 cities throughout the United States and is used by more than 120 companies, serving more than 7000 individual users. Through Telenet, a message can be sent from a display terminal in one office to a terminal in the same office or to one across the country. All the messages, regardless of where they originate and where they are sent, are processed by Telenet's central computer in Vienna, Virginia. The system is used by most offices as an electronic memo service for short communications between sales representatives and the home office.

Local Area Networks (LANs). Few things in life seem simpler than picking up the phone and making a call. However, even a local call requires a complex network of electronic equipment. Not surprisingly, it is even more difficult for computers to communicate. Computers not only must send and receive signals so that they know when to make connections, when to disconnect, and when one message has priority over another, but they also must perform many other functions. A system for computer communication over a short distance is called a *local area network*, or *LAN*. A LAN can link computers from distances of one-tenth of a mile to over eight miles.

Although there are differences, there are many ways in which a LAN is like a telephone system. Anyone who has a telephone in his or her house can talk to anyone else who has a phone connected to the system. A local area network is designed so that each computer connected to it can communicate with every other computer in the network. Sometimes a company builds a LAN solely for its own use; and sometimes other business organizations lease connections to the LAN, to share computer information.

It really doesn't matter to you to know how a LAN works any more than it does for you to know how a phone works when you place a call. What does matter is that you understand how to use the equipment and that it works properly. How you use a LAN depends on a number of things: the type of equipment that is connected, over what distance, what kind of communication it is used for, and the geographic or geometric arrangement of the computers and their peripherals.

The arrangement, or configuration, of the equipment is called the *architecture* or *network topology*. There are several basic LAN topologies.

Simple Network. Each place where a terminal, a printer, or a peripheral is located is called a *node*. Each node is connected to the LAN by a separate cable. The connecting path between two nodes is a *link*. The simplest network is a shared logic system linking three nodes to one CPU. An example of this is your terminal and a terminal in the next office sharing a printer, with each peripheral connected to a CPU across the hall. Even though this configuration is not typically referred to as a LAN, it illustrates how each node must be connected to the CPU by a separate link.

So far, this seems simple enough. But as nodes are added or removed it can get complicated. The terminals in this simple network do not need to communicate with each other. If they did, a cable would be needed to link each terminal. When more than one person tries to communicate at the same time in a larger network, messages can collide and cause traffic problems.

Star Network. To solve these two problems—too many cables and too much traffic—a different kind of network was designed. In this kind of network, a central switching device plays the role of telephone operator. The central controlling node is called a *hub* or *central controller*. Instead of people communicating with each other directly, their messages go first to the hub, and then the hub routes them to the receiving node. Be-

A star network.

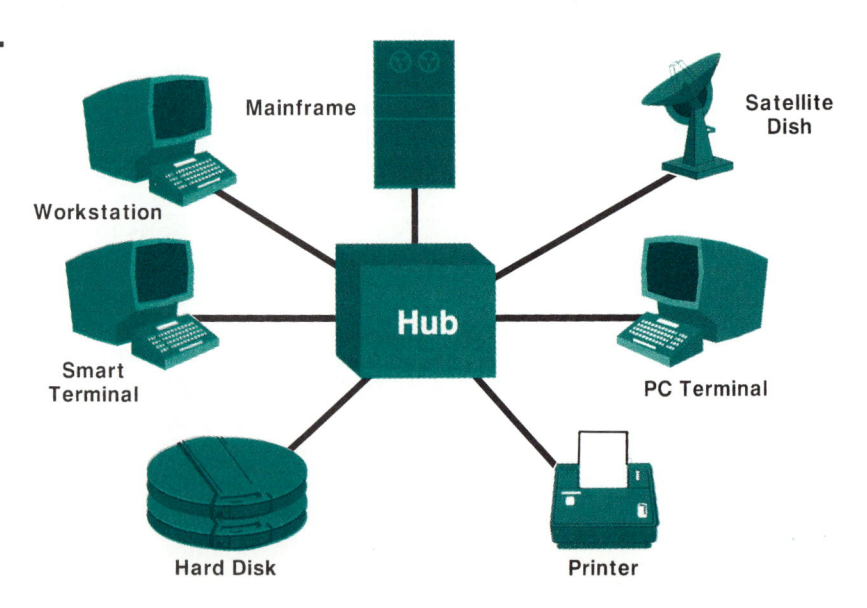

Information Systems

cause this network's topology is shaped somewhat like a star, it is referred to as a *star network*.

The star network has its drawbacks. In many star networks, the functions of the hub are handled by the CPU. This can mean that, when traffic is heavy, the CPU is so busy switching calls it has no time to handle other tasks. Moreover, a star network depends on the hub. If it fails, the LAN fails.

Ring Network. One way to eliminate the problem of relying too heavily on the hub is to link the nodes in a circle. This LAN configuration can look something like a ring. Picture a group of people passing a note from one person to the next at a round table. In a *ring network*, messages are communicated like this from one node to the next.

Some ring networks are designed so that when a node receives a message, it reads it and then sends it on to the next node. On other LANs, the node reads the address first. If the message is intended for another node, it is ignored and passed on. Eventually, the message is returned to the sender. If the message is received by the sender intact, it means the message was received intact by the addressee. One type of ring network is designed so that, before returning the message, the addressee can add a note showing that it was received. Some ring networks use a hub, or controller, to direct traffic, but the controller is not connected centrally, the way it is in a star network. It is simply another node in the ring.

The main disadvantage to a ring network is that, like a chain, it is only as strong as its weakest link. A ring network is, in a

A ring network.

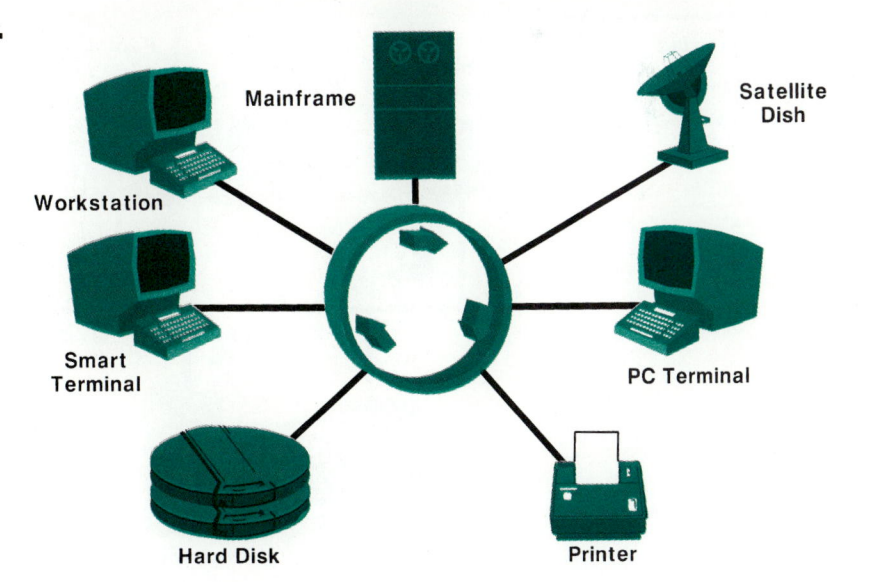

Distribution/Communication

sense, even more vulnerable than a star network. If even one node breaks down, no matter what node it is, the entire LAN will *crash*. "Crash" is a term often used by people who work with computers to mean that the system cannot function. A crash can be caused by a failure either in the computer hardware or software, or in the electric power supply.

Star-Shaped Ring Network. There are ways to get around the problem of a ring network breaking down. One approach is sometimes called the *star-shaped ring*. This type of LAN uses a hub to reroute calls if any of the nodes should fail. This keeps the rest of the LAN functioning, unlike a ring. A star-shaped ring may use a hub to switch calls.

Bus Network. The most flexible topology is the *bus network*. In a bus network, there is only one cable, and any number of nodes can be plugged into it, anywhere along its length. Individual nodes can be removed without affecting the LAN's operation. The bus will not fail if any of its nodes fail.

Xerox's Ethernet is probably the best-known bus network. There is no central CPU or hub in a bus network. The function of the hub is performed by a special software program which routes and exchanges messages. Each node in a bus network has its own CPU, therefore it can function independently of the other nodes. The messaging software can be stored in the disk drive of any node. Usually, more than one node stores a copy of the messaging software. This serves as a backup. If the CPU that is acting as the controller should fail, another CPU that is storing the messaging software can take over, and the system con-

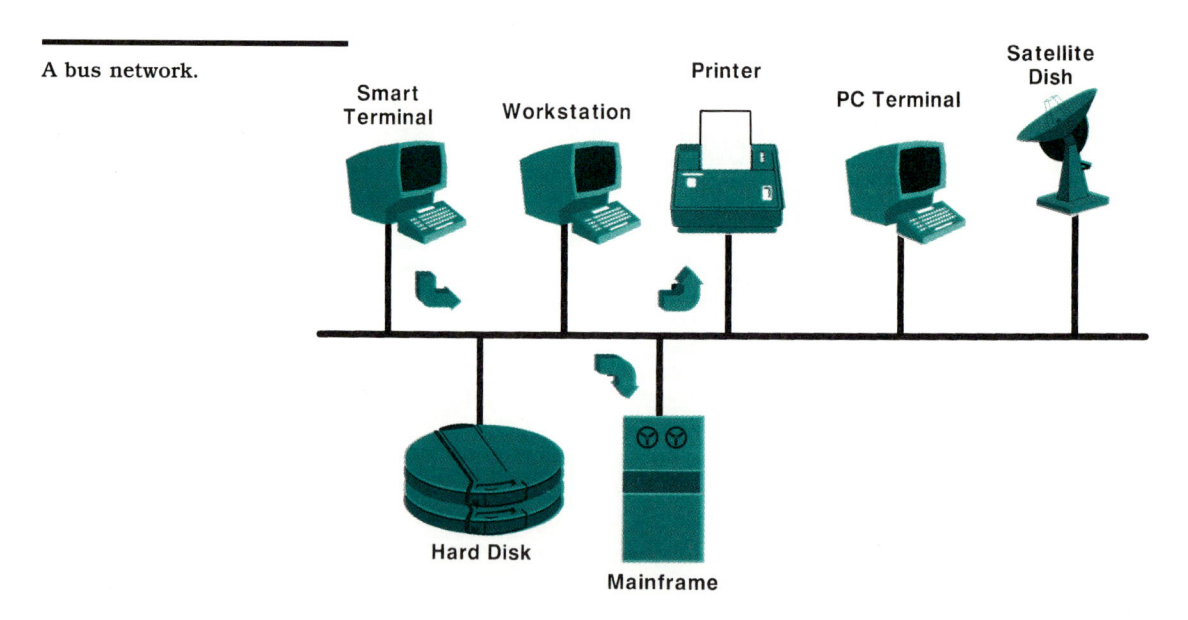

A bus network.

tinues running. Any user on a bus network can send a file to any other user.

All networks are prone to traffic congestion. Two methods are typically used for directing traffic. The first assigns a number to each node, in much the same way you would take a ticket with a number to get served at a bakery. Your number comes up electronically at regular time intervals. When it is your turn, you have a certain amount of time to use the LAN to send a message. This ensures that no one ties up the network for too long. With some networks, if you have a long message to send, you need to break it up into smaller segments, and take more than one turn to send it.

The second method of routing messages does not use "numbers." Instead, everyone gets a turn, and then the process repeats. If you want to send a message, you have to wait your turn. If you have no message to send you simply give up your turn, and wait for it to come around again.

LANs make it possible for people to use computers to communicate with each other from one office to another, or one building to another, whether in a plant, a corporate headquarters, a campus, or any other locally based organization. For communication at greater distances, a LAN can be connected by phone lines to other LANs. Communication by satellite makes it possible for one computer terminal to communicate with another terminal virtually anywhere in the world.

Transmission Systems

The enormous and growing amount of information requires us to find the best possible ways to transmit that information—to get it from one piece of equipment to another, from one place to another, from the person who has it to the person who needs it. You have already learned that information can be communicated by electronic means. Whether the machines are next to one another or thousands of miles apart, moving the information requires a *transmission system* of some sort. Transmission systems are vital to the creation of integrated information systems that link different computer-based functions and equipment—word processors, computers, Telex terminals, facsimiles, laser printers, and so on. Office automation means that machines involved in generating, processing, distributing, and storing information are part of one system.

When computers transfer data back and forth, they must talk the same language and at the same speed. Also, various other signals they exchange must be identical. Let us now look more closely at some of the transmission systems used to link data communication terminals and networks to make them operate as one system.

Distribution/Communication

Private Branch Exchanges. The most familiar use of a *private branch exchange*, or *PBX*, is to route telephone calls to the phone extensions within an organization. But a PBX can also be used to transmit text and data by telephone line from a terminal to any other equipment. The greatest appeal of PBXs for information processing is that the telephone lines they rely on are already in place.

However, until recently, PBXs could only carry the analog sound wave of the human voice. They could not be used to transmit the digital signal of a computer. (The difference between analog and digital is explained in Chapter 5, where we also describe a modem—a piece of equipment that converts a digital computer signal to an analog signal.)

In 1975, manufacturers developed a PBX that could convert digital signals to analog automatically, making a costly modem unnecessary. The most advanced of the recently introduced digital PBX systems is an *EPBX*, which stands for *Electronic Private Branch Exchange*. The device not only converts the signal automatically, but also makes it possible to connect telephone data transmission with LANs and other networks. The trend is clearly toward integration of voice and text—the telephone with the data terminal.

Interfaces. Data communications require special rules and procedures. Because communicating systems are not always compatible, special equipment must be designed to ensure that all codes, formats, instructions, speeds, and languages are recognized by both the sending and receiving systems. Manufacturers have agreed on standardized interfaces. An interface can be hardware, such as the plug used to connect equipment by cable, or it can be software.

Modem. The human voice has a wide range of varying frequencies that form a pattern called an *analog wave*. Telephone lines are designed to carry analog waves. Computers send information using only the binary language of *on* and *off*. This binary signal is called a *digital signal*. So in order for a computer to send data by telephone, you need to convert its signal from digital to analog. Then when the message is received, the analog signal has to be converted back to a digital signal, so the receiving computer can process the data that was transmitted. The device that does this is called a *modem*, short for *mod*ulator/*dem*odulator. Unless you are using some other equipment to convert the computer signal, such as an EPBX, you will need a modem to transmit data by telephone.

The modem links the computer and the telephone in either of two ways. If the modem is installed inside the CPU, it is called an

Modems come in different forms. This is an external modem.

This modem is an acoustic coupler.

internal modem. Usually you cannot see an internal modem. If the modem is a separate unit, it is called an *external modem.* For example, an external modem for a personal computer is usually placed on the desk between the phone and the PC. It may look like a box about the size of a typical hardcover novel. External modems are connected to the phone and CPU with cables and jacks. There may also be a cradle for the phone receiver.

The internal and external modems convert digital signals to analog signals, and vice versa. Another kind of external modem changes the computer's digital signal to an audible sound signal that you can hear. This audio signal is sent by telephone through the phone receiver, the same way your voice is transmitted when you make a phone call. This type of modem is called an *acoustic coupler.* The equipment itself has a plastic or foam rubber cradle that fits a phone receiver snugly enough so it does not pick up any room noise.

Acoustic coupling modems are especially convenient for businesspeople who use a microcomputer when they travel and often need to send computer data from the nearest phone. Other kinds of office equipment, such as copying machines, may be linked to acoustic couplers in an integrated information processing system.

Baud Rate and Bits Per Second. As we discussed earlier, the smallest piece of information a computer can recognize is a bit. A bit can be represented by either a one or a zero. A one lets the electric current pass through. A zero shuts it off. A byte is a group of eight bits which together represent one alphanumeric character. It is these bits that are sent from one computer to another in data communication.

The speed at which you send data can vary with the method of transmission, the equipment used, and the cost. Two ways that are used to measure how fast data travels over communication lines are *baud rate* and *bits per second (bps).* Although the terms are used interchangeably, the number of bits per second can differ from the baud rate, depending on the hardware and software used for the transmission. The trend is to use the term bps rather than baud rate. Personal computers typically exchange data at a baud rate of either 300 or 1200. The rates of 2400, 4800, and 9600 bps are common for communicating minicomputers and mainframes. The rate can go much higher—up to 10 million bits per second—when one CPU sends data to another without a modem.

Control Characters and Control Codes. When two computers communicate, they need to exchange other information besides the actual message that is transmitted. For example, it is not enough simply to send the text to a document or file in the form you see it displayed on the screen after keyboarding it on a word processor or computer. If the message is to be printed when it is received, your formatting keystrokes must also be sent to the printer at the receiving computer. These codes and instructions, and others like this, are sent before, during, and after the message itself is transmitted. They are called *control characters* or *control codes*.

Just as Samuel Morse devised a code for sending telegraph messages, in 1967 a code was devised for data communication. It is called the *American Standard Code for Information Interchange (ASCII)*, often pronounced *ask-ee*. There is an ASCII character for each alphanumeric character, all the punctuation marks, and the various control codes.

One of the control codes almost always used in data communication is the *parity bit*. Parity bits are sent along with the groups of alphanumeric bits. They give the receiving computer a way of checking whether the data received is identical to the data that was sent, or if an error occurred during the sending.

Modes of Transmission. There are two basic types, or *modes*, of data communication: *asynchronous* and *bisynchronous*. Let's look at how these control codes are used in each mode.

Asynchronous. Characters are sent one at a time during *asynchronous transmission* at uneven intervals rather than in a steady stream. There may be more of a wait between some characters than others. The receiving computer never knows when the data is coming. So it has to have some advance notice. For this reason, a *start bit* is sent immediately before each character, and a *stop bit* is sent immediately after. The stop bit tells the receiver when to look for the next character. Microcomputers generally exchange data asynchronously.

Bisynchronous. Instead of sandwiching each character between a start and a stop bit, the complete message is sent all at

Asynchronous transmission (as shown in the top illustration) uses start and stop bits when sending each *character*. Bisynchronous transmission (as shown in the bottom illustration) uses start and stop bits when sending each *word*.

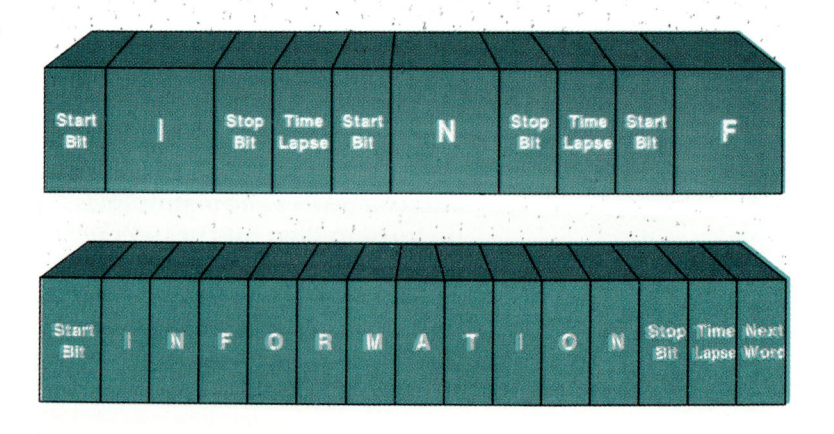

Information Systems

once in *bisynchronous transmission* (sometimes referred to as *synchronous*). The control codes that set up and begin the communication are sent first. Then the actual message is sent. Only after the entire message is sent does the receiving computer check for transmission errors.

Transmission Media. Data may be transmitted in the form of electricity, sound, light, or radio wave. If the data is transmitted by telephone, either by voice or with an acoustic coupler, then sound is also used. When the data leaves one computer on its way to another, it begins as an electric impulse. Like any form of electricity, it needs a medium, or conductor, to get from one place to the next.

Conductors vary according to how much information they can carry, and to the extent that they are susceptible to interference. The best conductor is silver, but it is too costly. So we use copper, another excellent conductor. Here are brief descriptions of some of the other kinds of transmission media used for communication links between computer systems.

Twisted Pairs. Uninsulated open wire was used first in the early days of electricity. As open wire was used more and more frequently, space became a problem. To save space, two insulated wires were twisted together to form one twisted-pair cable. Twisted-pair cable is now generally used for telephone lines. For other uses, *twisted pairs,* as they are called, are either placed in tunnels or buried underground. They are inexpensive and good for transmitting over short distances.

Noise caused by electrical interference is the greatest single problem in data communication. It can distort the transmitted signal so that information is lost. Another term for noise interference is *crosstalk*. More than one wire in close contact can cause noise. When several twisted pairs are wrapped together, they are wound at different angles to minimize crosstalk.

Coaxial Cables. Even *with* proper winding, crosstalk can be a problem on twisted pairs. Noise increases with distance and the number of messages carried by a single cable. *Coaxial cable* was developed to minimize noise interference. The copper wire in a coaxial cable is usually surrounded by an insulating layer of air or plastic. Covering the plastic insulation is often another layer of aluminum or copper mesh as an additional shield against interference. Then the entire cable is surrounded by a protective cover. This insulates each wire so effectively that up to 20 individual cables are often twisted together just like two wires are in twisted pairs. Coaxial cable can carry thousands of communications at the same time.

Fiber Optics. With fiber optics, data can be transmitted in

Coaxial cable.

Distribution/Communication

the form of light. The communication channel used to transmit light is glass fiber, hardly thicker than a human hair. When a transmission leaves the sending computer, it is an electric signal. This signal is changed to a laser beam and sent through the optical fiber. When it reaches the receiving computer, it is changed back to an electric signal. The information travels at the speed of light, so it is transmitted instantly. Light is not affected by electrical interference, so data is seldom lost. (See the illustration of fiber optics on insert page IV C.)

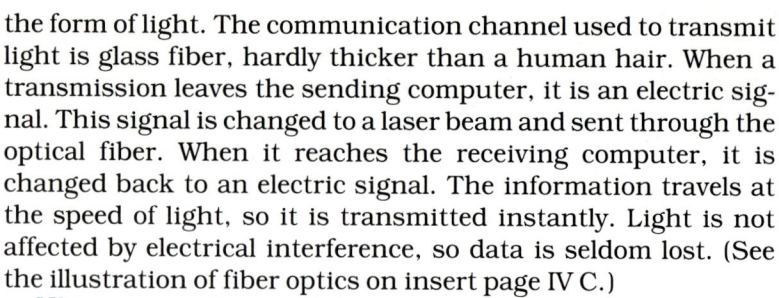

Microwaves. Text and data can also be transmitted by *microwave*. Microwaves are high-frequency radio waves. With microwaves, data is sent electrically from the sending computer to a microwave relay station. The data may also travel along optical fiber some or all of the distance between the sending computer and the relay station. When it reaches the relay station, the signal is beamed as a microwave a distance of 30 miles from one relay station to another station until it reaches its destination. At that point, it is changed back to an electric signal for the receiving computer. Microwaves can only travel through air, so relay stations are located on mountaintops, towers, and the tops of tall buildings.

This microwave relay station transmits high-frequency radio waves.

Satellites. When data must travel greater distances than is practical with relay stations, microwaves are beamed from a station on earth to a satellite in space, and back again to a different earth station. There are clear advantages with satellites: You do not need as many earth stations and, because of the speed of the signal, it is less vulnerable to noise and electrical interference. This reduces the likelihood of data errors.

Transmission Lines and Protocols. Two kinds of electrical circuits are generally used to transmit data: (1) a circuit with two wires, called *half-duplex*, and (2) a circuit with four wires, called *duplex* or *full-duplex*.

Protocols. A *protocol* is a technique or procedure for transmitting data that is agreed on by both the sender and receiver. There are three protocols that you can use to send data on either of these two circuits: A *simplex* protocol is used to transmit data in only one direction. The *half-duplex* protocol allows data communications between both the sender and receiver, but only in one direction at a time. With a *duplex* protocol, data can go in both directions at the same time, like a phone conversation when both people are talking at the same time and each can hear the other. *Echoplex* is a protocol often used with duplex transmission. With this protocol, the data you transmit is "echoed" back to your terminal after it is received, and displayed on your screen. This enables you to check whether it was received exactly as you sent it.

A protocol translator adapts the procedure of one machine to another.

Information Systems

Protocol Translator. Information processing manufacturers have created a number of software programs for data communication between otherwise incompatible word processing equipment and computers. These programs supply the necessary translation from the logic of one machine to that of another.

In addition to software conversions, devices known as *protocol translators* may be needed. (A protocol, as we explained, is a procedure.) The main reason equipment is incompatible is that one machine has different procedures from another. Protocol translators translate instructions of the sending machine into commands that the receiving equipment can understand.

Electronic Audio Communications

You have probably had the experience of calling a phone number and receiving prerecorded information such as the time of day, the weather forecast, a horoscope reading, or even a daily joke or recipe. The speaker's message has been recorded on magnetic tape and is transmitted over the phone wires to your telephone receiver.

Electronic audio communications, or *voice mail*, is a somewhat more sophisticated example of the same idea. Voice mail is just what its name implies—the electronic storing of telephoned messages (in a computer called a "voice mail box") so that they can be handled at the convenience of the person receiving them. A voice mail system can save time in large organizations where many employees, because of travel and business meetings, are often not available to receive direct phone calls. In a voice mail system, messages can be stored and forwarded at specific times, and outgoing calls as well as incoming ones can be recorded.

Teleconferencing

A *teleconference* is a meeting of people who are geographically separated but who are connected simultaneously by a telecom-

A teleconference is an electronic "meeting" with audio and video.

Distribution/Communication

munications system that uses two-way voice, text, or video communication. A person "attending" the teleconference can see and/or hear and respond to any of the other people attending the conference. Teleconferencing has the great advantage of permitting personal interaction, complete with sight and sound, without requiring the time and expense of travel.

STORAGE AND RETRIEVAL

Despite all the advances in storing and communicating information electronically, it is likely that nothing will ever completely replace paper-based filing systems, at least not for decades to come. A simple bound book with numbered pages continues to be one of the most efficient, portable forms of information storage. Nevertheless, new technology is changing dramatically the way businesses manage their records.

Storage of Paper and Magnetic Media

Until recently most of the information that exists in the world was stored on paper—in books, documents, newspapers, magazines, computer copy, punched cards, index cards, and so on. There are a number of common ways of storing paper. One of the most efficient is *open-shelf storage,* in which open shelves are stacked vertically and the stored documents are visible. But any kind of paper filing system takes up a great deal of costly space, and many companies have been interested in finding other methods of retaining information. One such method is storage on magnetic media. These media—such as magnetic cards, magnetic tape, floppy diskettes, and hard disks—lend

Information processing cycle (storage and retrieval).

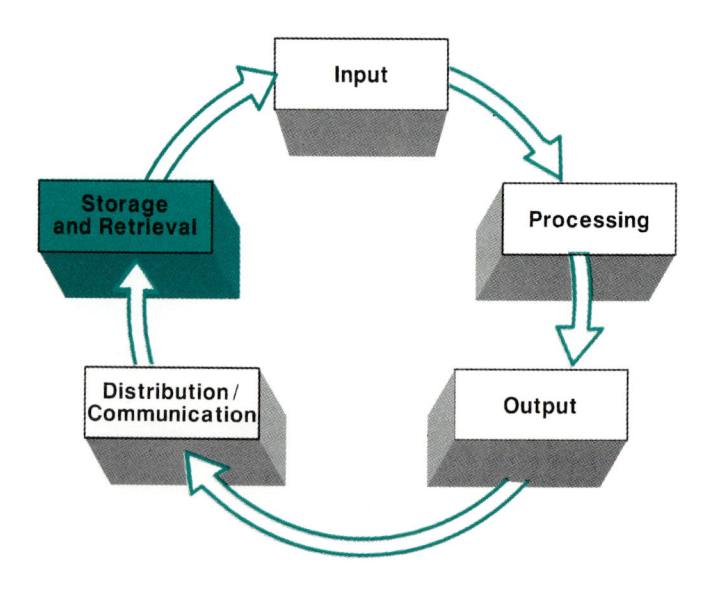

164   Information Systems

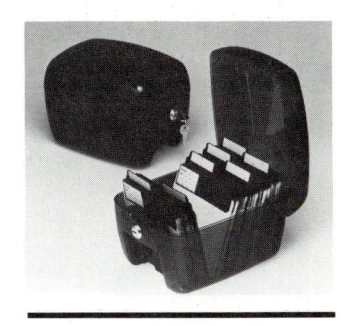

Desk-top storage units are often ideal for magnetic media.

Large offices may store magnetic media, such as these mag tapes, in special cabinets.

themselves to many of the same kinds of storage systems as paper does. However, magnetic media systems require far less office space to store the same amount of information.

Equipment for Storing Magnetic Media. In a small office, desk-top equipment—trays, binders, boxes, or tubs—may be sufficient for storage of magnetic media. Diskettes, for instance, can be stored in a plastic file box or in a three-ring easel binder with sleeves into which the diskettes fit. The file boxes may have suspension inserts or index tabs so that diskettes can be identified and retrieved easily. The boxes may also have covers that protect the diskettes from dust, smoke, and other potentially harmful substances. This type of equipment is portable and can be locked in desk drawers for security.

In large offices and in cases where many floppy diskettes are produced, rotary files offer easy access and may be the best choice for storage. Rotary files can be stacked one on top of the other to allow for more storage capacity in a limited space.

Cabinets are useful for storing large reels of computer hard disks, which are bulky and sensitive. The cabinets often have internal partitions that hold computer reel tapes, large folders of computer reel tapes and computer printouts, and hard disk containers. The cabinet doors, which open vertically or horizontally, offer protection against extreme variations of temperature and humidity, and they can be locked.

Some large organizations maintain computer tapes on open-shelf file systems within a controlled area such as an air-conditioned storage room. In these open-shelf files, tapes are kept in their protective cases and are easily retrieved.

How long do records have to be stored? Basically, the answer is: for as long as they are needed. Most companies have a records retention schedule that specifies how long certain documents should be held. When there is no further use for documents stored on magnetic media, they can be erased.

Micrographics

Film is another common storage medium. *Micrographics*, the fast-growing field of information storage on film, involves photographically reducing images of text and graphic information and recording them as tiny ("micro") images on film. The products that result from this process are generally referred to as *microforms*. Companies can save between 95 and 98 percent of the space needed for storing paper records by putting their records on microforms.

Microforms. A *microform* is a miniaturized image of a document. Information can be stored and retrieved on several kinds

Microfilm can be used to store old documents.

Microfilm jacket.

of microforms: microfilm, microfilm jackets, aperture cards, microfiche, or ultrafiche. To be fully retrieved, microform images must be magnified, of course, so that they can be read by people with normal vision. Microform readers or viewers, which you may have seen in libraries, are special machines that perform this function.

The oldest of the microforms, *microfilm*, is a continuous roll of film containing reduced images of graphic or textual material. Either 16- or 35-mm film can be used for photographing documents on microfilm. For documents on $8\frac{1}{2}$- by 11-inch paper, such as correspondence, invoices, and reports, 16-mm film is often used. Larger documents and graphic images—including newspapers, X rays, and blueprints—are usually photographed in sequence on 35-mm film. The number of pages that can be recorded on a standard 100-foot roll of 16- or 35-mm film depends on the degree to which the pages are reduced. At a ratio of 24 to 1, about 600 $8\frac{1}{2}$- by 11-inch pages can be photographed on one reel of 16-mm film. Nearly 3000 pages can be recorded on 35-mm film at the same reduction.

As office storage space becomes increasingly expensive, managers look to microfilm as a way to store more information for less. Microfilm can be kept in storage units such as reels, cassettes, or cartridge magazines. You will often find microfilm stored in desk-top files or carousels that hold 100 to 300 storage units.

Microfilm records can be updated or corrected by splicing new sections of film into the continuous roll. The film can also be cut into smaller segments—from one frame to a strip of several frames—producing what is called *unitized microforms*. Unitized microforms can be stored like index cards. They are a useful way to record and store one short document or one or more drawings. Microfilm jackets, aperture cards, microfiche, and ultrafiche are all forms of unitized microforms.

Microfilm jackets are two sheets of acetate or plastic, usually 6 by 4 inches, sealed at the top and bottom and divided into horizontal sections that will hold strips of microfilm. An *aperture card* is a form of keypunch card with a rectangular opening that holds one or more frames of microfilm. Because aperture cards are the same size as keypunch cards, they can be sorted by keypunch equipment. *Microfiche* is a small sheet of film about the size of an index card, most often 6 by 4 inches. The film contains reduced images of documents—anywhere from 50 to more than a 100 $8\frac{1}{2}$- by 11-inch pages, depending on the degree to which the original documents are reduced. The reduced images are arranged in rows and columns. The columns are numbered across the top, and the rows are lettered along the side.

Information Systems

Each microfiche shown here can contain as many as 98 pages.

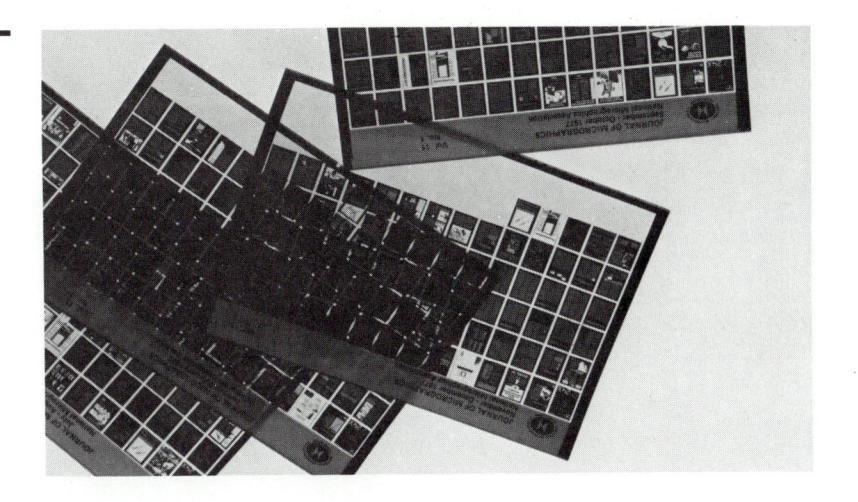

Ultrafiche is the most extreme form of image reduction. A 6- by 4-inch ultrafiche can contain as many as 4000 pages of information.

Computer Output Microfilm (COM). Microfiche can be created directly from documents by means of a planetary camera—one used to photograph large documents, such as architectural blueprints. Microfiche and other microforms can also be created by a special method known as *computer output microfilm*, or *COM*. As the name implies, COM represents an integration of computer and microfilm technologies.

In many computer operations output is produced on paper by means of a printer attached to the computer. With COM, instead of a paper printout you get microforms—usually in a microfiche format. The advantage of this method over the camera method of producing microfiche is that COM units can produce many microfiche at an extremely fast rate—200 to 300 full-page documents in a minute. The COM recorder can accept data directly from the computer or from computer tapes or disks. The COM recorder thus becomes an alternate to paper printers as a way of producing computer output.

Retrieval of Microforms. Microform retrieval involves getting microforms from files and finding specific documents on those microforms you have retrieved. Microfilm rolls, cassettes, and cartridges are usually retrieved manually from shelves or cabinets. Both microfiche and microfilm jackets, filed like index cards, can be retrieved by hand or, in automated filing systems, by machines in seconds. Aperture cards too can be filed like index cards. They can also be filed, sorted, and retrieved by keypunch equipment.

Microfilm readers enlarge and project the tiny filmed images.

Microfilm Readers. To find a specific document on microfilm, you need a *microfilm* or *roll-film reader*. This is a machine that enlarges and projects the microfilm image onto a screen. Specific pages can be located by means of whatever coding or indexing system the microfilm uses. Some microfilm readers advance the film mechanically, while others use computer technology to speed up the process of finding a specific page. Once a document is projected to its original size or larger, it can be read easily.

Microfiche Readers. To find a specific document on the microfiche, you first find the address of the document from whatever index is being used. You then move a pointer over a grid pattern attached to the reader. This grid pattern is similar to the pattern on the card. To locate a document whose address is C-5, you move the pointer to the C-5 position on the grid, and the carriage simultaneously moves the card in such a way that the document at C-5 is projected onto the screen in much the same way as in a microfilm reader. An aperture card reader works essentially the same way as the microfiche reader.

Reader/Printers. Some readers can also print copies of microfilm, microfiche, and aperture card documents. These machines are called *reader/printers*. Methods of producing copies may vary, but whatever method is used, the copy size is the same size as the reader screen, and the machines produce copies in just a few seconds.

Information Systems

Computer-assisted retrieval (CAR) gives instant access to files.

Computer-Assisted Retrieval (CAR). The computer can play an important role in the retrieval as well as the production of microforms through a system called *computer-assisted retrieval*, or *CAR*. Documents can be retrieved and viewed at terminals at almost any location as long as the terminals are electronically linked to a central filing system. Each document in the system is indexed with its own alphanumeric code. After finding the specific code number you need in a directory that resembles a phone book, you enter this code in the computer. The code is converted to a signal that rapidly scans filed microfiche until it finds the card with the matching code. That card is conveyed to an automatic microfiche reader, and the image is transmitted back to your terminal.

Computer-assisted retrieval is based on the computer's ability to access and update files instantaneously, and it reduces filing time and cost. In some instances, this may mean that you can change your filing system in ways that might have been so costly and time-consuming before that it was just not worth the trouble. You could use CAR, for example, to take advantage of the search and replace function in word processing.

Optical (Laser) Disks

If word processors have made us capable of producing documents in greater volume than we ever could before, they have also given us a greater need for storing information more efficiently and in less space. It is not enough simply to store a document. Even hard disks have their limits, especially for businesses that generate data in billions of bytes. With this in mind, scientists have worked for years to develop more compact and efficient means of information storage. One result of their research is the *optical disk*, or *laser disk*.

Storage and Retrieval

An optical laser disk.

Optical disks use light in the form of laser beams to write and read data. The laser records information by focusing heat that creates a small bubble on the disk surface. When the disk is read—that is, when you retrieve a document—light is bounced off the disk. If the disk has information stored on it, the angle of the reflected light changes in such a way as to transfer the data recorded on the disk.

The storage capacity of an optical disk is impressive. 3M Corporation's 12-inch disk has a capacity of about one gigabyte, or a billion bytes. 3M's $5\frac{1}{4}$-inch magneto-optical disk holds 300 to 550 megabytes which, depending on the equipment that you use it with, is equal to 50 hard disks, or 1500 floppy diskettes.

There are three different types of optical disks: With *read-only* disks, the user cannot write on the disk. You can write on *write-once* disks, but you cannot erase anything you have written. There are also *erasable* disks. They can be used for recording, erasing, and reading data. They combine laser/optical and magnetic technology.

Manufacturers are now taking the enormous storage capacity of the optical disk a step further by designing equipment that works like a jukebox to store and access hundreds of optical disks. Such a device would make it possible to store millions of documents inexpensively. Combined in a local area network with an electronic filing system, it would place staggering amounts of information within easy access of any terminal.

Information Systems

Image Processing

We learned about image processing in Chapter 3 as a form of input and image scanners earlier in this chapter as a form of output. This time let's look at image processing as a method of storage and retrieval. Often material such as handwritten applications, books and magazines, and pictures and graphic images need to be entered into a computer.

Often it is not efficient to keyboard the information. And, of course, you cannot keyboard a picture. However, image processing makes it possible to enter this material into a computer without keyboarding.

Equipment for image processing consists of a personal computer, image processing software, a scanner, and a laser or thermal printer. As we explain in Chapter 3, to copy any photo, illustration, or text, you place the image under the scanner. The image is converted into digitized bits for the computer. Once the image is copied, and you have enlarged or reduced it to the size you want, you can edit it. That is, you can use the image as an illustration in a page of text. You can merge it with another document, store it on disk, or transmit it to a communicating word processor.

Microimage Transmission

Perhaps one of the more interesting developments affecting the way in which information is managed is *microimage transmission*. Image technology has developed equipment that can scan a microfilm image and convert it to a digitized computer signal. This makes it possible to send a microfilm image from one computer to another at any location in the same way that we use computers to send alphanumeric data by telephone.

The same process that is used to convert a microfilm image to a digital signal can also be used to store microfilm data on a magnetic storage medium, greatly saving storage space. Microimage transmission is one more tool that can help to integrate text, image, and data into one system.

Data Base Management Systems

Computers allow us to store information in greater quantities than ever before. But to be useful, this information needs to be organized so that it is quickly and easily accessible to anyone who needs it. The concept of a data base arose out of this need. A *data base* is a collection of related information stored so that it is available to many users for different purposes.

A computer data base uses an electronic filing system with many cross-references that give you a tremendous number of ways to reorganize and retrieve data. Often, a data base is designed to operate with a software program that can access "unknowns" from data that is already stored. A data base can handle business inventory, accounting, and filing, and use the information in its files to prepare summaries, estimates, and other reports. It can store newspaper articles, magazines, books, and games. There are computer data bases that provide specialized information. In fact, a data base may contain any information that can be keyboarded.

The key to all this is how the information in the data base is managed. A *data base management system (DBMS)* is a combination of hardware and software that you can use to set up and maintain a data base, and to manage access to and retrieval of information you have stored in it.

The common four-drawer office file cabinet is like a personal computer. What's inside the cabinet is the data base, that is, a collection of related files. A *file* is a group of related pieces of information stored together. A *record* is a collection of information. A *field* is a single item of information. If you are familiar with manual filing, you can think of a field as a single filing unit.

Most data base management systems have the following capabilities:

1. Once files are created, data (information) may be added, modified, or deleted. Entire files may also be created, added, or modified.
2. All the information in the data base may be retrieved at will, either selectively or collectively.
3. Records may be sorted or indexed at the user's direction and discretion.
4. Reports may be produced in formats that are predetermined (standard) and/or user-defined.
5. Mathematical functions can be performed, and data can be moved and manipulated.

Data Banks.   A collection of data bases is called a *data bank*. A number of companies maintain data banks and permit their use by others, usually for a fee. Some data banks are based on numbers and consist of information such as economic statistics, stock market prices, and population figures. Others are based on words and may include such items as newspaper articles, court decisions, patents, or other documents that are indexed and cross-referenced according to key words.

Most data bases are structured with a similar purpose—to make information easily accessible to as many users as possible. However, these commercial data banks are entirely different from the applications software for managing a data base with a microcomputer that we talk about in Chapter 5. Just about any

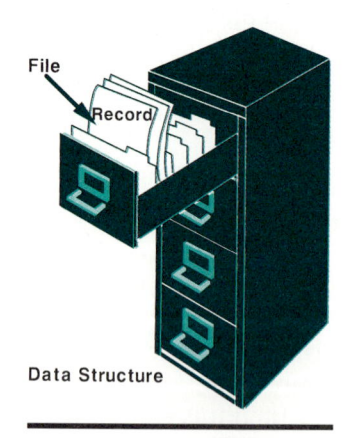

File
Record
Data Structure

Records make up the file which is part of the data base.

172   Information Systems

kind of business information you can think of is stored in a data bank somewhere. Gaining access to it by modem can save you hours and hours of searching in a library of printed documents—if, indeed, it even exists in a conventional library. In fact, you might think of data banks as libraries at your fingertips. Cuadra Associates of Santa Monica, California, data base specialists, reports that there are currently about 3000 computer data bases offered by nearly 400 data base services. The existence of a data bank, however, does not eliminate the use of in-house data bases. Very often it is necessary to use one or more in-house data bases as well as the resources of an outside data bank.

Online Information Services

Data base services are generally designed for use by companies, professional organizations, and libraries with heavy research needs. Their fees for online time are often beyond the reach of smaller businesses and most consumers. Online information services, however, can give you keyboard access to business, educational, recreational, and personal information at a moderate cost. An *online service* is a company that provides online access to one or more data bases. You can access an online service by connecting a personal computer to a telephone with a modem.

Records Management Systems

The storage and retrieval of information is a vital stage in the total information processing cycle. It is not enough just to generate useful information. That information must also be easily accessible. Otherwise, valuable time is lost. An efficient records management system can result in more efficient and more productive employees. There are two general systems of organizing office records—centralized and decentralized. Some offices adopt one system or the other, but a combination of both is possible.

In a centralized records management system, company records are in one place and are usually managed by a small staff of employees who control access to records, file and update records, handle requests for records, and generally keep track of the flow of records in and out of the centralized area. In a decentralized records management system, records are maintained in several areas throughout the company. Every company department, for example, may have its own filing system. A combined system usually consists of decentralized files with centralized control. Such a system ensures uniformity yet avoids excessive duplication of records.

Information Management

Technologically more advanced equipment will enable everyone in the office to participate in the information processing cycle at optimum efficiency. Fully integrated information management will speed and simplify the passage of information from one step in the cycle to another. The most useful equipment will be designed to accept information in any form from any user and transmit it instantly to any user, in a compatible medium.

In its more evolved stages, information management will combine word and data processing with film and electronic records management. Each person will have access to information at any location. Local area networks will link electronic filing systems and computer-assisted retrieval. The optical disk and other media will emerge in the years ahead to make sophisticated data base management a reality even for smaller businesses. Online information services will give us easy access to greater stores of information. People who choose a career in these areas will find it a challenge to create innovative capabilities for us, using these advances in hardware and software, and to coordinate the fully integrated electronic office into a system for information management.

CHAPTER SUMMARY

- One form of output not requiring the use of external printers or reprographics equipment is soft copy—text displayed on the screen of a display terminal.
- A printer for a word processor or microcomputer produces characters on paper by means of impact or nonimpact methods. Impact methods can produce carbon copies; nonimpact printers have the advantage of extremely high speed.
- Most printed information is some form of reproduced copy.
- Reprographics refers to several methods and kinds of equipment by which copies of written or graphic materials are made.
- The choice of reprographics method depends on the number of copies to be made, the desired quality, and the cost involved.
- Repetitive printing is an efficient method of producing original hard copies of a document by means of a word processing or microcomputer printer.
- Offset duplicating is an efficient means of reprographics when a large number of high-quality copies is desired.
- Photocopying does not require the preparation of a master. Photocopiers produce copies of uniform quality and offer

such capabilities as duplexing, reducing the image of an original document, copying in color or on colored stock, sorting, and stapling.
- Facsimile machines transmit and receive copies of documents by means of electronic signals that travel over telephone lines or through other electronic means.
- ZapMail, an electronic express document service, is the linking of state-of-the-art reprographics technology with satellite and telecommunication equipment.
- Electronic copier/printers can receive data from word or data processing equipment, producing multiple copies.
- Intelligent copier/printers store and manipulate data in various ways before committing it to hard copy form.
- Phototypesetting creates text by means of a light source that projects character images onto a film medium, which is then developed.
- Collating, binding, and folding are often needed to complete a copying job.
- Reprographics systems may be either centralized or decentralized. A centralized area serves the needs of an entire company or building. Decentralized areas serve the needs of groups of employees throughout the office.
- The U.S. Postal Service has developed two methods of meeting the increased need for speedy delivery of mail—Express Mail and International Electronic Postal Service (INTELPOST).
- Electronic mail is the method by which information is transmitted over telecommunications lines.
- Electronic mail makes it possible to send large amounts of information at high speed.
- The key to electronic mail is the ability of pieces of electronic equipment to communicate with each other via telecommunications lines or satellites.
- Telex and TWX, both services of Western Union, use telecommunications lines as a means of communication.
- A Mailgram uses capabilities of the telephone, telegraph, and U.S. Postal Service.
- Communicating word processors are being used increasingly to exchange information between workstations in the same building as well as between offices in distant locations.
- Types of equipment used in telecommunications include Telex, TWX, word processors, facsimile machines, and computers.
- A computer-based message system allows soft copy messages to be initiated, forwarded, and stored by means of a computer program and computer terminals.

- Public computer networks lease their communications channels to private companies, which use them to send messages from one terminal to another in the same office or across the country.
- Local area networks (LANs) link computer equipment for data communication up to eight miles. One LAN can communicate with another LAN at a different geographic location over telephone and other transmission lines.
- In a star network, several terminals are connected to a central controller that switches calls.
- A ring network connects each terminal to the next in a circle. A central controller is not essential, but many rings use one. Messages are passed from one node to the next until they reach the reader. If one node fails, the network crashes.
- A bus network is the most flexible in both topology and function. Any number of nodes can be connected or disconnected without affecting its operation. The main difference between a bus and other networks is that the bus has no central controller. Instead, call-switching functions are performed by a software program.
- Private branch exchanges (PBXs) route telephone calls within an organization and are used to transmit computer data by telephone.
- A modem converts a computer signal from digital to analog so it can travel over a telephone line. At the receiving end, a second modem changes the analog signal back to a digital signal for the receiving computer.
- Baud rate and bits per second (BPS) are both used to measure how fast data is transmitted. They are not always equal.
- During a data communication, both computers exchange control codes in addition to the actual message that is transmitted. The control codes are needed to send and receive data at precisely the right time and speed, to format and print it as hard copy when it is received, and to make sure it is transmitted without errors.
- In asynchronous transmission, data is sent at uneven intervals; in bisynchronous transmission, the entire message is sent all at once.
- Two types of cable commonly used are twisted-pair and coaxial.
- In fiber optics data is transmitted at the speed of light.
- Data can be transmitted in microwaves, which are high-frequency radio waves.
- A protocol is a technique or procedure for transmitting data that is agreed on by both sender and receiver.

- A half-duplex protocol can transmit data back and forth from sender to receiver, but only in one direction at a time.
- With a full-duplex protocol, data can travel in both directions at the same time.
- A protocol translator is a piece of equipment that converts the protocols of both the sending and receiving computers so they are compatible.
- Electronic audio communications, or voice mail, uses a company's phone system to initiate, forward, and store voice messages via a computer system.
- Teleconferencing involves the simultaneous back-and-forth exchange of information utilizing two-way voice, video, or text equipment.
- A good storage and retrieval system can result in more efficient and more productive employees.
- Magnetic media require considerably less storage space than paper for the same amount of information.
- Micrographics is the process of photographically reducing text and graphic images and recording them on film.
- Microforms include microfilm, microfilm jackets, aperture cards, microfiche, and ultrafiche.
- Microfiche can contain more than 100 pages of documents on a 6- by 4-inch card.
- Microfiche can be made directly from computer data by a process known as computer output microfilm (COM).
- Microfilm readers, microfiche readers, and aperture-card readers are machines which enlarge and project microform images for viewing.
- Hard copies of microforms can be produced by means of a reader/printer.
- No matter how a document is stored—whether on paper, microform, or a magnetic medium—it can be retrieved electronically with a system called computer-assisted retrieval (CAR).
- Optical disks use laser beams to store a tremendous amount of data in less than a fraction of the space used by magnetic media.
- You can convert a picture or other graphic information into digitized bits with image processing equipment, and then store or print the image on a word processor.
- Microimage transmission is a process that scans and then changes an image on microfilm into digitized bits that can be stored on disk or sent to a computer at another locaton.
- A computer data base uses an electronic filing system cross-referenced to give users many ways to access information.

- The hardware and software for setting up and maintaining a data base is called a data base management system (DBMS).
- A collection of data bases is a data bank. Data banks make their information available for a fee to subscribers, usually companies, that access the data bank by telephone using a computer and modem.
- An online information service provides access to one or more data bases. It is like a data bank but usually inexpensive enough for private individuals and smaller businesses to use.
- An office records system may be centralized or decentralized. In a centralized system company records are stored in one area. In a decentralized system company records are stored in several different areas.
- When word and data processing are combined with other electronic systems for records storage and transmission, they can form an integrated system for information management.

INFORMATION PROCESSING VOCABULARY

acoustic coupler
aperture card
baud rate
bits per second (bps)
bus network
centralized
  reprographics
character printer
coaxial cable
communicating word
  processor
computer-assisted
  retrieval (CAR)
computer-based
  message system
computer output
  microfilm (COM)
daisy wheel
data bank
data base
data base
  management system
  (DBMS)

data communications
decentralized
  reprographics
dot matrix
electronic copier/
  printer
electronic mail
facsimile
fiber optics
impact printer
ink-jet printer
intelligent copier/
  printer
International
  Electronic Postal
  Service (INTELPOST)
laser printer
line printer
local area
  network (LAN)
microfiche
microfilm
microfilm jacket

microform
micrographics
microimage
  transmission
microwave
modem
nonimpact printer
optical (laser) disk
photocomposition
photocopying
plotter
private branch
  exchange (PBX)
protocol
protocol translator
repetitive printing

reprographics
ring network
simple network
star network
telecommunications
teleconference
Teletypewriter
  Exchange Service
  (TWX)
Telex
thimble
topology
twisted pairs
ultrafiche
voice mail

CHAPTER QUESTIONS

1. What are the advantages that printers for word and data processors offer over standard typewriters for jobs that require repetitive printing?
2. In what ways has the photocopier changed office practices? Would life be more difficult without it? Explain.
3. What kinds of printing projects lend themselves to photocomposition?
4. In relation to speed and quantity of information, distinguish between distribution by electronic equipment and distribution by Express Mail.
5. How might teleconferencing be advantageous to a large corporation with branch offices throughout the country?
6. What are the similarities between the star, ring, and bus local area networks? What are the differences?
7. What function does a modem perform? Explain how a private branch exchange works. When can a PBX eliminate the need for a modem?
8. How can microforms increase the information-handling capability of most offices?
9. Give an example of a type of related information that could be grouped together in a data base. Describe how you would organize a data base management system for this information.
10. How might the use of optical disks for filing help a company that is pressed for office space?

CASE STUDY

The Bentix Corporation is a large national electronics manufacturing firm. Its headquarters are in Great Neck, New York, and it has branch offices in 20 major cities around the country. The company also has offices in Europe, including the Netherlands, and in Asia, Australia, and North Africa. Bentix sells a wide range of electronic equipment including computers, word processors, and facsimile machines. The company services machines purchased or leased by its customers and also provides data and word processing services for companies that do not wish to buy or lease their own equipment or who need to supplement their own equipment by having processing done at another site.

Bentix has a large in-house staff as well as a large sales staff and employees at its branch locations. Service and leasing customers are billed monthly.

Describe at least four methods of electronic communication that Bentix might use and what advantages those methods have.

Bentix, in a one-week period, handled the following requests. Read each request. Choose an appropriate method of reprographics for each. Select one of the following for each project: soft copy; repetitive printing; carbon paper; offset duplicating; photocopier; facsimile (analog or digital); electronic copier/printer; photocomposition. Explain your reasons for choosing a specific method. The requests are:

1. A two-page memo to be distributed in the office to three people.
2. A 40-page sales report to be distributed to ten key executives.
3. A 30-page company brochure describing the company pension plan, to be distributed to 1200 employees.
4. A reprinting of three copies of a 10-page proposal for the development of new equipment. This proposal is stored on a floppy diskette.
5. One copy of a purchase order to be sent as quickly as possible from the central office to a branch office in St. Louis.

CHAPTER 7

Integrated Information Processing and Office Environment and Organization

Lee Fong is a word processing specialist at Spangle Electric Company. The word processing center has many individual workstations, partitioned for privacy and efficiency. The center uses a shared logic system. Spangle has a computer in its Payroll Department. This machine is part of the data processing system that records payroll deductions, among other things. If Ms. Fong is asked to include information about payroll deductions for a report, she has to request a computer printout from Payroll. She then scans the printout for the figures she needs and keyboards them into her report. Spangle is thinking of integrating the data and word processing systems. If the company had an integrated system, Ms. Fong could obtain data by calling it onto her video screen. But to make best use of such a system, she will need to learn more about computers and communications.

Spangle Electric Co. is not unique in finding that it needs to rethink its information processing operation. Although both word processing and data processing involve computer technology, most companies originally treated them as separate systems. Recently, however, many offices have begun to join these systems together.

INTEGRATED INFORMATION PROCESSING

Some of the most recent improvements in information processing are based on the concept of integrated systems. The goal in joining systems is to make maximum use of the expensive and sophisticated electronic equipment and the information processed on it by combining the equipment in efficient ways. However, finding the appropriate solution is rarely easy.

Until recently, there were so many office systems and products to choose from that companies wanting to automate their offices became confused. The personal computer made things even more puzzling. Manufacturers introduced them without giving businesses enough of an idea of what they were for, or how to use them. In addition, corporations that already had word processing in one department and data processing in another found it difficult to justify the added cost of replacing their equipment with an office system that would integrate both.

The Systems Approach: Integrated Information Systems

This book began by explaining a word processor and a microcomputer. Then we showed you how terminals can be connected in communicating networks. Then we linked VDTs to other electronic equipment—data transmission, micrographics, and image processing are just a few examples. When offices are automated, many different types of equipment are joined electronically, so that an individual user at one terminal can have access to information from, and communicate with, any other user at a terminal connected to the system anywhere in the world. Office equipment connected this way is called an *integrated system*. This process of looking at the office as a whole—the sum of all these parts integrated as a system—is the *systems approach* to information processing.

Office managers use a number of terms to refer to *systems integration*. They may also call it *information resource management, networking*, or simply *office automation*. Systems integration does not mean just installing a lot of advanced equipment. It must be interconnected so that people working in the office can use the equipment to work with and share information more efficiently. As the use of the personal computer continues to grow, we will see other office systems and proce-

Every year a leading magazine in the office automation field presents awards for office design. Below and on the following pages are recent winners.

The "Office of the Year" award went to Moog, Inc., in East Aurora, New York. The new building for the Missile System Division blends well with the surrounding countryside.

The Personnel Department uses natural light to give a bright and open effect.

The Accounting Department is also well lit, using fluorescent and natural lighting.

The new headquarters of the J. M. Huber Corporation in Edison, New Jersey received a special merit award. This view of the reception and office area presents a modern, bright, and warm-looking work environment.

This room was especially designed for training.

Office workers have partitioned areas for privacy and quiet.

The law firm of Stone, Pigman, Walther, Wittman & Hutchinson, located in New Orleans, Louisiana, received a special merit award for its renovation of an old building. The open stairwell area is attractive and well lighted.

The space designed for the office worker retains the flavor of the original building while providing a modern workplace. Note the ergonomically designed desk and chair.

This conference room has the latest audiovisual equipment, which is stored behind the panels on the right.

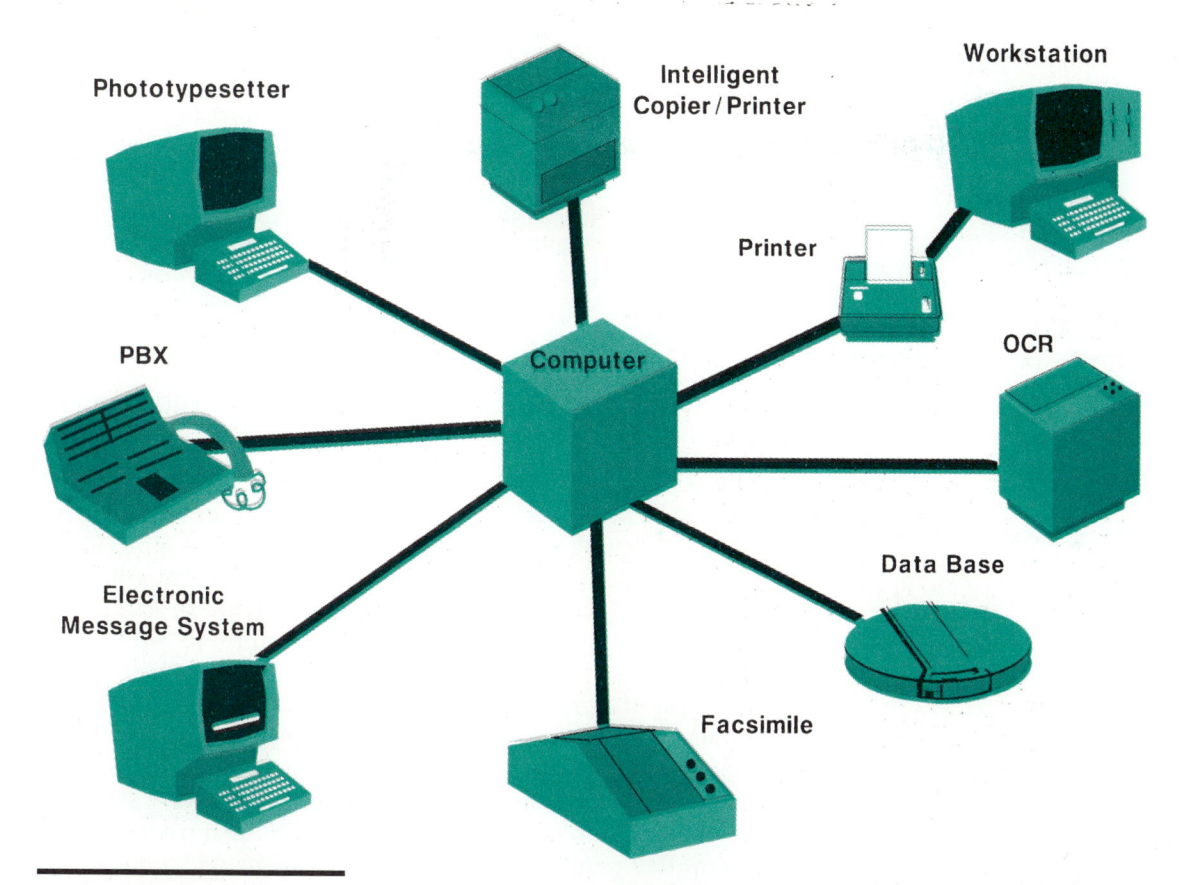

Integrated information processing.

dures change to become electronically integrated.

The overall interaction of equipment and systems will only increase as we move into the future. No piece of equipment or person in an office is isolated. You and the equipment you use are part of an integrated information system. Every bit of information, every task, every piece of equipment, and every person relates to all the others.

The Executive Workstation

An *executive workstation* is whatever the manager wants on her or his desk. It can be a word processor, a personal computer, or a "dumb" terminal. It could also be designed to perform any number of functions. The purpose of the executive workstation is to place within reach of the keyboard as much information as the manager needs to function effectively.

Until managers become thoroughly at ease with computers, manufacturers will continue to design workstations for executives that are simple to use and as user-friendly as possible. Generally this is accomplished through software with plenty of

Integrated Information Processing

183

An executive workstation is a manager's "control panel."

"help" screens to tell you what to do next. Executives with limited keyboarding skills will have the choice of either special function keys, a mouse, or a touch-sensitive screen.

Managers who can comfortably use a computer with many capabilities can input and extract data or text from data bases, or use data stored in a CPU or mainframe, often called the *host system*. The executive workstation may have a "windowing" capability, so that a manager can have access to several sources at the same time. Having access to a wide range of information, and the documents of many authors, an executive can manipulate raw data and create a report.

Some executive workstations, or *multifunction workstations*, can be specially designed to meet the needs of the user. An integrated system could include:

- *Access to Information*. Managers need text and data from a great many sources quickly, in a readable, usable form.
- *Communications*. The executive workstation will give managers keyboard access to person-to-person, person-to-group, group-to-group, person-to-computer, and computer-to-computer communications.
- *Document Generation*. Managers and professionals, especially those with keyboarding skills, may input their own documents. Graphics have already merged with text and data through image processing. Soon voice processing will make it possible for an executive to dictate a memo that a computer can translate into a document as easily as an OCR now reads a printed page.
- *Personal Computing*. Software packages, such as spreadsheets, are now available for use with personal computers. Eventually, it is expected that computers at executive workstations may be linked to time-sharing services and may have access to programs in a mainframe computer.

At the left is a windowed screen, which allows managers to view several items at once. At the right, a manager is checking his electronic calendar.

Integrated Information Processing

- *Personal Management.* With executive workstations designed to match their individual needs, managers will use software to perform numerous functions. *Calendaring* gives you a built-in alarm to remind you ahead of time when you have an appointment or something to do. *Electronic phone directory* enables you to keep your own personal list of phone numbers on a disk. By touching one key, the phone number is automatically dialed. *Electronic notebook* lets you interrupt whatever program you are working on and keyboard a random thought in a separate file. Then, with a single key, you can return to your original program.

The Changing Information Processing Cycle

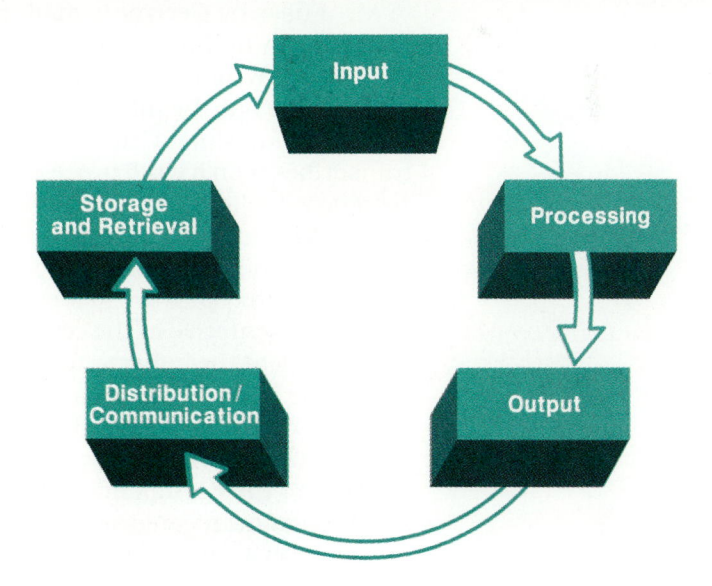

Everything we have talked about is part of information processing. You can see by now that information processing takes in a lot. It is comprised of data processing and word processing. It encompasses all the business and scientific operations performed on a computer. It is also a cycle that consists of five steps or stages: (1) input, (2) processing, (3) output, (4) distribution/communication, and (5) storage and retrieval.

The information processing cycle can differ from one office to another. For example, one office may use pencil and paper for input; another may use dictation equipment. One type of information may be stored on magnetic media, another on microfilm, and so on. Whatever equipment and media are used, the goal is to make the office a more productive place. The information processing cycle is flexible. We have streamlined information processing so effectively that, in some cases, we have

Information processing cycle.

Integrated Information Processing

185

blurred the line that separates one step of the cycle from another.

Imagine, for example, that Suzanne Wright is a finance executive at the Clearcut Lawn Mower Division of Multiregional Products, Inc. Each executive and key administrative employee at Multiregional has a terminal that can communicate with every other terminal at branch offices throughout the country in a system of local area networks linked by microwave relay to the company's headquarters in St. Paul, Minnesota. Robin Fuller, a sales representative in Idaho, keyboards a memo saying that he just sold 80 lawn mowers in a single day. That information is sent to two different places—the manufacturing plant in Detroit, where a supervisor takes the information into consideration in planning the production schedule and shipments to regional warehouses, and to the company's accounting office in St. Paul, where a computer automatically calculates the revenue received from the 80 lawn mowers, less expenses, including Fuller's commission.

Accounting sends the information to the finance division, which puts it into a report. The report is distributed to key executives. A copy is also sent to the corporation's Investor Relations Department in New York, so it can prepare Multiregional's quarterly earnings statement for Wall Street investors. So far, there was no need for hard copy.

The managers in the finance departments are so pleased that they decide to make Robin Fuller sales representative of the month. To do this, they will need more information. Suzanne Wright keyboards a memo to Robin Fuller. She sends the memo to Mr. Fuller by electronic mail. He responds by taking all the information he has about his great sales day and sending it back to Ms. Wright.

When she has the information she needs, she dictates a company announcement into a cassette recorder. Her secretary transcribes it on a word processor. Using image processing, the secretary includes in the announcement a photo of Robin Fuller. A soft copy of the announcement is sent electronically to every sales office. Then at each office, a copy is printed, and enough photocopies are made to distribute a hard copy to every sales representative in the company.

Let's look at the information processing cycle in this example. The same piece of information here becomes input for more than one document. Then the same information is processed in at least two or three different ways, which vary according to the purpose of the document. In the output stage, the same document is communicated as soft copy and as hard copy. The same information is stored and retrieved in different forms, on different equipment, in several offices. You can see by now that, as office systems and communications evolve, information is no longer processed in the simple cycle we describe at the beginning of this book. The illustration on page 188 shows that computerized technology has greatly affected each of the phases of information processing.

Computer Security

The security of computer information is a key element of information management. If an unauthorized person gains entry to a company's computer system and then alters confidential information, the company can lose a lot more than information. Millions of dollars have been illegally transferred in the computers of banks, and other financial and investment companies that store virtually all their records on magnetic media.

Computer Crime. What is computer crime? It is using a computer to commit a crime. Essentially there are three ways to use computer information illegally. Criminals can copy information to their own disk but leave the original intact; delete from someone else's magnetic media information valuable to the criminals or the business; and change computer information. In an attempt to prevent computer crime, many companies have set the following basic rules:

- Turn the system off when it is not in use.
- Install a lock that makes it impossible to use the system without a key. Strictly limit the number of keys.
- Keep disk and other magnetic media files locked.
- When the content of a disk is confidential, do not label the disk with a description of its contents.
- Label disks, stating who owns them. Put the company or firm name on a header or footer on every document.
- Security consultants sometimes recommend that you intentionally include an occasional spelling error in a valuable document, so that if it is illegally printed or photocopied, and not rekeyboarded, you can identify it.
- Make backup copies. Too often, nothing can replace information that is stolen, lost, or destroyed. Even if you could rekeyboard information, keep at least one backup copy of every disk.
- Monitor the use of your computer as closely as possible.
- Use passwords and encryption measures for added security. (These are explained on page 189.)
- Change locks, passwords, and encryption codes whenever a key employee leaves the company or when security is threatened in any other way.

The effect of computerized technology on the information processing cycle. Here the distribution/communication stage of the cycle is the electronic link to the other stages.

Input

- Paper & Pencil
- Shorthand
- Typed Rough Draft
- Machine Dictation
- Computer-Aided Transcription
- Optical Character Reader
- Keyboard
- Storage of Keyed Data
- Voice
- Image
- "Mouse"
- Light Pen
- Joystick
- Touch-Sensitive Screen

Processing

- Typewriter
- Electronic Typewriter
- Word Processor
- Computer:
  - Mainframe, Mini, Micro
- Software:
  - Operating Systems
  - Developmental:
    - BASIC
    - COBOL
    - FORTRAN
    - PASCAL
    - LISP
    - C
    - RPG
  - Applications:
    - Word Processing
    - Spreadsheet
    - Data Base
    - Communications
    - Graphics
    - Integrated
    - Personal Management

Distribution/Communication

- Express Mail
- INTELPOST
- TWX/Telex/Mailgram
- Communicating Word Processors
- Linked Equipment
- Computer-Based Message System
- Image Processing
- Facsimile
- Telephone
- LANs
- Twisted Pairs
- Coaxial Cables
- Microwave/Satellite
- Fiber Optics
- On-Line Information Services
- Bulletin Boards
- Teleconferencing

Output

- Soft Copy
- Printers:
  - Dot Matrix
  - Line
  - Ink Jet
  - Laser
  - Thermal
- Graphics Plotter
- Intelligent Copier/Printer
- Phototypesetter
- Carbon Paper
- Duplicator
- Photocopier
- Facsimile
- Scanner

Storage and Retrieval

- Paper Files
- Magnetic Media:
  - Floppy Diskette
  - Hard Disk
  - Mag Card
  - Tape
- Microforms:
  - Microfilm
  - Microfiche
  - Ultrafiche
  - Aperture Card
  - Microfilm Jacket
- Electronic Filing System
- Data Base
- Data Bank
- Optical Disk
- Image Processor
- On-Line Information Services

Here is an encrypted message before and after it has been decoded.

Passwords. A *password* is a secret alphanumeric combination, unique to each user, that you must keyboard in order to gain access to a computer. When you key in a password, the letters and numbers do not appear on the screen.

Frequently, each employee is assigned a *user identification code*, or *user ID*, in addition to the password. After you key in the password that allows you entry into the system, you keyboard your ID. This lets the system know more specifically whether you are entitled to use the system, what level of access you have, and what information you are permitted access to.

Encryption. Various techniques are used for *encryption*. A typical encryption technique is to keep switching the number of meaningless characters between the ones that count. Companies often use software programs that change their encryption code automatically at preset intervals, such as once a week. To read encrypted files, a user must not only log on with a proper password and ID, but must use a special password to unscramble the secret code.

"Softlifting"—Software Piracy. Unauthorized copying of commercially produced software is against the law. To prevent lawsuits, many corporations are now issuing statements for their employees to sign, saying that the company does not condone software copying. Once the company has a signed statement, disk copies become an employee's personal responsibility.

Since there are so many difficulties with current software copyright laws, many software companies have begun including special programs on their disks that make it impossible for anyone but a computer expert to copy. A number of program disks are sold that allow you to make one copy but no more. Other software companies give you one disk when you buy the package, and a serial number that identifies you as the purchaser. If the disk is damaged, stolen, or lost, you can contact the company and typically get a replacement disk free, and additional disks after that for a nominal fee.

Technology Takes a Quantum Leap

Information is one of the most valuable resources of the United States, and the technology for managing information one of our most marketable assets. Up to now, we have based our economy on manufacturing. If we are to keep leading in world markets, we will need to change our emphasis to information and service industries. In the coming years, information processing and management technology will move ahead in quantum leaps.

Here is the kind of growth we can expect in key sectors of the information industry:

- *Sophisticated Hardware.* Computer people tell us that by the century's end, we can expect computers to change both in their design and information processing capability as dramatically as they have from ENIAC to now.
- *Advanced Software.* Future software will make it possible for someone to sit down at a keyboard and operate a computer program the first time without even reading an instruction manual.
- *Integrated Office Systems.* Manufacturers are developing hardware and software that combine data and word processing, electronic mail, and other functions in one system.
- *Personal Computers.* It is estimated that by 1990, 50 percent of the work force will have personal computers.
- *Computer-Aided Instruction.* The computer has already found a place in the classroom. Computer-aided instruction provides support for teachers who cannot always give special drilling and remedial assistance. In the decades ahead, learning software could change the teaching process in ways we can only imagine now.
- *Productivity Packages.* Often referred to as decision-making software, it is currently used to increase productivity and lower costs in spreadsheets, graphics, data bases, computer-aided design, and communications. Business organizations will use these "what-if" programs to simu-

These students are working with computer-aided instruction.

late situations and choices. *Simulation software*, as it is also called, will find other applications in areas including finance and investment, marketing, urban planning, and manufacturing.
- *Electronic Mail.* Corporations have begun using electronic mail in local area networks. Soon data transmission networks will link corporations with each other and, through the U.S. Postal Service, with private citizens and businesses internationally.
- *Teleconferencing.* In addition to eliminating the stress, time, and cost of traveling, and making it possible to meet more often, teleconferencing will give executives a way to communicate ideas that are not easily keyboarded.
- *Robots.* Robots are best at doing things people cannot do, like cleaning up atomic waste. They are now used in educational settings. In Greenville, Ohio, for example, students from elementary to junior high school learn the languages and inner workings of computers by programming robots to speak French, draw designs on the floor, and retrieve objects from across the room.

Technology Changes Lives

The computer is moving us into a new world in which technology will free our minds to think about ideas that at this point we cannot even begin to grasp. But before we are overwhelmed by our own optimism, it is essential to remember that change does not always come easy. To change means to forget old ways and learn new ones. The Computer Revolution will remake our lives in a number of ways.

- *New Skills Are Required.* The U.S. Bureau of Labor Statistics predicts that, within the next five years, 65 percent of the work force will have to be retrained and the jobs of these people redesigned. Current jobs will have new specifications that reflect computerization. Old jobs will be phased out and new ones created. Managers and workers will need retraining.
- *Patterns of Communications Are Altered.* Managers using applications software at executive workstations will require new organizational procedures. Local area networks and communication software will have to be developed to centralize information and keep it uniform for top management.
- *Time Spans Between Communications Are Decreased.* Electronic audio exchanges and calendaring software help executives avoid the game of "telephone tag."

- *Roles, Work Relationships, and Reporting Responsibilities Are Modified.* Technology can make it easier for a secretary to perform more complex tasks. Furthermore, electronic information access will make it possible for managers to perform more independently in some areas, and yet interrelate more closely in other ways.
- *Data Ownerships Shift.* Companies will grow increasingly dependent on data banks, data bases, online information services, and other interactive systems rather than generating and maintaining data themselves internally. Data base management and electronic filing systems will make a company's information quickly and easily accessible internally to employees who need it.
- *Privacy and Security Concerns Increase.* Passwords, encryption, copy-proof diskettes, and strong copyright laws will become standard.
- *New Management Techniques Evolve.* Managers will make decisions and stay in touch with telecommunication systems. Top executives can communicate with employees at every level directly. Simulation software will make it possible for a company to consider options more carefully before bringing a product to market.

What this means is that the tremendous growth in electronic office technologies has generated a corresponding need to change not only the way we manage information but also many of our traditional business procedures. Computers can give the information needed to solve problems. But it is people who will solve the problems. In a computerized society, only a business that has the human resources to use information creatively will have the competitive edge.

ERGONOMICS

We have explained information processing hardware and software. But what about the most important element of an electronic office system—people? Office workers have sometimes found it difficult to adapt to automated equipment. Once automated equipment proved to have a clear cost advantage over nonautomated equipment, office experts focused their attention on designing equipment to fit the people who use it. People get more work done on well-designed equipment, and increased productivity means more profits.

The science of adapting working environment, conditions, and equipment to suit workers is called *ergonomics*. Ergonomics is sometimes referred to as *human engineering*. If a company plans to change over to, or enhance its current, electronic office equipment, managers need to look closely at how their people will interact with the equipment, and how the equipment will fit into their office environment. The psychological and physical well-being of the worker is the most important consideration in planning an ergonomically designed office.

In addition to purchasing equipment, managers must also consider appropriate furniture, lighting, layout, air conditioning, and work procedures. They must plan how and where equipment will be used. Otherwise, they are letting themselves in for employee complaints that range from eyestrain and blurred vision to numbness, headaches, and backaches. Ergonomists have approached all these problems associated with electronic information processing equipment, and have solved them in interesting and challenging ways.

Office Furniture

It does not matter how well designed a piece of equipment is—it will fail in its ultimate function if a person does not feel comfortable using it. This human interface with technology is essential. Only recently have designers begun to apply their expertise to office furniture.

The five-wheel chair is a good example of how ergonomic research can be applied. Designers in Europe learned that people like to lean back in their chairs, and that they tend to push themselves away from a desk suddenly. They found that a chair with four wheels toppled too easily. The solution? A five-wheel chair that rolls around just as well but does not tip over as easily.

At the left is an ergonomically designed desk. At the right is a backless kneeling chair.

Ergonomics

Researchers also determined that a backless kneeling chair relieves stress on your upper back. When you sit in a backless chair, your knees rest on a knee pad. When you want to lean forward, you are forced to arch your back at your hips. This eliminates pressure on your back.

Research will continue and office furniture design will improve still further.

Equipment Design

Equipment designers, like designers of office furnishings, strive to combine practicality, convenience, and comfort. They recognize that computerized equipment has a unique set of features that can be adapted to meet employee needs. For example, display screens may use white, green, or yellow letters against a dark background, or dark letters against a light background. They can be positioned at eye level or above or below it. Screens can also be set up at different angles and at varying distances from the user. Similarly, keyboards can be positioned at varying distances from a detached screen and at varying heights on a desk.

Lighting

Poor or inadequate lighting, or lighting that is too bright or glaring, can reduce both productivity and work quality and can even contribute to lower employee morale. Proper office lighting, on the other hand, can reduce glare from display screens and help avoid operator eyestrain and fatigue. Ideally, to be as readable as possible, the screen should be three to four times brighter than the light in the room. Screen glare can make keyboarding impossible. Where possible, screens should be positioned away from windows to prevent glare. Or users should be given the option of masking sunlight with curtains or venetian blinds.

One ergonomic problem is how to illuminate a paper copy and keep the light away from the user's eyes without causing screen glare. Dim ceiling light, and a desk lamp with a parabolic, or bowl-shaped, reflector will eliminate this problem.

Noise Control

The shield on this printer reduces the noise level.

Noise levels can be a problem when using electronic office systems. Open space with freestanding partitions and the sounds of printers and other automated equipment creates a noisy situation. Companies can take a number of steps to combat this problem. Specially designed sound-absorbing panels and partitions, for example, can be used to control noise. Carpeting and draperies perform a similar function. Noise-reduction devices, known as *shields*, can be attached to printers. Or this kind of

Integrated Information Processing

equipment can be kept in a separate area within noise-absorbing modular enclosures.

Temperature

Temperature control and ventilation are two very important factors that must be taken into consideration when automated office systems are laid out. High temperatures can accelerate the deterioration of equipment, magnetic tape, floppy diskettes, ribbons, print elements, printer paper, and various other materials. Rapid or extreme variations in temperature can have much the same effect.

In general, companies should avoid installing electronic systems in areas that receive a considerable amount of direct sunlight, near heating or cooling ducts, or near large windows.

Humidity

Much as temperature extremes can cause equipment to deteriorate, so can humidity that is too high or too low. High humidity leads to moisture absorption and dimensional changes in printer paper, floppy diskettes, and other magnetic media. Low humidity, on the other hand, allows static electricity to build up. This can cause logic errors in the memory of CPUs and permanent damage to sensitive control and logic circuits.

Office Landscaping and Design

Office landscaping refers to an open layout in which desks, files, partitions, and so on are arranged in freestanding clusters. To give workers a feeling of space while suiting their other work needs, office landscaping replaces permanent walls and fixtures with a large open area containing movable partitions, modular furniture, and other adaptable features. *Flexibility* is a

A landscaped office.

key word in office landscaping. Office furnishings and equipment are designed to be easily moved and can be rearranged to meet workers' changing needs. Overall layout is designed to promote the efficient flow of paperwork from one department or work area to another. Individual areas are partitioned off by acoustical panels to provide privacy while controlling the office noise level. Desk tops, cabinets, drawers, and storage units all may be attached to these panels in a variety of configurations. Office colors are chosen to create a pleasant and psychologically stimulating atmosphere.

Health Issues in the Office

The National Institute for Occupational Safety and Health (NIOSH) investigates the health and safety of workers. The institute has studied work conditions in mines, factories, and mills, and has set new standards for industrial hygiene. Perhaps its best-known recommendation is the hard hat at construction sites.

Recently, NIOSH has turned its attention to the office worker. It has looked into stress, fatigue, lighting, the effect of video display terminals, and air quality. We have already talked about some of these problems. Let's look now at the solutions NIOSH and others have offered in these areas.

VDT Safety. NIOSH found that the best way to use a VDT is to have your eyes level with the top of the screen. The angle from your eyes to the center of the screen should be no greater than 15 degrees, and you should sit from 14 to 20 inches from the screen. Harvard University's Health Services group suggests an even greater distance—17 to 30 inches—even farther if you can.

Frequent Breaks. Administrative employees, VDT operators, and secretaries at Verbatim Corporation indicated in a survey that they like regular rest breaks during their working hours. Studies show that breaks help keep you relaxed and increase your productivity. NIOSH recommends a break every hour for heavy keyboarders, and a break every two hours for more moderate work. Managers add one note of caution: Employees who are permitted breaks should not skip them.

Fatigue. Although information processing operators sometimes complain of eyestrain after keyboarding for several hours, NIOSH and the National Center for Disease Control have found no evidence that VDTs can harm your eyes or any other aspect of your health. Many of us feel some eyestrain after sitting at any kind of close work for a long time. For this reason, if you can keep from gazing at the screen nonstop while you are keyboarding, it can help to relax your eyes. Take visual breaks every few minutes by looking at something else.

Once a system is in place and operating, office supervisors should make certain that the VDTs are checked regularly. A flickering or blurred screen, for example, forces the eye to readjust continually, and this can cause fatigue.

How to Sit. In this country, colds and backaches are the two main reasons people stay home from work. Many different working conditions can contribute to backaches. Lifting something heavy, moving the wrong way, or sitting the wrong way or in the wrong chair can all give you a backache. Up to one-third of all lower-back injuries could be eliminated by giving workers ergonomically designed chairs. Here are several suggestions about sitting that could make your back feel more comfortable while you keyboard.

- If your chair does not support your lower back, use a pillow.
- Sit as straight as possible.
- Put your feet up on a small box or a phone book to take some of the weight off your lower back.
- When you need to bring your eyes closer to the screen, lean forward from your hips instead of bending your shoulders.
- Position your body so you are looking straight ahead at the screen. Try to avoid looking at the screen sideways.
- Do not keep anything in your pockets that would make you change the way you normally sit.
- If you use an adjustable chair, set it so your thighs are approximately horizontal, your calves vertical, and your feet resting squarely on the floor or a footrest.
- Position the keyboard so your upper arms are hanging straight down, and your forearms are horizontal or at a slight angle down.
- You can stretch, flex, twist, and perform many other standard calisthenic exercises at your desk.
- Just sitting still increases the pressure on your spine by 40 percent. Get up and walk around whenever you get the chance. It will vary the stress on your muscles and back.

The Balance Between People and Equipment

Electronic office systems are making it possible for us to process information more quickly and in greater quantities than we were capable of before. How people fit this new equipment physically and psychologically is most important to the managers, secretaries, and operators who are using the equipment in ever-increasing numbers. So it is also a key concern of manufacturers, office ergonomists, and designers.

Ergonomics

Many people have difficulty making the transition to electronic systems for a number of reasons. Ergonomists continue to study the physical and emotional stress experienced by many users of automated equipment. Their conclusions are reflected in the design of current office equipment and furniture.

Lois Verbrugge, Ph.D., at the University of Michigan analyzed national health statistics and concluded that administrative office workers are among the healthiest people in the country. Ergonomists are determined to make the office an even more comfortable, efficient, and productive place.

OFFICE ORGANIZATION

An ergonomically effective environment and integrated information processing are only two-thirds of a modern approach to a productive office. The third requirement is to find the office organization that fits the needs of the company and of the people working in it. The last part of this chapter looks at three settings for information processing—traditional, decentralized, and centralized.

Matching the System to the Need

Companies today understand that information processing will increase productivity and improve the quality of documents. It is essential in automating, however, to design and implement a system that will efficiently and productively fill a company's information processing needs. Too often, equipment is purchased without planning. Word processors and microcomputers sometimes appear almost mysteriously on people's desks for no reason except that someone found money in the budget to buy them.

A traditional office environment as compared to a more modern office setup.

Integrated Information Processing

Feasibility Studies. Designing a system takes careful consideration beforehand. Many companies find that a feasibility study is well worth the time and cost. A *feasibility study* is a detailed analysis—conducted either by company employees or specialized consultants—to determine whether it is worthwhile to put in place an electronic information processing system. If the study finds it is, then the next step is to decide exactly what equipment and procedures would best suit the company's specific needs. An office systems consultant is generally brought in to work with the company. Together, and often with an ergonomic specialist, they decide what kind of system the organization needs for optimum efficiency.

Information Processing in a Traditional Setting

Chris Sanchez is a secretary for A. Y. Rogers Educational Publishing Company. Recently, Ms. Sanchez transferred from the Marketing Department to the Editorial Department. The Editorial offices look similar to the offices in Marketing. The secretaries' responsibilities are basically the same. The only difference is the equipment.

In Marketing, there were two standalone word processors for keyboarding reports and budgets, and the secretaries all used electric or electronic typewriters. But almost everyone in Editorial has a display word processor or a microcomputer, and the secretaries are trained to use word processors and personal computers with word processing software. The authors who write the books published by the company usually submit their manuscripts on diskettes and as hard copy. The editors work on either. Sometimes an editor revises a document by keyboarding revisions at a terminal. At other times, the editor asks a secretary to transfer any typed or handwritten revisions to the diskette.

Many companies, like A. Y. Rogers, have chosen to integrate information processing equipment into a traditional office setting because having several word processors and microcomputers is precisely what is required to meet their needs.

Office Layout. In the traditional office, a secretary works for one or more managers or authors. Introducing information processing equipment into this kind of environment usually does not result in many major organizational or structural changes. The new equipment either replaces the old or is used in addition to it. In a traditional setting, secretarial stations (whether or not they have automated equipment) are typically located directly outside, or near, the manager's office. In some companies they are clustered together in one area, while authors are grouped

Information processing in a traditional office.

Work flow in a traditional office.

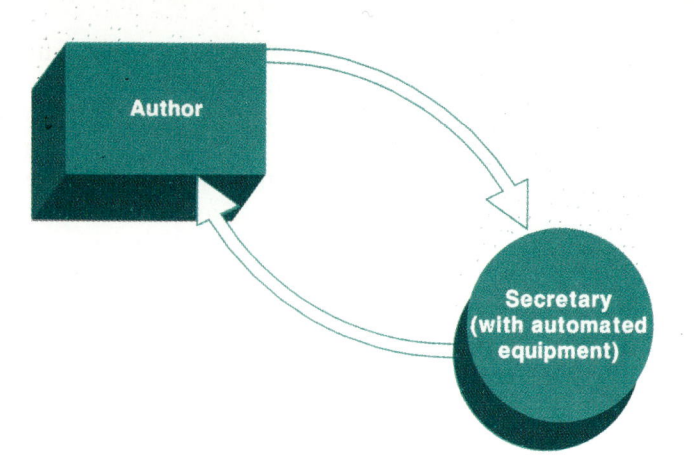

together in another. Each individual secretary may have a word processor, or a personal computer, or one or more units may be shared among several secretaries.

Work Flow in a Traditional Setting. In an office where word processing has been integrated into a traditional setting, input goes directly from author to secretary. Input may take the form of shorthand dictation, machine dictation, or a handwritten or typed rough draft.

If the equipment is shared, the secretary must decide whether to use the automated equipment or a typewriter. A three-line memo, for example, would probably be done most quickly on the typewriter, while a lengthy statistical report would be prepared on the automated equipment.

Secretarial Responsibilities. A secretary working in an office equipped with word processors and/or personal computers with word processing software has basically the same responsibilities as a secretary in an office that does not have automated equipment—the day-to-day tasks are similar. What *is* different, however, is that the electronic equipment generally enables the secretary to work more quickly and efficiently, and the department as a whole can be more productive.

Often the role of secretary extends beyond keyboarding. A secretary who operates a microcomputer can become involved in numerous other activities associated with, but not limited to, word processing. For example, many companies that give their secretaries a personal computer offer training in, and expect the secretary to be capable of, data base management and using a spreadsheet program.

Information Processing in a Traditional Setting: Pros and Cons. A business that integrates an information processing system into a traditional office usually needs no significant restructuring of its staff or procedures. Nevertheless, there are advantages and disadvantages. The following table lists some of them.

Pros and Cons of a Traditional Setting

Pros	Cons
Makes information processing available to offices that do not require a large-scale system.	May not appeal to employees who prefer specialized assignments.
Keeps turnaround time short.	Requires secretary to deal with a wide variety of office pressures.
Appeals to employees who like the diversified job responsibilities of a secretary.	Career path is limited and not clearly defined, often depending on promotability of employee's manager.
Permits development of a close working relationship with one or more authors.	
Offers the satisfaction of seeing jobs through from beginning to end.	
Emphasizes efficient and rapid information flow rather than quantity of documents produced.	

Decentralized Information Processing

Ben Daniels has worked at two different companies. At his previous firm, Northwestern Intercontinental Trust Company, he was secretary to three managers in the Accounting Department. He had many responsibilities, a heavy work load, and a lot of stress and pressure on the job. He saw no opportunity for advancement. Now Mr. Daniels works at Steger Electronics. After five months as a word processing operator at Steger, he has come to a definite conclusion: He much prefers working at Steger. Today he produces documents for one department. He does not have to deal with any of the administrative responsibilities associated with a secretary's job. He knows the authors, so he still feels involved.

A mini or satellite information processing center (at the left). At the right, work flow in a decentralized information processing system.

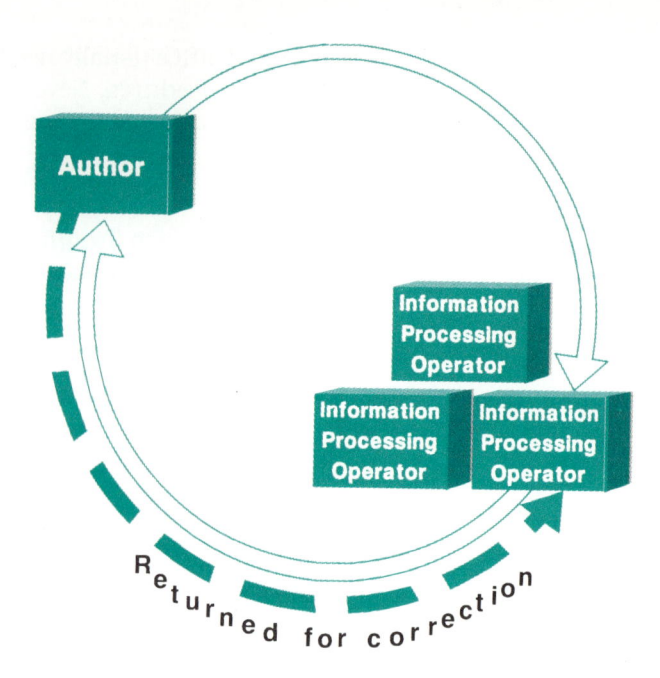

Satellites and Minicenters. A small information processing center that "reports to" or is an offshoot of a large center is called a *satellite*. A small center that works independently of any large centralized system is called a *minicenter*. (Some companies may have different names for these kinds of centers. However, we use these terms here.) A satellite or minicenter may be set up to serve one or more specific departments or floors. Operators prepare documents or other kinds of work for all the authors in the departments or floors served.

Work Flow in a Decentralized System. Input to a satellite or minicenter may occur in several ways. Dictation, through standard, mini-, or microcassette, is one method, especially in those departments where authors spend much time out of the office. Salespeople, for instance, are often on the road; they find cassette dictation very convenient. Some satellites or minicenters use an endless loop central recording system in addition to, or in place of, cassette dictation. Handwritten documents or typed rough drafts are generally accompanied by a *work order* or *document requisition form*. This form contains the author's name, the date, and specific instructions regarding document preparation. In order to control the flow of work, a supervisor, or designated lead operator, keeps a detailed log of all documents entering and leaving the satellite.

Integrated Information Processing

Document requisition form.

WORD PROCESSING CENTER — REQUEST FOR SERVICES			
Author	Author's Dept.	Ext.	Date

Type of Stationery:
- ☐ Letterhead
- ☐ Plain Bond
- ☐ Note-size
- ☐ Letterhead
- ☐ Report Paper
- ☐ Long Memo
- ☐ Short Memo

General Instructions
- ☐ Final Copy
- ☐ Rough Draft
- ☐ Single Spaced
- ☐ Double Spaced
- ☐ Special Format (indicate)

Handling
- ☐ Regular
- ☐ Priority (when needed?)
- ☐ Confidential
- ☐ Typed Envelope(s) (how many?)

Distribution
- ☐ Carbon Copies (how many?)
- ☐ Photocopies (how many?)
- Copies To (Names)

Special Instructions ____

Satellite or Minicenter Operators. People who work in satellites or minicenters are specialists, not only in equipment but also in the terminology and formatting of documents of the particular department or floor served. This can greatly aid efficiency and productivity, especially in those departments where technical vocabulary, complex formatting, or specialized software is the rule rather than the exception. An operator with heavy experience in compiling tables of medical data, for instance, finds keyboarding such material much easier than would an operator with little or no experience.

The role and functions of satellite or minicenter operators vary from one center to another. In some departments, for example, there may be quite a bit of direct contact between operators and authors. In others there may be almost none at all.

The size of the satellite or minicenter is another factor that determines what tasks an operator handles. For example, in a smaller department, besides word processing a worker might also handle an author's mail and take telephone calls. In Chapter 8 we explain how companies keep a record, or log, of work. These functions can be assigned to one operator or shared on a rotating basis.

Each satellite usually has a supervisor. A minicenter can have a supervisor or a lead operator. Depending on how the company's offices are organized, the supervisor or lead operator of a satellite or minicenter may report to the manager of the department where the center is located or to the person who supervises the company's main information processing center.

Decentralized System Design and Equipment. Offices are usually organized so that the satellite or minicenter of a department is located in a special area on the same floor or in a nearby room. Workstations may be surrounded by partitions in keeping with the overall office layout and design, or if the department's documents are confidential. In satellites or minicenters where there is very heavy document processing, it is most likely that dedicated word processing equipment is used. In situations where the work of the center is varied, microcomputers may also be used.

Decentralized Information Processing: Pros and Cons. Like electronic equipment in a traditional environment, a decentralized information processing system has both advantages and disadvantages. The following table lists some of them.

Pros and Cons of Decentralized Information Processing

Pros	Cons
Keeps turnaround time low because of proximity of authors to operators.	Costs more than purchasing one type of equipment for centralized system.
Permits selection of equipment and software for special departmental needs.	Results in boredom if the same kinds of documents are worked on day after day.
Increases efficiency by making operator thoroughly familiar with department documents and vocabulary.	Allows operators to learn the technical vocabulary of only one particular department.
Lessens production pressure found in centralized system.	Limits career opportunities to positions available in the individual satellite or minicenter.
Offers leeway in determining how a document should be handled.	

Centralized Information Processing

A *centralized information processing system* is normally found in a large organization rather than a small office. The core of such a system is the *information processing center*, sometimes called a *document production center*, or *word processing center*, which is a centrally located room or area in which a group of information processing specialists handle all or most of the document preparation for an entire company.

Specialization. *Specialization* is a key word in centralized information processing systems, as it is for decentralized systems. While in a traditional office setting several secretaries may perform a variety of tasks, in an information processing center the workers do *only* information processing. Each operator may have a different degree of responsibility within the center. In

204 Integrated Information Processing

A centralized information processing center.

some companies, information processing operators specialize in handling certain types of documents or subject matter.

As might be expected, the specialization that comes with centralized information processing tends to increase efficiency and productivity. Note, though, that operators in an information processing center, no matter how specialized, handle the work of many authors and managers in all of the company's various departments. This way, if one of the managers is away from the office, no operator's work comes to a standstill. Furthermore, since operators prepare documents for such a large number of authors, there is a fairly continuous flow of work and operators don't have to spend much time waiting for assignments.

Specialization also allows better matching of employee skills with assignments. Someone who is adept at preparing legal documents may be assigned to do just that; and the person who is skilled at producing general correspondence will handle this work.

Equipment Selection. A centralized information processing system must have equipment that can meet the needs of the particular company. For example, a company that produces several 100-page financial reports each month needs a system that allows operators to share the preparation of such large, tightly scheduled jobs. A company that regularly distributes lengthy documents updating repetitive statistical information requires a system that makes it possible for operators to share prestored text, mailing lists, and data bases. As companies grow, information processing centers can upgrade their equipment and add more sophisticated technology.

Work Flow in a Centralized System. Documents may be transmitted to an information processing center through machine dictation, or input may be handwritten or typed rough drafts. A

Office Organization

Work flow in a centralized information processing system.

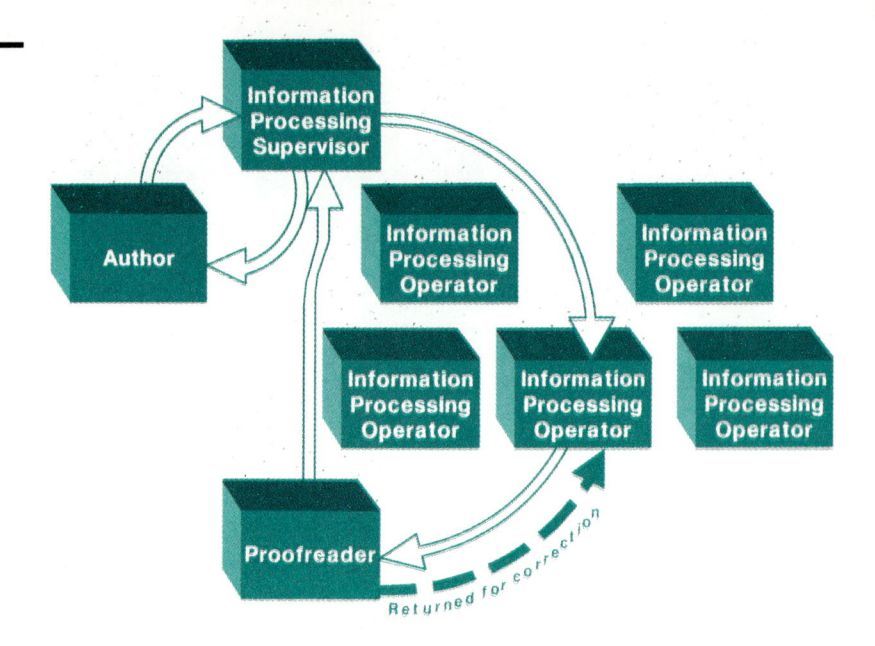

[Diagram: Author → Information Processing Supervisor → Information Processing Operators → Proofreader, with "Returned for correction" arrow back to Operators]

center may employ an endless loop centralized dictation system or a centralized cassette recording system. Centralized systems are generally accessed by telephone. (Some are accessed by microphones.) Just as in a decentralized word processing system, handwritten or rough draft input is usually accompanied by a document requisition form or work order.

The Center Supervisor and the Operator. In addition to logging documents in and out of the center, the supervisor is in charge of scheduling and overseeing the work. This entails assigning work to the various operators, establishing priorities, and solving problems. In some centers the supervisor has a proofreader check finished documents to spot any errors that may have slipped through. Final proofreading, however, is usually the author's responsibility.

The center supervisor must also keep careful records. For example, if company policy calls for limiting the amount of time documents may be stored, the supervisor must keep an up-to-date record of all prerecorded and stored documents in the center. The supervisor may also maintain productivity records and charts of each operator's output.

As we have seen, information processing operators who work in a center are specialists in operating information processing equipment. They must know how to use the equipment to the fullest capacity, and they must know how to care for it.

Unlike traditional secretaries, who work for managers in one particular department, information processing operators can

Integrated Information Processing

work for people throughout the company. They learn not only about the working procedures of the center itself but also about the procedures of the entire organization.

Operators often must keep records, too, such as logs of their documents and backup copies.

Office Design. A centralized information processing area can look different from a traditional office. The workstations in a large information processing center are usually located near each other. In some companies, individual workstations are enclosed with partitions; others prefer one large, open area for easy access to both employees and equipment.

Centralized Information Processing: Pros and Cons. Centralized information processing has advantages and disadvantages. The following table lists some of them.

Pros and Cons of Centralized Information Processing

Pros	Cons
Works best for a company that needs to produce a large volume of documents rapidly and efficiently.	Often located at a considerable distance from authors, which may lead to problems in revising long, complicated documents.
Permits the storage in central location of thousands of repetitive paragraphs for use throughout the company.	Creates danger that inept management of center will result in delays, misplaced documents, and other inefficiencies.
Makes it possible for several information processing operators to work simultaneously on a long, urgent document.	Restricts employees' advancement opportunities within the information processing center environment.
Allows equipment too costly for one department to be purchased for central use.	Causes some workers to feel isolated from authors, resulting in diminished pride in work.
Appeals to employees who find specialized keyboarding tasks more challenging than generalized tasks.	Makes some employees view their work as too repetitive; they may resent not doing a variety of tasks.

Pros and Cons of Centralized Information Processing (*cont.*)

Pros	Cons
Offers employees advancement opportunities because of varying levels of positions and titles.	Sometimes leads to high rate of employee turnover.

Peopleware

Up to now, we have talked mostly about information processing for secretaries and operators, but very little about how it may change the structure of a business organization. Will there be changes in the traditional relationship between the employee and the manager? Will the employee's opportunity to make a contribution to the company increase or decrease?

Although we can measure how many lines or documents an operator keyboards in a day, at what point do these keystrokes stop being alphanumeric combinations transferred by rote and emerge as a new idea? It must become our responsibility to protect the rights of the employee who takes data, changes it into information, and expresses it as an idea. It remains for us to maximize the return to the individual from information technology.

CHAPTER SUMMARY

- Systems integration is a way of looking not just at individual tasks but also at how those tasks go together, how they fit in with other related tasks.
- Integrated information processing refers to the tying of word processing and data processing operations, a situation in which nothing is isolated—in which every person, every task, every piece of equipment relates to all the others.
- An executive workstation is an electronically equipped work space designed to help a manager or executive generate, process, distribute, store, and retrieve information as rapidly and efficiently as possible.
- A multifunction workstation is designed to match an executive's computer capabilities. It can combine any number of word and data processing features including access to information, communications, document generation, personal computing, and personal management.
- Information processing and management technology is so advanced now that it is hard to pinpoint where one step of

the information processing cycle ends and another begins.
- Computer security systems keep unauthorized users from accessing information. Typically, users are asked to keyboard passwords and other identification codes.
- A more sophisticated computer security system is one that relies on encryption, or the translation of confidential files into secret codes.
- "Softlifting," the unauthorized copying of software, accounts for millions of dollars in lost revenues each year for software manufacturers.
- In an information society, human resources are the competitive edge; they're the key to any organization's growth.
- Ergonomics is the science of adapting working conditions, environment, and equipment design to meet the needs of workers.
- Backaches, stiff muscles, stress, and fatigue can result from badly designed office chairs.
- Temperature and humidity can adversely affect the performance of electronic systems and magnetic media.
- Designers try to plan an office landscape with as much open space as possible to give people a feeling of roominess. Modular systems have an advantage over permanent ones because they change more easily as an organization changes.
- Automated equipment generally enables a secretary in a traditional office setting to work more quickly and efficiently and enables the department to be more productive.
- Secretaries are usually assigned to one or a few authors and handle both keyboarding and nonkeyboarding tasks. Information processing operators only keyboard but may work for any number of authors.
- Decentralized information processing systems are made up of satellites or minicenters.
- Information processing operators who work in a satellite or minicenter become specialists in the terminology and formatting of the documents produced by their particular department or floor.
- Satellites and minicenters are located close to authors so there is more personal contact. This tends to reduce turnaround time.
- The core of a centralized system is the information processing center, a centrally located area where operators handle all or most of a company's document preparation.
- Specialization is a key word in centralized information processing because in an information processing center the workers do only information processing and, in some cases, work only on specific kinds of documents.

- Operators in an information processing center work for authors throughout the company.
- Centralized information processing has proved to be an efficient and cost-effective system for companies that need to produce a large volume of documents rapidly.

INFORMATION PROCESSING VOCABULARY

centralized information processing system
decentralized information processing system
document production center
document requisition form
encryption
ergonomics
executive workstation
feasibility study
information processing center
integrated information systems
minicenter
multifunction workstation
National Institute for Occupational Safety and Health (NIOSH)
office landscaping
password
satellite
"softlifting"
software piracy
systems approach
word processing center

CHAPTER QUESTIONS

1. Why is the integration of information processing equipment regarded as an extension of the systems approach?
2. What is an executive workstation? Name some benefits.
3. In a company fully equipped with an electronic office system, it may be difficult to distinguish between one step of the information processing cycle and another. Show how this can happen by tracing a document as it might move through a large corporation with many branch offices.
4. What major factors do ergonomists consider when they plan an office environment? Describe the problems that an employee might encounter in an office that is not ergonomically designed.
5. What can be done to reduce the amount of noise created by printers?
6. What are the three basic ways of organizing information

processing equipment and employees? Which of these would you generally recommend to a large company? A small one? Explain.
7. How might workers in a satellite be even more specialized than those in a large center? Give an example.
8. Do you think a secretary who transfers from a traditional office to a centralized system would find her or his new job more or less pressured? Why?
9. Which of the three office settings described in this chapter provides the greatest career opportunities? Explain your answer.
10. If your company has just hired a consultant to conduct a feasibility study, what kinds of information would you expect to learn from the study?

CASE STUDY

Michelle Blake is an experienced secretary who left the office to raise a family. When she returned to work, she took a job as word processing operator in a small word processing center. The primary function of the center is to handle large mailings, correspondence, and reports. The center has been in operation a very short time. Two microcomputers, two dedicated word processors, and two character printers were purchased. Standard office furniture, already on hand in the company, was used. The equipment is set up in a small open area right in front of a big picture window.

Ms. Blake enjoys using the automated equipment, but is glad when the work day is over. Aside from the pressure of producing documents all day long, she and the other operators in the center complain about headaches, eyestrain, and backaches. The center has experienced high turnover and high absenteeism.

As fate would have it, Ms. Blake has been offered two new jobs. One would be as the new center supervisor where she would have to improve working conditions. The other is as a secretary to a business executive. (The salaries are about the same.) Ms. Blake enjoyed being a secretary and is having a difficult time making a decision? What factors should Ms. Blake take into account before she makes a final decision? How might she go about improving conditions in the center if she accepts the job of supervisor?

CHAPTER 8

Careers

Jack Morrow checked himself in the mirror for the sixth time. Hair...okay. Tie...fine. Jacket...looking good. He gave his reflection a big smile. "Good morning, Mr. Morrow. Welcome to the L. S. Norton Conover Company." He glanced down at his shoes. Not new, but they had a decent shine. "I think you're ready, kid," he told his reflection. As Jack left the house, he wondered what his first day on the job would be like. Would he like his coworkers in the information processing center? Would they like him? He felt a little anxious, but he was determined to do well. After all, this was the career he chose and went after. What was it that his former instructor always used to say? "Keep a positive frame of mind, and you can do anything." As Jack boarded the bus on his way to work, he told himself, "I can do it!"

Like Jack Morrow, most people approach a new position hoping to like their job and do well at it. Jack made his decision to work in an information processing center. There are many other options open in the field of information processing that are available to you now. After you have worked in the job for a while, you may consider being promoted or changing from one kind of job to another in the same field. This chapter provides an introduction to productivity measurement and work procedures. It then surveys the kinds of job situations and careers that are available in information processing. It also takes a look at the ways in which employees can do well in this field.

PRODUCTIVITY

Throughout this book the word *productivity* has come up many times. There is good reason for this. Productivity has become one of the catchwords of the modern office, particularly in light of the amount of work that needs to be done daily in offices across the country.

Work Procedures and Methods

One way that companies try to increase productivity and efficiency is by setting up work procedures. Following these procedures can improve your personal productivity and help you do well on the job. Good procedures can benefit both you and the company. Most companies have found that without set procedures, the overall cost of document production—in time as well as money—tends to go up. When there are no procedures, it makes the individual employee's job more difficult. Some of the more common work procedures and methods follow:

- Standardized formats establish guidelines for the creation of a document that everyone can follow, saving authors and information processing operators time and trouble.
- Document/media coding systems enable standard paragraphs, forms, and other prerecorded documents to be retrieved whenever required. As we saw in Chapter 2, by combining variable information with coded (boilerplate) paragraphs, an author can work with an operator to create an almost infinite number of documents.
- Procedures manuals are used to explain to employees how to perform certain office tasks. These manuals provide step-by-step directions, demonstrate workflow, improve work quality, and cut down on questions.
- Vendors' manuals are supplied by manufacturers to help you know how to use their equipment. They are also called *user's manuals* or *documentation*.
- In-house training can take several forms. A company orientation program informs new employees about the company

Many companies provide in-house training for their employees.

Productivity 213

as a whole, its various parts, and its services. Training programs deal with job performance, such as the use of equipment, work procedures, and skills training.
- Documentation is prepared by many companies to supplement or replace vendors' documentation. It tailors procedures so that they are specific to that company's needs or use of equipment or software.

Measuring Productivity

While there is little doubt that productivity can be increased through standardized formats, coding, standardized procedures, training, and efficient documentation, there remains the question of *how much* it can be increased. This is an issue that company managers must address if they are to justify the large dollar outlay required to purchase equipment.

Reasons for Measuring Productivity. Computing and recording the amount of work produced by employees can help managers operate their business and plan ahead. Measuring productivity helps managers evaluate how effectively an information processing system is serving the company and whether upgrades of hardware or software are required. It identifies any workflow irregularities. It measures whether additional staff is needed (and whether additions should be part time, full time, or temporary), which less productive employees would benefit from additional training, and the cost of the center for "chargebacks" to other departments for information processing time spent in preparing their documents. Measuring productivity also helps managers set job performance standards, and identify those operators who meet or exceed standards.

Methods of Measuring Productivity. Companies use several methods of productivity measurement. Perhaps the most common measurement instrument is the document log.

Document Log. A *document log* is a chart that records the work coming into and going out of an information processing center (or, in some cases, a satellite or minicenter). It usually includes the name and department of the author of the document, the kind of document (letter, report, or memo), and the form in which the document was given to the center (dictation, typed draft, handwritten draft, or the like). It will also include the date and time the document was received by the center, the date and time it was completed, and by whom, and the number of pages in the final document. Document logs may be tabulated on a daily or weekly basis and then summarized in production reports.

In addition to measuring productivity, document logs are

Advances continue to be made in technology. Electronic office equipment has become smaller and more powerful. Now portable equipment and telecommunications make it possible to have an electronic "office" anywhere.

This portable computer is a helpful tool anywhere the user chooses to take it.

This portable computer has a pop-up screen.

This portable microfiche reader is invaluable at meetings in or outside the office.

Airfones make it possible for business people to remain in contact with the office, even in a plane.

IV B

As we discuss in the text, fiber optics is a transmission medium that sends data through glass fibers in the form of laser beams.

CREDITS FOR COLOR INSERTS

The photographs in the four color inserts are courtesy of the following:

INSERT I
Page I A, *top to bottom:* Honeywell; Mohawk Data Services. Page I B, *clockwise from upper right:* Sperry Corporation; Texas Instruments, Inc.; International Business Machines Corporation. Page I C, *top to bottom:* Wang Laboratories, Inc.; AT&T. Page I D: PPG Industries.

INSERT II
Page II A, *clockwise from upper right:* International Business Machines Corporation; ISSCO; SAS Institute, Inc.; Graphic Media N/Y. Page II B: Koala Technologies Corporation. Page II C: Datapoint Corporation. Page II D: Steelcase, Inc.

INSERT III
Pages III A and III B: Moag, Inc. Pages III C and III D: Stone, Pigman.

INSERT IV
Page IV A, *top to bottom:* Radio Shack, a Tandy Corporation; Will Faller. Page IV B, *top to bottom:* Micro Design, Bell & Howell Company; Airfone, Inc. Page IV C: Martin Dohrn/Photo Researchers, Inc.

used to manage workflow in and out of a center, to locate individual documents, to keep track of work for "chargebacks," and to provide a record of a company's or a department's document production. Logs also measure the output of each operator in lines, pages, or documents. And they measure the overall productivity of a center, satellite, or minicenter.

Document and Line Counting. A number of different methods are used to count documents. If all the documents produced are similar in format and type of input, keeping a record of the total number of lines keyed per operator per day should be sufficient. But in other cases, documents vary greatly—from brief notes to complicated statistical reports. They may be dictated, in rough draft, or handwritten. Some may be completely new, some may require minor revisions, some may be largely boilerplate with only a few variables to be inserted. In these cases, merely counting lines would not give a complete picture. The supervisor and the manager have to develop a system that distinguishes these different tasks. In any case, increasing production is not the only measure of an information processing center. As a center supervisor once put it: "Better to produce 100 perfect documents than 200 imperfect ones."

CAREERS

It is now time to examine more closely some of the different job situations and career opportunities that are available in the information processing field. There are a number of factors that will affect how well you will do on the job. Some of them will have to do with the company. Some of them will mainly have to do with you. And some of them will depend on finding the right slot—the job that closely matches what you can do, and where you want to go.

Differences That Affect the Employee

The size of a company as well as the kind of business it is will have an impact on your job and the kind of working conditions you will find. Furthermore, how comfortable you are in a job will depend on the particular information processing environment in which you work—a word processing center or satellite, or a more traditional office setting.

Self-Evaluation. In addition to knowing about the environment in which you will work, you must know about yourself, your skills and attitudes. Can you keyboard accurately at a reasonable speed? Do you have sharp proofreading skills? Solid language skills, and the ability to think abstractly and to organize material are essential. How well do you relate to others? How mature and flexible are you? What do your personal appearance, your approach to the job, and your attitude tell others about you? A positive approach, promptness and reliability, and a team spirit will all be helpful to you.

Careers in Information Processing

When you are considering any new job, you should ask yourself certain questions. For instance: Do the skill requirements of the job match my abilities and training? Has the employer spelled out the duties I will be expected to carry out? Would I feel comfortable, and yet reasonably challenged, performing these duties, or is there another job within the organization that would be better for me? What advancement opportunities are available within the company? What jobs outside the company might this position prepare me for?

You will be able to answer such questions more easily if you have good general knowledge of the opportunities within the information processing field.

Job Titles in Word Processing. The following titles and job descriptions for word processing personnel are based on survey results published by the Association of Information Systems Professionals (AISP), 1015 N. York Road, Willow Grove, PA 19090. The AISP is a professional organization founded in 1972 to develop and disseminate information/word processing ideas, methods, and techniques. The descriptions that they have developed will give you a general idea of what to expect.

Operators. In a centralized word processing system, operators can be classified according to a number of different levels and specialties based on an operator's degree of skill, seniority, and special aptitudes or interests.

The *word processing trainee* position is for people who have worked in word processing less than a year or not at all. It requires keyboarding skills; a good knowledge of grammar, punctuation, spelling, and formatting; and the ability to use dictionaries and other reference materials. A trainee should like working with machines and should have a spirit of teamwork.

Trainee duties include routine transcription and manipulation of text from dictation, rough drafts, and other raw material. Trainees usually keep their own production records and may be required to proofread their own work.

The job of *word processing operator* is for people with six months to two years of word processing experience. In addition to meeting all the requirements and performing all the duties of a trainee, an operator handles special documents, meets established quality standards, uses all the text-editing functions of a word processor, and is familiar with any special terminology or practices associated with the organization.

Your ability to work well with others will be the key to your success.

Careers

A *word processing specialist I* is an operator with at least 18 months of experience. The specialist is skilled at formatting and producing and revising complicated documents, such as lengthy technical and statistical reports. The specialist may have to assemble these documents from complex sources, sometimes retrieving information from electronic files. Specialists must understand proofreading and editing symbols, too.

This job requires the ability and confidence to act independently when interpreting instructions. A specialist assumes full responsibility for the accuracy and completeness of a document. An employee at this level is fully acquainted with the procedures of the word processing center and knows how to maintain records. Word processing specialists sometimes operate telecommunications equipment.

A *word processing specialist II* knows how to operate all the equipment and perform all the jobs within a word processing center. As the supervisor's assistant (or *assistant supervisor*), the specialist II may be responsible for coordinating and assigning work, compiling production statistics, and recommending changes in procedure. A specialist II may also help train new employees.

An operator who keyboards and revises text for use in a photocomposition system, such as that used to print magazines, is called a *phototypesetting specialist.* This job requires a knowledge of type sizes and typefaces and other aspects of printing and typesetting, as well as general proficiency on the word processor.

A *word processing trainer's* chief responsibility is to teach new operators to use word processing equipment. A trainer may also help authors learn machine-dictation skills and other techniques for making the best use of a word processing system. Before purchasing new word processing equipment, managers may ask a trainer to make recommendations based on personal experience or knowledge of what equipment is available. This job requires at least two years of experience.

A *proofreader* checks documents for content, grammar, spelling, punctuation, and typographical errors. Proofreaders may also be asked to set standards for grammar and format and to guide authors and secretaries in their effort to meet them.

Secretaries. Even in a completely centralized word processing system, a need for secretaries exists. There are not nearly as many secretaries in a centralized system as in a traditional system, but the ones who are there have important duties.

An *administrative secretary* works as part of an administrative support team to handle word processing as well as taking dictation, filing, photocopying, scheduling, and other tasks for a group of executives. If you work in the smallest of offices, of course, the support team may consist of one person—you!

The team's *senior administrative secretary* is qualified to compose and edit documents for the executives. She or he also handles special projects, sometimes assists the supervisor, and may help executives with research. This job requires an exceptional secretary who is fully aware of the organization's practices and standards.

Managers. Just as there are different levels and specialties among operators, so are there among managers. Some managers are concerned only with word processing. Others oversee the administrative support services. Still others, at the highest level, are involved with both.

The *word processing supervisor* is responsible for the day-to-day operation of the word processing center. The supervisor is responsible for training, makes assignments, establishes and maintains quality standards, sets priorities, and helps operators process documents. Supervisors also analyze production procedures and suggest ways of improving them. They sometimes make recommendations for equipment purchases, and they may work on budgets.

The *word processing manager* is responsible for the entire word processing center, including the design of the system. The manager is in charge of staffing decisions and budgets. He or she coordinates the work of authors, operators, and the administrative support staff. The manager may also oversee the operation of photocopying, printing, mailing, and graphics services.

The *administrative support supervisor* coordinates the secretarial team's work flow and acts as a go-between for the secretaries and the executives. The supervisor evaluates staffing requirements and recommends improvements in the administrative support system.

The *administrative support manager* is responsible for the development, maintenance, and evaluation of all administrative support services, such as filing, telephone staffing, mail handling, and paraprofessional aid. The support manager works closely with the word processing manager to coordinate the work of their staffs. In addition, the support manager may be in charge of other administrative functions, such as printing.

The responsibility of the *staff analyst* is to consult and assist word processing and administrative support supervisors and managers. In doing this, the staff analyst conducts studies, reviews operations, and recommends appropriate staffing, procedures, and equipment.

The *director of information support systems* has total responsibility for all aspects of an organization's office system, includ-

A supervisor helps a word processing operator.

ing word processing, administrative support, and other information processing functions.

Jobs in Information Processing. With offices everywhere using more computers, new job opportunities are developing. Let's look at some of the new jobs that have been created.

In-House Trainer. More computers mean more computer jobs, and employees need training. Larger companies often have their own in-house training department. An in-house trainer is responsible for setting up the training programs.

A typical program offers instruction at various levels from beginning to advanced. Subjects typically include word processing, spelling verification, spreadsheets, and data base management. The in-house trainer tells employees what courses are offered and when.

In addition to teaching skills, an in-house trainer needs to understand how computers work, and should have hands-on experience with hardware and software.

Applications Specialist. Purchasing applications software is a significant expense for companies that furnish many of their employees with personal computers. These businesses often hire an applications specialist whose job is to test applications packages and decide which ones work best for the company. Applications specialists also teach employees to use software packages. If you like working with new software and showing people how to use it, you may find this an interesting position.

Systems Analyst. As we mentioned earlier, a large company does not simply go out and buy a computer system. Selecting the appropriate system is a job for a systems analyst. As a systems analyst, your responsiblities would include first working closely with managers and employees to design a system that fits their needs precisely. Then you decide on the hardware and software, and what kind of operators and how many are needed. Once the system is in place, you train the operators and orient the employees who will use the system, and continue to make changes until the system is operating smoothly. Many large companies employ a full-time systems analyst in each department who reports to someone in management information systems (MIS), or a part-time analyst on a project basis. If you like solving computer problems logically, and can communicate orally and in writing about computers in a business environment, you many want to learn more about this career area.

Programmer. Organizations that use mainframes, minicomputers, or a sizable number of microcomputers often cannot find prepackaged software that satisfies exactly what they need for their particular business operation. They hire a programmer, full time or part time, to design and write programs that will perform specific functions. Programmers often work with systems analysts as part of a team.

Programming is difficult, precise work. Many programmers have mathematics backgrounds in addition to computer training, and may know a number of programming languages including BASIC, COBOL, FORTRAN, Pascal, and Assembler. If you like working with computers and appreciate detail and concentration, you may want to look into programming as a career.

Records Manager/Data Base Specialists. If a company's data bases are large enough, or if many or widely located sources are used to update them, then data base management becomes a job in itself. Larger companies that create and maintain their own data bases often find it necessary to employ a full-time records manager, also called a data base specialist. If you like organizing and managing data, networking, and online communication, look into records and data base management. New positions will continue to open up in this growing career area.

Other Job Possibilities. The expansion of information processing and office technology has created many career options outside the office. These jobs range from selling and maintaining computerized equipment to providing services for organizations that do not have their own systems. Experience in information processing may qualify you for one of these positions. Let's look at these now.

Vendor's Sales Representative. *Vendors* supply equipment but do not always manufacture it. The increasing number of vendors and their expanding product lines mean that sales jobs are opening up all the time. As a sales representative, you must be able to deal with many kinds of people in a variety of business settings, and you may have to travel extensively. In addition, you need a thorough knowledge of the vendor's product line and of how its products compare with those of the competition.

Vendors are especially eager to hire sales representatives who can operate their equipment and who have learned from experience how the equipment performs during routine use. If you are aggressive and knowledgeable, you can earn excellent money as a vendor.

Trainer for Vendor. Unlike a trainer in a word processing center, a trainer for a vendor works for a company that sells word or information processing equipment. This job requires considerable technical expertise as well as supervisory experience. It also requires the ability to tailor instructions to individuals in many professions, people who have widely different levels of education and degrees of experience with electronic equipment.

A vendor's sales representative demonstrates the product.

Some trainers work at the vendor's headquarters. Others, often referred to as support personnel, spend most of their time visiting companies that have purchased equipment. Support personnel may make frequent visits to new customers, and they go back now and then if problems arise. Sometimes they help companies set up their own in-house training programs.

Many stores that sell microcomputers employ people to demonstrate equipment and to train customers. For this position you need technical expertise about a variety of equipment, and about the software packages designed for microcomputers. You may train customers in the store or on-site, that is, in the office where the equipment will be used.

Free Lancer. Many personnel agencies specialize in temporary office help. They look for, and supply companies with, people who know word processing and can work with microcomputer applications programs. The assignments often involve working as a secretary or operator, usually for a day or two, sometimes longer. Some companies hire free-lance workers on a temporary basis to train their employees in using the equipment.

Temporary assignments may pay well, but you will probably not receive fringe benefits. Because you can choose from the assignments that are offered, your work hours may be more flexible than if you worked full time for one employer.

If you are uncertain about what kind of environment you want to work in permanently, signing up with a temporary agency could give you a chance to sample the possibilities. Occasionally a temporary assignment leads to a full-time job offer.

Electronic Workstation Specialist. A company planning to purchase a word processing or microcomputer system may first hire an electronic workstation specialist to try out different kinds of equipment. What this specialist does is to push the equipment to its limits, to see which equipment best suits the needs of the company.

This job is for someone with a thorough understanding of information processing concepts who loves working with the equipment. Depending on the employer's needs, the job may be temporary (although it could last for several months), or it may be part of a permanent position that also includes other duties.

Consultant. Consultants work on temporary but usually long-term assignments, sometimes at high fees, for vendors and for organizations that purchase information processing equipment. Companies hire consultants when they are thinking about automating or enhancing their current office systems, but are not yet ready for a systems analyst.

To succeed as a consultant, you must be thoroughly acquainted with all equipment currently on the market in your area of expertise. You also need to know how to solve problems analytically, working closely with people and equipment. In addition, you must understand the work flow in an office and be able to recommend cost-saving improvements.

A company might hire a consultant to help determine how it should organize its information processing system or to help it establish guidelines for authors who use the system. Vendors sometimes hire consultants for assignments such as writing training manuals.

Service Company Operator. If you have enough experience, you can buy one or more word processors or personal computers and start your own service. Your customers can include individuals and smaller companies that cannot afford their own equipment, or companies having work flow that at times is too heavy for their operators or equipment to handle.

Service companies may offer a number of services, or word processing for only one field, such as law, or special computer services such as accounting and spreadsheets.

Owning your own service company requires self-discipline, confidence, and a number of other attributes. You must be able to solicit clients, keep financial records, and manage various other aspects of a business—all in addition to having a thorough knowledge of information processing. The rewards can be high, but so are the risks. Owners usually start out working alone, often in their homes.

A service company that succeeds and gets enough business may purchase more equipment and hire other operators.

The Electronic Cottage. If you use a personal computer at work, why can't you use it at home and communicate with the company's offices by modem? In fact, many workers have already turned their homes into "electronic cottages."

Professionals such as lawyers, writers, and editors can easily keyboard outside a typical office environment. *Telecommuting*, as it is called, also provides work opportunity for people who cannot get to an office—new mothers, for example, and permanently disabled people who may otherwise be considered unemployable.

Some people prefer telecommuting because they find the daily events in an office distracting for certain tasks requiring heavy concentration. Others like it because they can set their own hours. Telecommuting gives management the opportunity to employ more people and pay less rent for office space. By the end of this century, it is estimated that about a third of all workers will telecommute full time or part time.

Onward and Upward

After you have been in a job for a year or two, you will probably want to develop your skills further, to acquire more knowledge, to maximize your potential. The question is *how*.

Knowing what your options are is the first step toward making wise decisions about your career. In addition, talk to as many qualified people as you can to find out what they think are your strengths and abilities. Once you have a realistic sense of yourself, you will be equipped to choose intelligently from among your career options.

Education. Education can help you attain your goal. Many companies recognize the value of advanced or continuing education, and, to encourage their employees to take courses, they will pay part or all of the tuition fees.

Performance Appraisals. Periodically your supervisor will review how well you are doing on the job. This *performance appraisal* is an excellent way for you to learn more about your strengths and weaknesses. To get the most from performance appraisals, view them as an opportunity. For example, if your supervisor suggests that you improve your performance in certain ways, ask for specific recommendations on how to accomplish such improvements. Try to come away from appraisal sessions with a clearer idea of where you are headed on the job.

Performance appraisals are opportunities to learn.

Making the Most of Your Company. If you are happy working at a particular company but want to move to a new or more challenging position, don't assume that you must change employers. In most companies, especially larger ones, there may be more job opportunities than you imagine. And if you have a good work history with the company, you may find yourself one step ahead of the competition.

Some businesses have a policy of *job posting*, or listing job openings on a bulletin board or in the company newspaper several weeks before outside applicants are interviewed. In any case, you can also investigate in-house positions by talking to a personnel specialist. This person can make you aware of what is required to climb various job ladders, what skills and how many years of service are required to move to another job in the company. In addition, you may find that your best source of assistance is your supervisor.

Toward Change and Growth

Over the past decade, word and information processsing systems have developed at an amazing rate that shows every sign of continuing for years to come. Already we see electric typewriters being replaced by electronic typewriters, word processors, and microcomputers. It is a familiar process, one repeated with each new wave of information technology: Things we did by hand, we can do automatically; functions we performed electrically are made more efficient and productive with electronic tools.

As offices have become increasingly automated, office systems have become more integrated. Networked microcomputers and telecommunications blur the line that once separated word processing and data processing. Comprehensive office systems will have only one purpose: information processing.

Just as the carpenter's hand tools were replaced by power saws and drills, we now have a new set of tools in the office that, like the carpenter's, will enable us to perform the old functions better and many new ones that were not possible or feasible using earlier methods. The electronic systems that we will see introduced in the years ahead will make the office an exciting, stimulating, and challenging place to work, a place where modern technology gives us the opportunity for professional as well as personal growth.

CHAPTER SUMMARY

- Standardized formats for documents save time and trouble for information processing operators and authors by establishing a set style of document preparation for everyone.
- Document coding enables operators to retrieve prerecorded documents quickly and easily.
- Office procedures manuals are designed to guide and assist employees in performing their assignments.
- Measuring the productivity of information processing workers helps management evaluate current equipment and make plans to add equipment according to need.
- Productivity measurement provides management with important information that can be used in planning and scheduling work and in identifying high and low producers.
- Productivity measurement is also used in financial recordkeeping and planning.
- Calculating and recording employee work production helps managers and supervisors set performance standards tailored to the individual company or department.
- A document log is a chart that records work coming into and going out of an information processing center, minicenter, or satellite. Although they have other purposes, document logs are commonly used to measure productivity.
- The size of a company, the type of business, and the specific

information processing environment in which you work all help determine whether the position is right for you.
- Proofreading skills, and the ability to think in abstract terms and organize material, increase chances for career success.
- Success on the job results from a combination of factors: the ability to carry out assignments and relate to others, good judgment, maturity, flexibility, discretion, good personal appearance, a positive attitude, and a conscientious approach to the job.
- When you apply for a job, try to find a position that fits your skills, offers opportunity for advancement, and challenges your career goals.
- Some operators eventually leave the office to pursue related careers, such as selling word processors.
- Many large companies offer their employees a full program of in-house training to improve their current information processing capabilities and help them learn new ones.
- An applications specialist tests application programs to see which software works best for a company, and may also teach employees how to use it.
- A systems analyst designs a system, selects the hardware, works with programmers to develop appropriate software, trains employees, and continues to modify a system until it is operating smoothly.
- Organizations with large information processing systems may not be able to use prepackaged software, so they hire a programmer to write specific programs they need. A programmer should know at least one programming language, and may know several.
- Free-lance, or temporary, office assignments are usually for a day or two but can last much longer. Temporary work gives you a chance to explore a number of different organizations, and may lead to full-time employment.
- Consultants are hired to analyze a company's information processing system and make recommendations to enhance current equipment, purchase a new system, or make other cost-saving improvements.
- A service company offers information processing services to individuals and smaller businesses that cannot afford their own systems. Operators sometimes purchase equipment and start their own service companies.
- Telecommuting means to work at home on a word processor or microcomputer and communicate with your company by modem.
- Education and job training can help you in getting ahead. It is also important to understand the value of performance

appraisals in preparing for career advancement.
- Employees should make the most of the opportunities in their company before changing employers. Reading posted job descriptions, talking to personnel, and consulting with supervisors are three ways to explore in-house options.

INFORMATION PROCESSING VOCABULARY

Association of
  Information Systems
  Professionals (AISP)
documentation
document coding
document log
electronic cottage

in-house training
job posting
performance appraisal
procedures manual
standardized format
telecommuting

CHAPTER QUESTIONS

1. Why are employers so concerned with productivity? Do you think their concern is justified? Why or why not?
2. Why can productivity measurement be considered a good thing for employees as well as for management?
3. Knowing your own temperament and qualifications, do you think you would be happier working for a large or small company? In a large or small office? Explain.
4. What are some advantages of working in a large information processing center?
5. What stresses might employees in an information processing center experience?
6. Contrast the opportunities for advancement in a typical traditional office with those in a large information processing center. Which situation do you think might offer a beginner a better opportunity to master basic skills?
7. Would you enjoy working at home in an electronic cottage? Give your reasons, including both advantages and disadvantages.
8. How can employees use performance appraisals to their advantage?
9. What are some arguments in favor of staying with an employer rather than switching companies?

10. Following are eight career categories in information processing. Pick four and briefly discuss the responsibilities and functions performed in each.

    Applications specialist   In-house trainer
    Consultant   Programmer
    Data base specialist   Systems analyst
    Free lancer   Vendor sales representative

CASE STUDY

Stephanie Leone has worked as a word processing operator in Royal Furnishings' Marketing Department satellite for over three years, ever since she graduated from business school. Ms. Leone enjoys many aspects of her job. She works with fine people for a reputable company, earns decent wages, and enjoys excellent benefits. But lately she has begun to feel restless.

    She is considering changing jobs. Royal has three other satellite centers, but Ms. Leone isn't sure that she merely wants to transfer to another satellite. She has begun looking at newspaper want ads for openings at other companies. At the same time, she has ordered the current catalog of her old community college and is studying course offerings in management training.

    Ms. Leone has not yet approached her supervisor to discuss her feelings. At her last performance appraisal, she was told that she was "outstanding in most respects," especially in organizational ability. However, she was told she could still improve the speed at which she works.

    Last week during lunch break, Ms. Leone noticed an opening for an administrative assistant on the company's "Jobs at Royal" bulletin board. She wondered whether she would qualify for that job and whether she should apply for it.

    Based on what you have read in this chapter, what advice would you give Ms. Leone, speaking as one friend to another? What would *you* do if you were Ms. Leone?

Glossary

Acoustic coupler A communications device that converts electrical data signals to tones for transmission over a telephone line by using a conventional telephone handset. The tones are converted back to electrical signals at the other end of the line.

Alphanumeric Combining alphabetic and numeric symbols.

American Standard Code for Information Interchange (ASCII) A code devised for data communication between incompatible equipment; each alphanumeric character, all punctuation marks, and various control codes are represented by an ASCII character; the standard code for digital asynchronous communications over telephone lines.

Analog facsimile A copy produced by a scanner that converts every part of a document, including blank spaces, to electric signals.

Aperture card A type of keypunch card with a rectangular opening that holds one or more frames of microfilm.

Applications software Computer programs designed for a specific purpose: business, recreation, or education; applications software is available for word processing, spreadsheets, data bases, graphics, communications, integrated tasks, and desk organizers.

Architecture See **Topology**.

Archive Storage of backup, or duplicate, text on disks or diskettes.

ASCII See **American Standard Code for Information Interchange**.

Asynchronous transmission During data communication, characters are sent one at a time at uneven intervals; a start bit is sent immediately before each character, and a stop bit is sent immediately after.

Author The creator of a document, who in a sense "writes" it; a *word originator* or *principal*.

Automated office An office that has adopted the systems approach through the use of electronic equipment to make office work faster, thus improving productivity.

Automatic gain control A feature of some dictation units that controls the volume when voice fluctuations occur.

Automatic measured review A feature of some dictation units that permits a controlled repetition of recorded dictation; also called *automatic text repetition*.

Automatic recalculation A procedure in a programmed spreadsheet whereby once one number in one cell is changed, all entries in the other related cells are automatically refigured to conform to the new information.

Automatic sheet feeder A device that feeds sheets of paper into a printer automatically.

Automatic text repetition See **Automatic measured review.**

Automatic word wraparound At the end of a line of keyboarding, the cursor automatically drops down to the beginning of the next line without the use of the carriage return; if the last word won't fit on a line, that word is automatically "wrapped around" and entered as the first word on the next line.

Automation A system of production that uses "self-acting," or automatic, machines.

Background printing A feature of some word processing systems and microcomputers using word processing software enabling the user to work on one document while another is being printed.

Backup Duplicate text that is magnetically stored.

Band printer See **Line printer.**

BASIC The simplest of all computer languages.

Baud rate A measure of transmission speed at which data is sent through communication lines; also called *bits per second (bps)*.

Bidirectional printing A method of printing in which the type element moves from left to right and from right to left.

Bidirectional tractor A continuous-form tractor that can move the paper in two directions to make it possible to print charts and graphs as well as subscripts and superscripts.

Bisynchronous transmission During data communication, characters are sent in a steady stream; control codes that set up and begin the communication are sent first, followed by the message; also called *synchronous transmission.*

Bit The smallest unit of information recognized by a computer, represented by a single one or a single zero; stands for BInary digiT.

Bits per second (bps) See **Baud rate.**

Blind word processor A word processor not equipped with a video display terminal.

Boilerplate Stored paragraphs that can be arranged in different ways or combined with new material to produce tailor-made documents.

Buffer memory See **Temporary memory.**

Bulletin board services (BBS) An electronic computerized service, accessible to the user by modem, that provides different kinds of information, such as announcements, schedules, notices, and the like.

Bundled software In a dedicated word processor DOS and the word processing program are built into the ROM of the machine; bundled software works automatically when the machine is turned on.

Burster A device that separates continuous-form paper into individual sheets.

Bus network The most flexible local area network, with only one cable and any number of nodes plugged into it anywhere along its length.

Byte A group of bits strung together to form a character (letter, number, symbol, etc.); programmers string bits to form characters just as people string letters to form words.

Cassette A magnetic recording tape permanently encased in a small plastic container.

Cassette-tape text editor A blind word processing machine in which storage is on a large-capacity tape cassette.

Cathode-ray tube (CRT) An electronic vacuum tube that can be used to display text and graphic images; often used interchangeably with *video display terminal.*

Cell The location where a row and a column intersect on a spreadsheet.

Cellular radio A low-cost, wireless communications system.

Central controller See **Hub.**

Central processing unit (CPU) The component of a word or data processing system containing the operating instructions; acts as the "brains," "logic," or "intelligence" of the unit; sometimes called *internal processor.*

Central recording system A system in which all dictation is channeled (usually over telephone lines) into a central location, where it is recorded and transcribed.

Centralized information processing system The concentration of information processing services in a single area within an organization to make maximum use of personnel and equipment, thus improving productivity.

Centralized records management system A management system in which the records of a company are kept in one place.

Centralized reprographics The grouping of reprographics staff and equipment in one area in order to duplicate and assemble documents for an entire company.

Centralized word processing system The concentration of word processing services in a single area within an organization so as to make maximum use of personnel and equipment, thus improving productivity.

Character printer An impact printer that prints one letter, symbol, or figure at a time.

Chip An integrated circuit or circuits on a thin slice of supporting material, usually silicon, used as the central processing unit.

Clustered system An arrangement in which word processing units (or microcomputers) share one or more components, such as a printer or hard disk.

Coaxial cable A transmission medium developed to minimize noise interference; copper wire surrounded by an insulating layer of air or plastic, covered again by another layer of aluminum or copper mesh, and then surrounded by a protective cover.

COBOL A computer language mainly used for business.

Coded word processing system A word processor that has no menu to guide the user through its operation but rather requires the user to keyboard commands with a code, either with function keys or with combinations of function and character keys.

Combination unit A machine that can be used for both dictation and transcription.

Glossary

Communicating word processor A word processor that can send text to and receive text from another word processor via telephone lines or other electronic communications links.

Communications software A software program that allows compatible but independent equipment to exchange information.

Computer-aided transcription The use of a computer to transcribe sound impulses recorded on magnetic tape by a shorthand machine.

Computer-assisted retrieval (CAR) The retrieval of documents stored on microform through the use of computer terminals linked to central file systems.

Computer-based message system A system of person-to-person communications using linked computers; the computer screens contain message blanks.

Computer crime Use of a computer to commit a crime, such as the illegal copying of information from a copyrighted disk, deleting valuable information from another individual's disk, or changing computer information.

Computer graphics Output in the form of images, such as drawings, charts, figures, or graphs, converted from data input.

Computer output microfilm (COM) A process in which a data processing printout is produced directly on microform; an integration of computer and microform technologies.

Configuration The components and peripherals of a word processor or microcomputer and the manner in which they are arranged.

Constant A part of a document that does not change for each recipient; repetitive text.

Continuous-form paper A roll of single-ply or multiple-ply paper with horizontal perforations separating each sheet.

Control characters Codes and instructions sent before, during, and after a message is transmitted to indicate some kind of mechanical activity such as spacing, carrier returns, formatting keystrokes, and printing directions; control characters do not print but only indicate; also called *control codes*.

Control codes See **Control characters.**

CPU See **Central processing unit.**

Crash When a computer system cannot function; can be caused by a failure in either the computer hardware or software or in the electric power supply.

Crosstalk A noise problem during data communication caused by electrical interference which distorts the transmitted signal so that information is lost.

Cursor A spot of light on a display screen that indicates the point in the text at which the user is working.

Cursor keys Keys generally marked with arrows used to move the cursor up, down, and to the right or left on the display screen. See also *Cursor.*

Cycle time The time a computer takes to execute one instruction, such as moving a piece of information from one location in the computer's memory to another; today's microcomputers vary in cycle time from 2 to 12 million instructions per second.

Cycles per second (cps) The number of cycles a computer can perform in one second; used to evaluate CPU speed; also called *hertz.*

Daisy wheel A type element on some character printers on which the characters are engraved at the ends of bars or spokes, thus resembling a daisy.

Data Facts or figures that are assembled and processed to produce needed information.

Data bank A collection of databases.

Data base A collection of related files (items) stored in a computer system and available to many users for different applications.

Data base management system (DBMS) A combination of hardware and software that allows a user to set up and maintain a data base and to manage access to and retrieval of information stored.

Data processing Information in numeric form; the mathematical or other logical manipulation of numbers or symbols, usually done by a computer.

Decentralized information processing system Distribution of information processing facilities among departments or floors of an organization to increase personal involvement and better serve specific needs; also called *minicenter* or *satellite center.*

Decentralized records management system A management system in which records are kept in several areas throughout the company.

Decentralized reprographics The placement of reprographics equipment in several areas throughout a company to make duplicating more convenient.

Decentralized word processing system Distribution of word processing facilities among departments or floors of an organization to increase personal involvement and better serve specific needs.

Dedicated word processor Electronic equipment used specifically and only for word processing.

Desk-top dictating unit A dictation machine using standard or minicassettes that records spoken words; usually larger than a portable dictation unit.

Development software A program that automatically converts programming language into machine language. See also *Programming language.*

Dictating machine An office machine that records spoken words.

Digital facsimile A copy produced by a scanner that converts information in a document to binary signals.

Digitizer Scanning device used to change words, graphs, images, etc., into signals that a computer can understand.

Discrete media Recording media, such as cards, disks, and cassettes, that can be detached easily from dictation machines and used on other dictation or transcription equipment.

Disk See **Floppy diskette** and **Hard disk.**

Disk drive The unit in a word processor or microcomputer in which the floppy diskette is inserted so that the machine is programmed.

Disk operating system (DOS) The system software that manages the resources and handles all the functions of the computer such as the keyboard and the transfer of information from soft copy to diskette.

Display screen The televisionlike screen on a video display terminal (VDT).

Display terminal See **Video display terminal.**

Display word processor A word processor equipped with a video display terminal (VDT).

Distributed processing A word processing system configuration using intelligent workstations; also called *distributed logic system.*

Distribution/communication The fourth stage of the information processing cycle; the purpose of this step is to make sure that the information is communicated to the people who need it; today you can distribute information in different ways, depending on the form in which it is needed and the location of the recipients.

Document Any business communication that contains information; includes correspondence, reports, statistical tables, and forms.

Document assembly The creation of a document by combining stored paragraphs, sometimes with new material added.

Document production center See **Centralized information processing system.**

Document requisition form A work order accompanying a document requiring word processing services; also known as a *work order.*

Documentation The operating instructions prepared by a manufacturer of equipment or software; also called *user's manual* or *vendor's manual.*

DOS See **Disk operating system.**

Dot matrix A printing pattern made by some printers, in which a group of closely spaced dots resembles the shape of a character.

Dual display A feature of some word processors whereby two different video screens can appear at the same time; also referred to as a *split screen.*

Dual pitch A feature of printers enabling them to print either pica (10 characters to an inch) or elite (12 characters to an inch).

Dual-recording track A feature of some endless loop systems permitting the author to dictate onto one track of the tape and switch to the other track to make insertions or revisions or add special instructions.

Dual-sheet feeder A device that feeds paper automatically into a printer from two separate stacks.

Dumb workstation A workstation in a shared logic system entirely dependent on the central processing unit for operating instructions and storage.

Duplex A protocol that allows data to be communicated between the sending computer and the receiving computer in both directions at the same time; also referred to as *full-duplex.*

Duplicator A copying machine that requires the preparation of a master.

Dvorak keyboard A keyboard alternative to the standard QWERTY keyboard, which relocates the most commonly used letters to the "home row," where typists can reach them with the least finger movement. See also *QWERTY keyboard.*

Echoplex A protocol often used with duplex transmission in which the data transmitted is "echoed" back and displayed on the sending terminal after it has been received, thus enabling one to check whether the data was received exactly as sent.

Electronic audio communications A technology by which telephone calls can be recorded, stored electronically, and delivered at designated times; also known as *voice mail.*

Electronic copier/printer A machine combining the technologies of printer, office copier, and facsimile machine. "Intelligent" copier/printers can manipulate data. "Dumb" copier/printers are limited to the execution of printing instructions.

Electronic cottage See **Telecommuting.**

Electronic cuing A feature of some dictation units that enables the author to insert special instructions for the transcriptionist.

Electronic data communication See **Electronic mail.**

Electronic mail The transfer of documents over communications channels at very high speeds without the physical movement of paper; sometimes referred to as *electronic data communication.*

Electronic private branch exchange (EPBX) An advanced digital PBX system that not only converts digital signals automatically but also makes it possible to connect many other products that are used for telephone data transmission with local area networks and other networks.

Electronic spreadsheet See **Spreadsheet.**

Electronic typewriter (ET) A blind word processor with all components—keyboard, CPU, storage unit, and printer—housed in one unit; has many of the advantages of a display word processor and can print in a wide range of typestyles; some ETs offer slim displays, and others can be upgraded to include a disk drive for floppy diskette storage.

Electrostatic A printing process whereby images are burned into paper electrically.

Emulation Programming a terminal to carry out instructions from another computer; for example, a PC can be programmed to perform as a mainframe terminal.

Encryption Putting confidential computer files into code so that only receiving terminals with the correct decoding program can unscramble the message.

Endless loop A long recording tape connected at both ends and housed in the tank of some dictation machines; often used in central recording systems.

ENIAC Electronic Numerical Integrator and Computer; one of the first computers developed.

Envelope feeder A device that automatically feeds envelopes into a printer.

EPBX See **Electronic private branch exchange.**

EPROM See **Erasable programmable read-only memory.**

Erasable programmable read-only memory (EPROM) Chips developed to allow the user to erase programs and program the system to fit specific needs of the user.

Ergonomics The science of adapting working environment, conditions, and equipment to suit workers; also called *human engineering.*

Ergonomist A person who specializes in ergonomics.

Executive workstation A self-contained, electronically equipped work area designed to help managers generate and retrieve information as efficiently as possible.

Expandable memory board A computer board containing memory chips; can be purchased independently from the hardware when the memory capacity of a system needs to be upgraded.

Express Mail The U.S. Postal Service overnight delivery system.

External modem The modem is a unit separate from the computer and may be placed on a desk or table between the computer and the telephone and connected to the phone and CPU with cables and jacks. See also *Modem.*

External storage A storage facility separate from the computer itself, or part of the system unit of a microcomputer, that retains text or information in a form acceptable to the word processor or computer.

Facsimile A copy of a document transmitted electronically from one machine to another, usually via telephone lines.

Feasibility study A detailed analysis undertaken by a company to determine how it might be reorganized or equipment might be used to increase productivity.

Fiber optics The use of light-conducting glass or plastic rods to transmit information coded as light signals.

Field A single item of information stored in a data base.

File A group of related pieces of information stored together in a data base.

Firmware The operating instructions or programs of a computer that are permanently installed as a basic part of the hardware.

Fixed disk A hard disk for a microcomputer encased and fixed in its drive.

Floppy diskette A magnetic storage medium for word processors and microcomputers that looks like a small phonograph record in its protective jacket.

Format The page margin, spacing, and indentation requirements of a document.

Format keys Function keys that control the physical layout of a document, such as margins, page length, vertical line spacing, printing requirements, tabs, indentations, centering, underlining, and page breaks.

FORTRAN Computer language, primarily for scientific and mathematical use.

Full-duplex See **Duplex.**

Function key A special key on word processing and microcomputer keyboards used to communicate instructions to the CPU.

Function menu system The selection procedure in some word processing programs to perform relatively simple tasks such as centering a line or inserting a word.

Graphics Information in the form of numbers and words that is entered into a computer and displayed on the screen as a graph, chart, table, or in other graphically illustrated form.

Half-duplex A protocol that allows data to be communicated between the sending computer and the receiving computer, but only in one direction at a time.

Hard copy The paper copy of a document; also called *printout*.

Hard disk A magnetic storage medium with a large storage capacity; used with word processors and microcomputers.

Hardware The physical equipment of a computer or word processor.

Hertz See **Cycles per second.**

Host system The central computer to which smaller computers, minicomputers, or microcomputers are connected.

Hub The central controlling node in a star network serving as a central switching device through which all messages are routed to the receiving node; also called *central controller.*

Image processing Information in the form of pictures; an actual picture or photograph is taken, entered into the computer, and shown on the display screen.

Image scanner State-of-the-art technology that scans information, regardless of form (letters, memos, graphs, illustrations, etc.), for electronic reproduction, transmission, and/or storage.

Impact printer A printer that strikes type against a ribbon and paper.

In-house training Orientation and hands-on equipment programs provided by companies to maximize employee knowledge, ability, and productivity.

Information The orderly and useful arrangement of facts, or data, so that they are accurate, timely, complete, and concise.

Information management The combining of word and data processing with film and electronic records management to speed and simplify the passage of information from one step in the information processing cycle to another.

Information processing The coordination of people, equipment, and procedures to handle information, including word and data processing; administrative support; and the distribution/communication, and storage and retrieval of information.

Information processing center See **Centralized information processing system.**

Information processing cycle A sequence of five steps or stages—input, processing, output (including printing and reprographics), distribution/communication, and storage and retrieval—that occurs frequently in the processing of information in an office.

Information resource management See **Networking.**

Information sharing The free passing of information between tasks (word processing, spreadsheet, data base, graphics, etc.) in an integrated software program.

Ink-jet printer A nonimpact printer that sprays tiny electrically charged ink drops onto paper, forming characters.

Input Facts or data that are entered into an information processing system; the first stage in the information processing cycle.

Inscribed media Voice storage media, such as plastic belts, cylinders, and disks, that cannot be erased or reused.

Integrated information system A system in which different computer-based functions and equipment—such as word processing, data processing, and telecommunications—are linked electronically.

Integrated software An applications program designed to interface or link more than one application so that a variety of tasks can be performed without changing the software.

Intelligent copier/printer Electronic copier/printer that can manipulate data.

Intelligent workstation A workstation that is equipped with its own CPU and storage; also called a *smart workstation.*

INTELPOST See **International Electronic Postal Service.**

Interface An electrical or mechanical link connecting two or more units or systems.

Internal modem A modem installed inside the CPU; usually you cannot see an internal modem. See also *Modem.*

Internal processor See **Central processing unit.**

Internal storage The storage of text or data inside the word processor or microcomputer; also called the *CPU.*

Internal storage media Recording media kept inside dictation machines, such as an endless loop, not usually touched or handled by the author or transcriptionist.

International Electronic Postal Service (INTELPOST) An electronic system of the U.S. Postal Service using communications satellites to transmit mail.

Joystick A hand-held input device that allows the user to manipulate characters on the display; used most frequently with video games.

Keyboard The component of a computer or word processing system resembling a typewriter keyboard but usually having additional keys for special functions.

Keyboarding The entry of words and numbers into the memory of word processing, microcomputers, and other electronic equipment by pressing keys on a keyboard.

LAN See **Local area network.**

Laser disk See **Optical disk.**

Laser optical disk See **Optical (laser) disk.**

Laser printer A printer using a laser beam, a narrow beam of pure red light, that burns characters onto light-sensitive paper.

Light pen An input device used to enter or create data and graphic illustrations on a display screen; resembles a standard writing pen with a light-sensitive cell at the end of the pen to identify a point on the display when the two come into contact.

Linear display A feature of some word processing machines enabling the user to view illuminated characters in a single line of type; sometimes referred to as a *thin screen* or a *window into memory.*

Line printer A printer that prints one entire line at a time rather than one character at a time; sometimes called a *band printer.*

Link The connecting path between two nodes in a local area network.

Local area network (LAN) A system that uses cables or other means to allow communication among various kinds of electronic equipment within a small distance, usually 3 to 8 miles.

Logic The basic operating instructions of a computer.

Machine language The language understood by computers, written in combinations of ones and zeros (bytes); the language into which programs are translated.

Magnetic card A plastic card coated with magnetic material that permits recording and storage of information.

Magnetic media Media, such as cards, disks, and cassettes, that record dictation or keystrokes by means of electric impulses and magnetism.

Magnetic tape Tape coated with magnetic material on which information may be recorded and stored.

Mailgram A form of electronic mail sent via Western Union's telecommunications equipment and delivered the following day as regular first-class mail.

Mainframe The largest and most costly type of computer, having a vast storage capacity and operating at the highest speeds.

MC/ST (Magnetic Card Selectric Typewriter) Automated typing system, developed by IBM, that records keystrokes on a magnetic-coated card; also called the *Mag Card*.

Mechanical word processor A blind word processor that has a keyboard, internal processor, and printer in one console and a primary storage medium in another. A mechanical word processor lacks some of the sophisticated functions of an electronic typewriter.

Media The recording supplies commonly used with information processing equipment, such as cards, diskettes, and cassettes.

Media compatibility When different memory devices can share each other's diskettes, disks, or tapes.

Megahertz (MHz) One million hertz (cycles per second). See **Cycles per second.**

Memory An integral component of computers in which keystrokes are stored; sometimes called *internal storage*.

Menu A list of processing options (tasks or functions) displayed on some word processors, as well as microcomputers using certain word processing software packages, to guide the user with selection procedures throughout the entry and editing of text.

Microcassette The smallest type of tape cassette (voice storage medium), which records 30, 60, or 90 minutes of dictation time.

Microcomputer The smallest type of computer powered by one or more microprocessors that can be programmed to perform a variety of tasks for home and office use. Also called *personal computer, professional computer, PC,* and *micro.*

Microfiche A small sheet of film on which reduced images are arranged in rows and columns; used in records management.

Microfiche reader A device that locates images stored on microfiche and projects them onto a screen for viewing.

Microfilm A continuous roll of film containing reduced images of graphic or textual material; used for records storage and filing.

Microfilm jacket A set of plastic or acetate sheets that holds strips of microfilm.

Microfilm reader A machine that enlarges and projects a microfilm image onto a screen for viewing.

Microform A miniaturized image of a document.

Microform reader A device for viewing microform images.

Micrographics The technology by which images of text and graphic information are photographically reduced and stored on film.

Microimage transmission Technology that can scan a microfilm image and convert it to a digitized computer signal to transmit the image from one computer to another at any location.

Microprocessor A tiny digital computer, usually just a very small silicon chip.

Microwave relay A transmission medium similar to high-frequency radio wave signals, that can be used to send computer data between relay stations.

Miniaturization The re-creation of large objects in a smaller size.

Minicassette A cassette smaller than a standard cassette, with a recording capacity of 30 minutes to a side.

Minicenter See **Satellite center** and **Decentralized information processing system.**

Minicomputer A medium-sized computer less costly and less powerful than a mainframe.

MIPS Millions of instructions per second; the method by which electronics engineers measure the information processing capabilities of a microchip.

Glossary

Modem Short for *modulator/demodulator*. A device that converts electrical signals into tones for transmission over telephone lines.

Modular Consisting of interchangeable or compatible plug-in items or other "building blocks" for expanding capacity.

Mouse An input device a few inches long and an inch or so high, which is small enough to fit in the hand; a magnetic ball on the bottom allows the device to roll around on a desk while moving the cursor on the screen; menus are displayed and files are opened and closed by pressing a button on the device.

MT/ST (Magnetic Tape Selectric Typewriter) Developed by IBM, the first automated typing system to record keystrokes on a magnetic storage medium.

Multifunction workstation See **Executive workstation.**

Multiple cassette system A central recording system in which dictation from a number of authors may be recorded on cassettes at the same time.

Multitasking The ability of integrated software to perform a variety of tasks uniformly and without the need for changing programs.

Network topology See **Architecture.**

Networking The linking together electronically of computer and other office equipment for processing data, words, graphics, images, and voice; networking the equipment of various technologies, so that people and machines can communicate and interact, further expanding the possibilities for processing and managing information.

NIOSH (National Institute for Occupational Safety and Health) An organization that investigates the health and safety of workers.

Node Each place where a terminal, a printer, or a peripheral is located in a local area network; each node is connected to the LAN by a separate cable.

Noise shields Special noise-reduction devices attached to printers.

Nonimpact printer A printer that has no printing device striking the paper or ribbon.

OCR See **Optical character reader.**

Office landscaping The design of office space using desks, files, screens, or movable partitions within large, open areas to create free-standing clusters.

Offset duplicating A duplication process in which the inked image on a metal plate is transferred, or "offset," to a rubber-surfaced roller, which then transfers the image to blank paper.

Offset lithography See **Offset duplicating.**

Omnifont optical character reader An optical character reader capable of reading any standard typeface.

On-line information service A company that provides on-line access to one or more data bases by connecting a word processor or microcomputer to a modem; often called *electronic library.*

Open-shelf storage Storage units that are open and stacked vertically without drawers or doors.

Operation keys Special keys on a word processor that control other components such as the storage unit, printer, or other terminals (for sending and receiving keyboarded documents).

Optical character reader (OCR) A device or scanner that reads printed or typed characters and converts them into signals for input into a data or word processor.

Optical (laser) disk A recordlike device on which information is stored (recorded) by the use of light in the form of laser beams to write and read data.

Output The production of soft copy or typed or printed copies in an information processing system; the third stage in the information processing cycle.

Paper shredder A device that destroys large amounts of paper at one time.

Parity bit A control code used in data communication as a check bit, sent along with the groups of alphanumeric bits, to determine the accuracy of data during transmission.

Password An identification code known only to authorized users of a computer.

Peripheral Any device that extends the capabilities of a word processing system or microcomputer but is not necessary for its operation.

Permanent memory The set of instructions, or program, built into a word processor or microcomputer by the manufacturer; also called *read-only memory (ROM).*

Personal computer See **Microcomputer.**

Photocomposition See **Phototypesetting.**

Photocopying A reproduction process in which copies are produced directly from an original by photographic means.

Phototypesetting The process of setting text into type by using a printing device that generates characters under the control of a computer and records them photographically on film or paper.

Pinfeed platen A platen that controls the movement of a continuous roll of paper during printing by engaging marginal perforations on the paper with sprockets.

Plotter A printer containing pens of a variety of colored inks used to highlight graphic illustrations, data, and other types of artwork.

Point-of-sale terminal (POS) A cash register with a keyboard to key in the price of the merchandise as well as additional coded data printed on the price tag and a screen for displaying the information.

Portable computer A lightweight, battery-powered computer.

Portable dictation unit A small, hand-held recording device using minicassettes or microcassettes.

Portable microcomputers A microcomputer that ranges from pocket-size to those that can fit in an attaché case. Also called *transportables* or *lap-size computers.*

Principal See **Author.**

Printer The device that produces copy on paper.

Printout See **Hard copy.**

Privacy lockout A feature of some central recording systems that prevents anyone other than the author, transcriptionist, and supervisor from hearing the dictation.

Private branch exchange (PBX) An in-house telephone network, also used to transmit data or text between other electronic equipment in the system.

Procedures manual A book containing descriptions and explanations of office jobs, tasks, or systems prepared by a company for its employees.

Processing The sorting, classifying, or editing of input to organize it into information; the second stage of the information processing cycle.

Productivity The output per employee.

Productivity measurement The computing and recording of the amount of work produced by employees.

Program A sequence of instructions used by a computer to process data.

Programmable read-only memory (PROM) Chips developed to allow the user to program ROM for applications used frequently.

Programming language Language in which software is written; a set of rules that provides a way of instructing the computer to perform operations to solve a problem. See also *Development software.*

Protocol A technique or procedure for transmitting data that governs the format and control of data transmitted.

Protocol translator A device that enables machines with different sets of operating procedures to communicate with each other.

Public computer network An electronic person-to-person communications service available to companies or individuals who do not own a computer.

QWERTY keyboard The standard typewriter keyboard arrangement of letters, number keys, a space bar, and shift keys occupying the part of the keyboard closest to you so that you can reach them most easily; the keyboard used most frequently on word processors and microcomputers.

RAM See **Random access memory.**

Random access A storage technique enabling direct retrieval of stored data or text elements regardless of their location on the storage medium.

Random access memory (RAM) The temporary memory of a word processor or microcomputer.

Read-only memory (ROM) The permanent memory of a word processor or microcomputer.

Read/write head A device contained in the disk drive that reads, writes, or erases data on a storage medium.

Glossary

237

Reader/printer A microform reader capable of printing hard copies of documents stored on the microform.

Reading When information is transferred from some external storage medium (for example, a floppy diskette) into a system.

Record A collection of information stored in a data base.

Records management Planning, organizing, and controlling the creation, protection, use, storage, and disposition of records.

Repetitive printing The printing of more than one original hard copy by means of a word processing or microcomputer printer.

Repetitive text Duplicate information contained in documents intended for different recipients; also called *constant text*.

Reprographics The methods and kinds of equipment by which copies of written or graphic materials are made.

Ring network A local area network topology resembling a ring with a completely closed loop where messages are passed from one node to the next until they reach the addressee; some ring networks use a hub to direct traffic, but the hub is not connected centrally.

ROM See **Read-only memory.**

Rotary file A storage unit for paper or magnetic media that either rotates, thus saving space, or encircles a desk or workstation.

Row The divided vertical sections of a spreadsheet.

Satellite center A small concentration of information processing operators and equipment (linked administratively to a large center) to serve specific departments or floors of an organization. See also *Minicenter* and *Decentralized information processing system*.

Satellite communications The transmission of information to geographically distant locations by using earth stations consisting of terminals and connecting facilities.

Screenload The amount of text that can appear on a video display terminal at one time.

Scroll To move stored text vertically or horizontally so that it can be viewed on the video display terminal.

Serial access A retrieval technique requiring a search through one item after another on the storage medium.

Shared logic system A system consisting of a number of word processors or microcomputers sharing the processing and storage capabilities of one central processing unit.

Shared resource system A clustered word or information processing system in which workstations with their own internal processors share resources such as printers and central storage.

Sheet feeder A device that automatically feeds sheets of paper into a printer.

Shorthand A method of rapid handwriting using symbols that designate letters, words, or phrases.

Shorthand machine A portable device with keys that are pressed in combinations to produce printed or sound-recorded abbreviations for words.

Simple network A network in which a small number of terminals share a central processing unit. See also *Shared logic system*.

Simplex A protocol used to transmit data in only one direction.

Small business system A sophisticated microcomputer, more expensive and having greater capabilities than a personal computer.

Soft copy Text displayed on the screen of a video display terminal.

Softlifting The illegal copying of commercially produced software packages; also called *software piracy*.

Software The operating instructions or programming of a computer.

Software piracy See **Softlifting.**

Sonic search A feature of some dictation units that enables rapid scanning to find beginnings and endings of recorded documents.

Split screen A feature of some word processors and microcomputer software whereby two documents can appear on the screen at the same time. The documents may be reduced.

Spreadsheet An electronic program based on an accountant's pad or ledger sheet, in which the screen contains rows and columns to form cells; the user programs the meaning and value of each cell, and the program automatically recalculates any affected values when a cell is changed. Also called *electronic spreadsheet*.

Standalone A self-contained word processing system, not linked to any other equipment or to a central computer.

Standard cassette A 2½- by 4-inch cassette, usually with a recording capacity of 60 or more minutes; some cassettes allow recorded dictation up to 180 minutes, 90 minutes on each side of the tape.

Standardization The process by which equipment manufacturers agree on a basic design for a specific piece of equipment, such as the arrangement of letters on a typewriter keyboard.

Standardized format An established style of document preparation.

Star network A local area network whose topology is shaped like a star with all lines converging into a hub (central controller).

Star-shaped ring network A local area network using a hub to reroute calls if any of the nodes should fail; used as a technique to solve the problem of a ring network's breaking down.

Start bit A binary digit sent immediately before each character in asynchronous transmission to indicate to the receiving computer that a character is coming.

Stop bit A binary digit sent immediately after a character has been sent in asynchronous transmission, informing the receiving computer to look for the next character in the data stream.

Storage unit The component of a word processing system or microcomputer that holds the media on which information is stored.

Synchronous transmission See **Bisynchronous transmission.**

Systems approach The examination not only of individual tasks but also of the way those tasks go together, the way they fit in with other related tasks.

Telecommunication lines Telephone and other communications lines used to transmit information from one location to another.

Telecommuting Working at home but being linked electronically to the office through the use of a word processor or personal computer and a modem.

Teleconference A meeting of geographically separated participants connected via a telecommunications system using two-way voice, text, or video communication; sometimes called *videoconference*.

Teletypewriter A keyboard terminal used in the transmission of hard copy over telecommunications lines.

Teletypewriter Exchange Service See **TWX.**

Telex An automatic switching service provided worldwide by various carriers by which information is transmitted over telecommunications lines between teletypewriters.

Temporary memory The area of storage in a word processor or microcomputer temporarily reserved for keyboard characters and instructions; also called *buffer memory* or *random access memory (RAM)*.

Text editing A general phrase that covers a wide variety of word processing systems and procedures.

Thermal transfer A nonimpact method of printing using an ink, heat, and matrix technique; output is clear and sharp, resembling a photocopy.

Thimble A thimble-shaped type element on some character printers.

Tiling A windowing technique that limits the size of each window in proportion to the total number of windows on the screen.

Time-sharing system A system in which an organization pays a fee for using time on a computer owned by another organization.

Topology The arrangement, or configuration, of electronic equipment in a local area network; also called *architecture*.

Touch-sensitive display An input method which allows the user to touch the screen to operate the system and the application programs.

Tractor A device that guides continuous-form paper through a printer.

Transcriptionist Someone who produces keyboarded copy from dictated, handwritten, or recorded material.

Transmission system A communication device that transfers information from one location or piece of equipment to another.

Transparent When the software and hardware are meshing well, the user is not aware of what is happening; the function or operation is "invisible."

Glossary

Transportable microcomputer See **Portable microcomputer.**

Turnaround time The time information takes to be processed and returned to the author.

Twisted pairs A transmission medium used for communication links; two insulated wires twisted together to form a cable; generally used for telephone lines; twisted pairs are placed in tunnels or buried underground and are inexpensive and good for transmitting data over short distances.

TWX (Teletypewriter Exchange Service) A system operated by Western Union in which teletypewriter stations are provided with lines to a central office for access to other such stations throughout the United States, Canada, and Mexico.

Ultrafiche A small sheet of film containing extremely reduced images.

Unified command structure When using integrated software, the ability to perform all tasks (word processing, spreadsheet, data base, etc.) in a similar way by using the same commands.

Upgrade To enhance or add to the features and capabilities of information processing equipment.

User's manual See **Documentation.**

Variable An item that differs from document to document.

VDT See **Video display terminal.**

Vendor A supplier of office equipment, often the manufacturer.

Vendor's manual See **Documentation.**

Video display terminal (VDT) A component of word processing or microcomputer equipment that displays text on a screen for ease in manipulation or editing before production of printed copy.

Video screen See **Video display terminal.**

Voice generation The capability of a computer to produce the sound of a human voice.

Voice mail See **Electronic audio communications.**

Voice-operated relay (VOR) A feature of some dictation systems in which the voice activates the recording mechanism.

Voice processing The processing of information in the form of spoken words; voice recognition equipment changes human speech into signals that a computer translates into words that are displayed on screen.

Volume The total amount of text retained in an external storage center.

White noise A low-level, continuous background sound, such as the hum of an airconditioner, that effectively masks other minor noises in an electronic office environment.

Winchester disk The type of hard disk most often used with word processing and microcomputer systems.

Window A thin-line screen; also called a *thin window.* In some instances, the entire screen is referred to as the *window.* When integrated software is used, *window* refers to the separate areas or boxes on the screen which can display different aspects of work.

Word processing A total system of personnel, procedures, and equipment designed to handle business communications efficiently and economically; the manipulation, by machine, of alphabetic and numeric characters to serve various communication purposes.

Work flow The path from the start to the finish of a task. Work flow in word processing follows this logical path: from input to processing, to output, to distribution/communication, to storage and retrieval.

Work order See **Document requisition form.**

Work procedures A variety of procedures that are used to control the work flow in information processing systems.

Word processing center See **Centralized information processing system.**

Workstation The place where an employee performs most of his or her job functions; includes all the equipment, furnishings, and accessories required to perform the work.

Writing In recording new text, the information is transferred from the keyboard by "writing" it onto the storage medium (for example, a floppy diskette).

ZapMail An electronic express document service which links state-of-the-art reprographics technology with satellite and telecommunication equipment; offered by Federal Express as an alternative to facsimile systems.

INDEX

Acoustic coupler, 159
Address, 118
AISP (Association of Information Systems Professionals), 216
Alphabetic data, 15
Alphanumeric data, 15, 64
American Standard Code for Information Interchange (ASCII), 160
Analog facsimile, 146
Aperture card, 166, 168
   reader for, 168
Applications software, 123–132
   communications, 130–131
   data base, 129
   graphics, 129–130
   integrated, 131–132
   spreadsheet, 127–129
   word processing, 124–127
Architecture, 153–154
Archive, 83
ASCII (American Standard Code for Information Interchange), 160
Assembling documents, 148–149
Association of Information Systems Professionals (AISP), 216
Asynchronous transmission, 160
Author, 48, 52–54, 59–62, 72, 199, 202, 206
   (*See also* Input)
Automatic gain control, 60
Automatic measured review, 59
Automatic recalculation, 128
Automatic sheet feeder, 143, 145
Automatic text repetition, 59
Automation:
   definition of, 9
   effect of, on jobs, 12–15
   office and, 9–11, 15
   productivity and, 13–15
   systems of, 9

Background printing, 141
Backup, 83
Band printer, 142
Baud rate, 159
BBS (Bulletin board service), 131
Bidirectional printing, 141
Binary digit, 118, 159, 160
Bisynchronous transmission, 160–161
Bit, 118, 159, 160
Blind word processing equipment, 90–95
Boilerplate, 33–35
Buffer memory, 78–79
Bulletin board service, 131
Bundled software, 121
Burster, 144
Bus network, 156–157
Business communications, 27–36
   classes of, 32–36
   dictation machine and, 28, 29
   distribution and, 27
   importance of proper handling of, 26–27
   kinds of, 27–36
   (*See also* Documents)
Byte, 118

CAR (computer-assisted retrieval), 169
Carbons, 10, 18, 145
Careers, 215–224
   factors to consider in choosing, 215
   job options, 219–224
   job titles, 216–219
   (*See also* Working in word processing)
Cassette tape text-editor, 92
Cassettes, 53, 55–57, 60–63, 65, 202, 206
Cathode-ray tube (CRT) (*see* Video display terminal)
Central controller, 154
Central processing unit (CPU), 73, 76–79, 91,

Central processing unit (CPU) *(continued)*: 104, 117–119
Central recording system, 54, 60–62
Centralized records management, 173
Centralized reprographics, 149–150
Centralized word processing, 204–208
Character printer, 141
Chip, 6, 117
Clustered system, 104–106
Coaxial cable, 161
Coded system, 100–101
COM (computer output microfilm), 167
Communicating word processor, 152
Communication/distribution (*see* Distribution/communication of information)
Communications, business (*see* Business communications)
Communications satellite, 151, 162
Computer-aided transcription, 63
Computer-assisted retrieval (CAR), 169
Computer-based message system, 152–153
Computer crime, 187–189
Computer language, 122
Computer output microfilm (COM), 167
Computer security, 187–189
Computers, 5–7, 113–119
   mainframe, 113
   microcomputer (*see* Microcomputer)
   minicomputer, 114
Constant, 32, 34–35
Continuous-form paper, 143
Control character, 159–160
Control code, 159–160

241

Correspondence, 28, 32–35
CPU (central processing unit), 73, 76–79, 91, 104, 117–119
Crash, 156
Crosstalk, 161
CRT (cathode-ray tube) (*see* Video display terminal)
Cursor, 75, 96
Cursor key, 75
Cycle time, 119

Daisy wheel, 141
Data, 11, 15–16
Data bank, 172–173
Data base, 129, 171–173
Data base management system (DBMS), 171–173
Data processing, 17–21, 182
  (*See also* Integrated information processing)
Data transmission media, 161–163
Decentralized records management, 173
Decentralized reprographics, 150
Decentralized word processing, 201–204
  (*See also* Minicenter; Satellite center)
Dedicated word processor, 121
Dictation machine, 7–8, 28–29, 52–63, 202
  advantages of, 8, 52–53
  business communications and, 28–29
  central recording system, 54, 60–62
  desk-top, 59–60
  kinds of, 53, 57–63
  media for, 53–57
  portable, 58
  secretary and, 52–53
  transcription machine and, 57–63
  word origination and, 52–53, 202
Digital facsimile, 146
Digitization, 65, 171
Discrete media, 54–57
Disk (*see* Floppy diskette; Hard disk; Optical disk)
Disk drive, 82–83

Disk operating system (DOS), 120–122
Display screen (*see* Video display terminal)
Display word processor, 96–103
  capabilities of, 101–103
  characteristics of, 96, 98
  coded system of, 100–101
  components of, 96
  keyboard, 98–103
  linear, 95
  menu-driven, 98–99
  printer and, 140–144
  software for, 124–127
  storage and retrieval, 79–83
  uses of, 101–103
  using, 98–101
  varieties of, 98
  (*See also* Video display terminal)
Distributed logic, 106
Distribution/communication of information, 18, 27, 150–164
  importance of, 150
  networking, 134–135, 153–157
  transmission media, 161–163
  transmission systems, 157–163
  U.S. Postal Service, 150–151
Document log, 214–215
Document production center, 204–206
Document requisition form, 202, 206
Documentation, 213
Documents, 26–45
  assembly of, 34, 148–149
  classes of, 32–36
  counting, 215
  creation of, 48–53, 200
  definition of, 27
  kinds of, 29–34
  standardized format, 213
  (*See also* Business communications; Input)
DOS (disk operating system), 120–122
Dot-matrix printer, 141–142

Downloading, 133
Dual display, 88
Dual-sheet feeder, 143
Dumb copier/printer, 147
Dumb workstation, 105
Duplex, 162
Duplexing, 146
Dvorak keyboard, 115–116

Echoplex, 162
Electronic communication (*see* Distribution/communication of information; Teleconference; Voice mail)
Electronic copier/printer, 147–148
Electronic cottage, 222
Electronic cueing, 58
Electronic integration, 182–183
  (*See also* Integrated information processing)
Electronic mail, 151–163
Electronic Private Branch Exchange (EPBX), 158
Electronic spreadsheet, 127–129
Electronic typewriter (ET), 9, 93–95
Encryption, 189
Endless loop, 53–54, 57, 60–62, 202, 206
ENIAC (Electronic Numerical Integrator and Computer), 6
Envelope feeder, 143
EPBX (Electronic Private Branch Exchange), 158
EPROM (erasable, programmable, read-only memory), 78
Ergonomics, 192–198
  climate control, 195
  health issues, 196–197
  lighting, 194
  noise, 194–195
  office furniture, 193–194
  office landscaping, 195–196
  (*See also* Office equipment configuration)
ET (electronic typewriter), 9, 93–95

Ethernet, 156
Executive workstation, 183–185
Expandable memory board, 118
Express Mail, 151
External storage, 79–83, 119
(See also Magnetic media)

Facsimile, 146–147, 151
Feasibility study, 199
Fiber optics, 161–162
Field, 172
File, 172
Firmware, 120
Floppy diskette, 21, 63, 79–81, 114, 119, 148, 164–165
  care and handling of, 80–81
  storage of, 165
Format keys, 76
Forms, 29–31
Function keys, 74–76, 92, 96, 115
Function menu, 99
Furniture, 193–194

Graphics, 16, 129–130

Half duplex, 162
Hard copy, 21, 83, 85, 114, 145
Hard disk, 81–82, 114, 134, 164
Hardware, 73–90, 115–120
Hertz (unit), 119
Host system, 184
Hub, 154

Image processing, 64–65, 171
Image scanner, 147
Impact printer, 141–142
In-house training, 213–214, 219
Indexing, 58, 60, 166, 168
Information:
  definition of, 11–12
  office and, 11–15, 26
  (See also Information processing)
Information processing, 15–22, 26
  business applications of, 36–44

Information processing (continued):
  careers in (see Careers)
  data processing and, 17–21
  definition of, 15
  integrated (see Integrated information processing)
  steps in cycle of, 15–19, 185–187
  word processing and, 17, 19–22
  (See also Word processing office systems)
Information sharing, 131
Ink-jet printer, 142
Input, 15–16, 48–68, 202
  author and, 48–49
  dictation machine and, 52–63, 202
  methods of, 48–53, 63
  transcription machine and, 57–63
  voice storage media for, 53–57
Inscribed media, 55, 57
Integrated information processing, 182–192
  executive workstation, 183–185
  systems approach to, 182–183
  (See also Information processing)
Intelligent copier/printer, 147–148, 152
Intelligent workstation, 105
INTELPOST (International Electronic Postal Service), 151
Interface, 183–186
Internal processor, 73, 76–79, 91, 104, 117–119
Internal storage, 53–54, 72, 77–79, 90–93, 121
  (See also Random-access memory; Read-only memory)
International Electronic Postal Service (INTELPOST), 151

Job posting, 223
Job titles in word processing, 216–219

Joystick, 116

Keyboard, 74–76, 91–93, 98–103, 115–117
  display word processor, 98–103
  Dvorak, 115–116
  microcomputer, 115–117
  QWERTY, 74, 115–117
Keyboarding, 17, 28, 29, 51–52, 65, 74–76, 98–103
Keypunch card, 166, 167

LAN (local area network), 153–157
Laser disk, 169–170
Laser printer, 142–143
Letter, 28, 32–35
Light pen, 117
Lighting, 194
Line counting, 215
Line printer, 142
Linear display word processor, 95
Linked equipment, 152
Local area network (LAN), 153–157
Logic (see Central processing unit)
Longhand, 28, 49, 202, 206

Machine dictation (see Dictation machine)
Machine language, 122
Mag Card II, 92
Magnetic card, 164
Magnetic media, 21, 55–57, 80, 165
  care of, 80
  storage of, 165
  (See also Floppy diskette; Hard disk)
Magnetic tape, 164
  (See also Cassettes)
Mailgram, 151
Mainframe, 113
MC/ST (Magnetic Card Selectric Typewriter), 91–92
Mechanical word processor, 93
Media (see Magnetic media; Voice storage media)
Media compatibility, 57
Megahertz (unit), 119

Index 243

Memo, 28
Memory, 53–54, 72, 77–79, 90–93
   (*See also* Internal storage; Random-access memory; Read-only memory)
Memory Typewriter, 92–93
Menu, 98–99
Menu-driven system, 98–99
Microcassette, 56–59, 202
Microchip, 6, 117
Microcomputer, 114–139
   components of, 115–119
   CPU, 117–119
   external storage, 119
      (*See also* Floppy diskette; Hard disk; Magnetic media)
   keyboard, 115–117
   networking, 134–135
      (*See also* Local area network)
   portable, 115
   software (*see* Microcomputer software)
Microcomputer software, 119–132
   applications (*see* Applications software)
   development, 122
   operating system, 120–122
Microfiche, 166–168
   reader for, 168
Microfilm, 166–169
   CAR, 169
   jacket for, 166
   reader for, 168
Microforms, 165–169, 171
   indexing of, 166, 168
   readers for, 168
   retrieval of, 167
   transmission of, 171
   unitized, 166
   (*See also* Microfiche; Microfilm)
Micrographics (*see* Microforms)
Microimage transmission, 171
Microprocessor, 6, 117
Microwave, 162
Miniaturization, 6
Minicassette, 55–59, 202

Minicenter, 202, 203
Minicomputer, 114
Modem, 158–159
Mouse, 117, 132
MT/ST (Magnetic Tape Selectric Typewriter), 19, 91
Multiple cassette system, 61–62
Multitasking, 131

National Institute for Occupational Safety and Health (NIOSH), 196
Network, local area (LAN), 153–157
Network topology, 154
Networking, 134–135, 153–157
NIOSH (National Institute for Occupational Safety and Health), 196
Node, 154
Nonimpact printer, 142–143
Numeric data, 15

OCR (optical character reader), 63–64
Office:
   automated, 9–11
   automation and design of, 15
   (*See also* Ergonomics)
   information and, 11–15, 26
   productivity in, 13–15, 213
Office equipment configuration, 103–109
   clustered system, 104–106
   shared logic, 104–106, 152, 154
   shared resource, 106
   standalone, 103
   time-sharing system, 106–107
   (*See also* Ergonomics; Word processing office systems)
Office landscaping, 195–196
Office organization, 198–208
   feasibility studies and, 199
   (*See also* Word processing office systems)
Offset duplicating, 145
Omnifont reader, 64

Online data base, 36, 173
Online information service, 173
Open-shelf storage, 164
Operator (*see* Word processing operator)
Optical character reader (OCR), 63–64
Optical disk, 169–170
Output, 18, 140–150
   hard copy, 21, 83, 85, 114, 145
   printer (*see* Printers)
   reprographics and (*see* Reprographics)
   soft copy, 21, 85, 140, 145

Paper shredder, 144
Paperless typewriter, 95
Parity bit, 160
Password, 189
PBX (Private Branch Exchange), 158
PC (personal computer) (*see* Microcomputer)
Performance appraisal, 223
Peripheral, 79
Permanent memory, 77–78
   (*See also* External storage)
Personal computer (PC) (*see* Microcomputer)
Photocomposition, 148, 152
Photocopying, 8, 145–146
Phototypesetting, 148, 152
Plotter, 143
Point-of-sale (POS) terminal, 40–41
Principal (*see* Author)
Printers, 74, 83, 140–144
   character, 141
   devices used with, 143–144
   display word processor and, 140–144
   dot-matrix, 141–142
   impact, 141–142
   ink-jet, 142
   laser, 142–143
   line, 142
   nonimpact, 142–143
   reprographics and, 145
   thermal transfer, 142
Printout, 21, 83, 85, 114, 145
Private Branch Exchange (PBX), 158

Procedures manual, 213
Productivity, 13–15, 213–215
　automation and, 13–15
　definition of, 13
　measurement of, 214–215
　office and, 13–15, 213
　work procedures and methods, 213–214
Programs:
　computer, 17, 77, 120
　for data processing, 17
　(See also Microcomputer software)
PROM (programmable read-only memory), 78
Protocol, 162–163
Protocol translator, 163
Public computer network, 153

QWERTY keyboard, 74, 115–117

RAM (random-access memory), 78–79, 121
Random access, 91
Random-access memory (RAM), 78–79, 121
Read-only memory (ROM), 77–78, 121
Reader, 168
Reader-printer, 168
Record, 172
Records management, 173
　(See also Microforms; Storage and retrieval)
Repetitive printing, 145
Repetitive text, 32–33, 38–39
　(See also Boilerplate)
Report, 28–29
Reprographics, 18, 144–150
　centralized, 149–150
　decentralized, 150
　definition of, 144
　document assembly and, 148–149
　methods of, 144–148
　printer and, 145
　systems of, 149–150
Retrieval (see Storage and retrieval)
Ring network, 155–156
ROM (read-only memory), 77–78, 121

Rotary file, 165
Rough draft, 51

Satellite center, 202, 203
Satellite communications, 151, 162
Screenload, 78, 86–88, 119
Scroll, 78, 87–89
Secretary, 13–15, 28–29, 48–50, 52–55, 60–61, 200, 204, 206, 217–218
　careers open to, 217–218
　compared with word processing operator, 200, 204, 206
　effect of automation on, 13–15, 60–61
　machine dictation and, 52–53
　responsibilities of, 200
　shorthand and, 49–50
　transcription and, 55
　word origination and, 48–49, 200
Serial access, 91
Shared logic, 104–106, 152, 154
Shared resource, 106
Sheet feeder, 143, 145
Shorthand, 8, 28, 49–50, 63, 200
　advantages of, 8
　dictation machine compared with, 8
　as method of document creation, 49–50, 200
Shorthand machine, 63
Simple network, 154
Simplex, 162
Soft copy, 21, 85, 140, 145
Software (see Microcomputer software; Programs)
Software piracy, 189
Sonic search, 58
Specialization, 204–205
Split screen, 88
Spreadsheet, electronic, 127–129
Standalone, 103
Standardization, 5, 33, 43
Standardized format, 213
Star network, 154–155
Star-shaped ring network, 156
Start bit, 160

Statistical keys, 76
Statistical table, 29
Stop bit, 160
Storage and retrieval, 19, 53, 62, 79–83, 91, 164–174
　computer-assisted, 169
　dictation machine and, 53
　display word processor, 79–83
　electronic mail, 151–163
　magnetic media (see Magnetic media)
　micrographics and (see Microforms)
　OCR and, 63
　of paper, 164
　random access and, 78–79, 91
　records management system, 173
　serial access and, 91
Supervisor, 62, 206–207, 218, 223
Synchronous transmission, 160–161
Systems approach, 182–183

Technology:
　business applications of, 36–44
　documents and new (see Documents)
　impact of, 2–24
　individual and, 2–3
　inventions and, 3–7
　office and, 3–11
　uses of, 8–9
Telecommunications, 151–164
Telecommuting, 222
Teleconference, 163–164
Telegraph, 5, 151
Telenet, 153
Telephone, 5, 107, 151, 163–164, 206
　electronic mail and, 151, 163
　machine dictation and, 5
　teleconference, 163–164
　telegraph compared to, 5
　uses of, 5, 107, 206
Teletypewriter, 151
Teletypewriter Exchange Service (TWX), 151
Telex, 151

Index

245

Template, 115
Temporary memory, 78–79, 121
Text:
  definition of, 17
  editing of, 36–44
  electronic mail and, 151–163
  hard copy, 21, 83, 85, 114, 145
  repetitive, 32–33, 38–39
  soft copy, 21, 85, 140, 145
Text-edited document, 35
Thermal transfer printing, 142
Thimble, 141
Tiling, 132
Time-sharing system, 106–107
Topology, 153–154
Touch-sensitive screen, 117
Tractor, 143–144
Traditional office environment, 199–201
Training, 213–214, 219–221
Transcription machine, 57–67
  dictation machine and, 57–63
Turnaround time, 62
Twisted pair, 161
TWX (Teletypewriter Exchange Service), 151
Typewriter, 3–5, 7–9, 72, 93–95, 145, 148
  electronic, 9, 93–95

Ultrafiche, 167
Unified command structure, 131
U.S. Postal Service, 150–151
  Express Mail, 151
  INTELPOST, 151
Unitized microform, 166
Upgrade, 94–95
User's manual, 214

Variable, 32
VDT (see Video display terminal)
Vendor's manual, 213
Video display terminal (VDT), 21, 38, 62, 83–90, 96, 119, 148, 196
  configuration, 86

Video display terminal (VDT) *(continued)*:
  safety, 196
  screen size, 86–88
Videoconference, 163–164
Voice mail, 163
Voice-operated relay (VOR), 60
Voice processing, 65–67
Voice recognition, 65–67
Voice storage media, 53–57
  (*See also* Dictation machine)
VOR (voice-operated relay), 60

Winchester disk (*see* Hard disk)
Window:
  in executive workstation, 184
  in integrated software, 132
  (*See also* Dual display; Split screen)
Word origination (*see* Author; Input)
Word processing:
  applications software, 124–127
  business applications of, 36–44
  centralized, 204–208
  classes of documents in, 32–36
  decentralized, 201–204
  definition of, 17
  development of, 19–21, 90–93
  efficiency through, 31, 43
  equipment for (*see* Word processing equipment)
  information processing and, 17, 19–22
  productivity and (*see* Productivity)
  (*See also* Integrated information processing)
Word processing center, 204–206
Word processing equipment, (*see* Word processor)
Word processing office systems:
  centralized, 204–208
  configurations, 103–107
  decentralized, 201–204

Word processing office systems *(continued)*:
  traditional environment, 199–201
  (*See also* Office equipment configuration)
Word processing operator, 200, 203, 204, 206–207, 216–217
  secretary compared to, 200, 204, 206
  in word processing systems, 206
Word processing supervisor, 62, 206–207, 218, 223
Word processor, 16–17, 19–21, 72–107, 117–119, 121, 152
  blind, 90–95
  communicating, 152
  components of, 73–90
  dedicated, 121
  definition of, 72
  logic of (*see* Central processing unit)
  mechanical, 93
  memory of, 77–79
  microcomputer as (*see* Microcomputer)
  portable, 95
  standalone, 103
Work flow, 15–19, 200, 202, 205–206
Work order, 202, 206
Work procedures and methods, 213–214
Working in word processing:
  advancement, 223
  approach to job, 215–216
  performance appraisal, 223
  personal appearance, 215–216
  personal qualities, 215–216
  productivity (*see* Productivity)
  (*See also* Careers)
Workstation, 103, 105, 183–185
  dumb, 105
  executive, 183–185
  intelligent, 105

Xerography, 8, 145–146

ZapMail, 147